THE MAKEUP ARTIST HANDBOOK

Second Edition

THE MAKEUP ARTIST HANDBOOK
Techniques for Film, Television, Photography, and Theatre

Second Edition

Gretchen Davis and Mindy Hall

AMSTERDAM • BOSTON • HEIDELBERG • LONDON
NEW YORK • OXFORD • PARIS • SAN DIEGO
SAN FRANCISCO • SINGAPORE • SYDNEY • TOKYO

Focal Press is an imprint of Elsevier

Illustrators: Robert Revels (www.robertrevels.com), Devon Keene
Drawings for shapes: Dan Gheno
Drawings for color: Don Jusko
Cover design: Mary Birchler

Focal Press is an imprint of Elsevier
225 Wyman Street, Waltham, MA 02451
The Boulevard, Langford Lane, Kidlington, Oxford, OX5 1GB, UK

Notices

Knowledge and best practice in this field are constantly changing. As new research and experience broaden our understanding, changes in research methods, professional practices, or medical treatment may become necessary.

Practitioners and researchers must always rely on their own experience and knowledge in evaluating and using any information, methods, compounds, or experiments described herein. In using such information or methods they should be mindful of their own safety and the safety of others, including parties for whom they have a professional responsibility.

To the fullest extent of the law, neither the Publisher nor the authors, contributors, or editors, assume any liability for any injury and/or damage to persons or property as a matter of products liability, negligence or otherwise, or from any use or operation of any methods, products, instructions, or ideas contained in the material herein.

Library of Congress Cataloging-in-Publication Data
Davis, Gretchen.
  The makeup artist handbook: techniques for film, television, photography, and theatre / Gretchen Davis, Mindy Hall. – 2nd ed.
    p. cm.
  Includes index.
  ISBN 978-0-240-81894-8
1. Film makeup. 2. Television makeup. 3. Theatrical makeup. I. Hall, Mindy. II. Title. III. Title: Techniques for film, television, photography, and theatre.
  PN1995.9.M25D38 2012
  792.02'7–dc23

                                                                                    2011038123

British Library Cataloguing-in-Publication Data
A catalogue record for this book is available from the British Library.

For information on all Focal Press publications,
visit our website at www.elsevierdirect.com.

12 13 14 15   5 4 3 2 1

Printed in China

CONTENTS

The Makeup Artist Handbook has become our journey into writing about what we do, how we do it, and why we do it. The Second Edition gives updated information, with new artists and products, and the latest in innovations and techniques. Our pro tips and artist quotes will inspire you and give you an advantage on the job. Our new addition of on-the-job, professional examples written from the set, gives you insight into a moment, or day, in the life of a professional Makeup Artist, with invaluable lessons from the field.

Our goal has always been to pay it forward and share the experience and knowledge of our careers in makeup, to provide the next generation of artists with the most real, timely knowledge from many points of view. The original idea was simple: think outside the box, include as many of our colleagues as possible to share their expertise and knowledge, and give the book as many "voices" to learning as possible. We had no idea how rewarding this experience would be, not only for you but for us—we have been inspired. Our global group brings knowledge rich with talent, skill, and innovation. This community's generous nature to share and mentor from their phenomenal experience is your gain, and to your advantage. You are learning from some of the best of the best!

Learning from one standpoint puts the students at a disadvantage and our global base gives you more insight into working as a freelance Makeup Artist, with all the skills, knowledge, and protocol that are required of you. By exposing you to as many different approaches as possible you will learn to work outside the box and be able to handle the flow of your first day on any job. There are countless ways to go about creating and applying makeup, so we have included examples from different artists to develop your hand, your instincts, and open your mind.

The innovations within our industry keep us constantly learning, evolving, and moving forward with our talents. This is a career where you never stop learning, so for us, this time of updating products, techniques, and added information is exciting, necessary, and an opportunity to continue sharing the experience.

We assure you that all product references, lists of industry standards, and the techniques in this book are genuine working examples in today's market. The lists are a culmination of our 25-plus years of experience, interviews with our colleagues in all mediums, and done without bias or favoritism. No endorsements or promotional fees by any company or individual were paid to us or our colleagues in the preparation of this book. We are part of an international community: Sharing knowledge, product information, and techniques are all part of the lessons learned and shared with each other through our travels and our commitment to the art.

ACKNOWLEDGMENTS

Once again, we could not have done it without our amazing pros, who continued to share, update, and inspire us. We are very grateful to have all of the original contributors and designers from the first edition join us again on the second edition, and we are thrilled to include new artists and pros to this global group. Their vast contribution of knowledge, talent, and experience to this edition is humbling.

Tremendous thanks to Darla Albright, Matiki Anoff, Gary Archer, Mary Birchler, Fred Blau, J.C. Cerville, Debra Coleman, Richard Dean, Ken Diaz, Daniela Eschbacher, Kris Evans, Kim Felix-Burke, Dan Gheno, Steven Horak, Don Jusko, Devon Keene, Erwin H. Kupitz, Bradley M. Look, Gerd Mairandres, Randy Huston Mercer, Gil Mosko, Michele Mulkey, Matthew Mungle, Kenny Meyers, Dina Ousley, Christina Patterson, Robert Revels, Susan Stone, Joseph N. Tawil, Christien Tinsley, Nancy Tozier, Kazuhiro Tsuji, Jenny King Turko, Paul Wheeler, and Patty York.

To S.E. Radich, there would be no text without you. You kept us sane and organized with our crazy schedules, multiple time zones, locations, and our long hours on set. Your amazing patience, support, and input have made this book complete. Unending thanks to you for your invaluable contribution in getting us to the final manuscript. Once again, we could not have done it without you.

Much thanks to Mary Birchler Design, for our beautiful book covers and elegance throughout both editions of this book. Thank you to Robert Revel and Devon Keene, whose illustrations give visual inspiration and life to our text.

Thank you to Focal Press and Elsevier for recognizing the need for this book. Specifically, thank you Elinor Actipis for your continued support, guidance, and encouragement through two editions.

We thank our friend, Jeffery J. Dicks, Esq., and colleague, Ashley C.L. Brown, Esq., for the support, guidance, and care in all things legal, and their wonderful enthusiasm for this book and the future.

Thank you to the Academy of Art University, San Francisco, and to filmmaker and innovator, David Oliver Pfeil, who was the first to approach Gretchen about starting a makeup program for the Academy of Art University. Without his vision and understanding of the importance of makeup in the film department, both as an art form and a career, students would not have had the opportunity to experience and witness what a Makeup Artist does. Thank you to Dan Burns and Jack Isgro for their support in the success of the makeup program at the Academy. Jack, your input to Elsevier made this all happen. Many thanks to Elisa Stephens who encourages instructors to teach students how it really is in the working world.

Much love and thanks to our families, friends, and mentors, who over the years have cheered us on in our careers, supported us in our travels, and offered unwavering, unconditional love, no matter how many times our schedules changed. You made it possible for us to give back, sharing all that we know and do.

Lastly, to all those actors, models, and performers whom we have touched throughout our years, thank you. You have allowed us to do "that thing we do" with you as our canvas!

Thank you.

—Gretchen Davis and Mindy Hall

1

SHAPES

Proportions of the Face and Body in Art

Makeup Artists are masters at illusion. We manipulate the shapes and features of the face and body with our artistry. We cannot achieve this without understanding how to correctly determine proportions, shapes, and the anatomical structure of the body.

In studying anatomy drawing, you learn, for example, individual skeletal or muscular size, shapes, and functions. The functions and proportions are key in creating realism. There are fundamental drawing skills that teach you value, form, light, and shadows, as well as how these elements fall onto the surface of the face and body. For example, if you do not understand the shape and function of a muscle, your placement of highlight and shadow, a tattoo, body paint, or prosthetic will be off and therefore unsuccessful.

Painting, drawing, and understanding the body will give you the skills and ability to understand how to change facial features and alter an individual's features to look like something or someone else. Your artistry will move with the subject, making it look more authentic. This is a very important lesson used in all areas of makeup artistry. "Anatomy is an applied science which underpins fine art, the study of structure is essential for artistic representation. The skeleton, joints and muscular system of a creature determine its proportions and the movement of the body." (Fehér 7)

Value, Shadow, and Light

by Dan Gheno

The study of values is a complicated subject. When trying to draw in a tonal manner, it helps your ability to see value changes on the model if you learn the terminology of the subject.

Values: Each object, whether simple like a sphere or complex like the human figure, is composed of millions of tonal "value" changes. These range from the brightest bright (where the object most directly faces the light) to the darkest dark (where the object is turned away from the light source).

Halftones: A generic term that refers to all of the value variations within the light side of the model. The halftones are brightest where the form turns most directly toward the light source, and are darkest just before the form falls into complete shadow.

Dark and Light Halftones: To keep things simple, artists should class their halftones into two different categories: "light halftones" and "dark halftones." Things can go wrong if these two types aren't kept separate. Some artists make all of their halftones equally dark, creating muddy-looking drawings, while others insist on making their halftones equally bright, creating washed-out drawings. Note in the Watcher picture (Figure 1.1) that the halftone shapes

FIGURE 1.1: THE WATCHER WOMAN

are distinctly lighter on the side of the forehead most directly facing the light source, while they are dramatically darker near the shadow shapes on the forehead. Try squinting to test the validity of the value renditions. When you squint, the light halftones should fade away and disappear into the overall light shape, while the dark halftones should visually melt into the adjacent, general shadow shapes.

Shadow: As the form of the model turns completely away from the light source, the dark halftone shapes get darker and darker, until the light completely terminates and the big shadow shape begins. Literally called the "terminator" by those who deal with light as a science, this shadow edge can look abrupt and contrast at times, or soft and fused at other times. It all depends on the amount of reflected light bouncing into the shadow side of the model.

Reflected Light: Shadows are simply the absence of light. The only reason anything can be seen within the shadow shape is because of reflected light. The light source illuminates not just the model, but also the surrounding environment. The light bounces off the walls, floor, and ceiling, ricocheting into the shadows, and lighting (or filling) the dark side of the model. Indeed, even various body parts reflect light onto the other shadowed parts of the model. One very important rule to know: no reflected light in the shadow shape can be as bright as the direct light hitting the model.

Core Shadow: When the dark side of the face turns away from any source of reflected light, the shadow gradually darkens until the darkest part of the shadow, called the "core shadow," is reached. This term refers to an area of the form that gets no direct light and very little reflected light. Even when drawn subtly or in a barely visible manner, the core shadow creates a cornering effect that helps to magnify the plane changes of the model.

3

Movement of the Head: To determine the correct proportions of facial features when the head has moved in different angles, use the vertical and horizontal axes (Figure 1.2). The centerline is the vertical axis. This line determines the movements made by the face from side to side. The horizontal axis defines the brow line.

FIGURE 1.2: HORIZONTAL AND VERTICAL AXES

If the human head is turned in any direction, the main vertical and horizontal axes become elliptical curves (Figure 1.3).

FIGURE 1.3: ELLIPTICAL CURVES

If the head turns in any direction, the parallel horizontal lines become parallel elliptical curves (Figure 1.4).

Body and face measurements help the artist correctly achieve the right proportions. Artist Leonardo da Vinci calculated the parts of the body that could be used as units, and was the first to adapt the head for units of measurement. He used the length of the face, but not the length of the whole head. His methods are still in use today.

Proportions for the Face and Body

by Don Jusko

The skull is the basic division of the human body (Figure 1.5). To draw the head, start with an oval (3 × 4). Divide the head into three parts:

1. Top of the skull.
2. Pupils are the middle.
3. Bottom of the nose to the bottom of the chin.

Add the lips a third of the way down, below the nose. Add the chin crease below the nose.

Profile View: The height of the side head is one head length. The width equals one head length. The top of the ears are in line with the eyebrows. The ear hole is in line with the bottom of the nose and the occipital bone (the hindmost bone of the skull, which forms the back of the skull above the nape). The bottom of the earlobe always varies with each individual.

The face triangle (Figure 1.6) is from the center of each pupil, through the nostrils, to the point between the top front teeth. This is an important trait, as every person's triangle is different.

A smiling mouth lines up under the pupils. The two irises usually equal the maximum smiling width of the mouth. The space between the eyes is an average of 2-½ inches. One eye width equals the space between the eyes (Figure 1.7).

FIGURE 1.4: PARALLEL ELLIPTICAL CURVES

FIGURE 1.5: FRONT VIEW OF DIVISION OF HEAD

FIGURE 1.6: FACE TRIANGLE

FIGURE 1.7: ILLUSTRATION OF PUPILS WITH CORRECT SPACE BETWEEN THE EYES

The Body: A perfect body is eight heads high. The neck is a quarter of one head length, starting under the chin with the top of the head. The second head starts at the neck mark.

The shoulder-line mark is a quarter of one head down. This leaves space for the chest above the clavicle and for the neck-support muscles.

The Torso Triangle: The shoulder line is two head lengths (not widths) wide, and is the top line of the torso triangle that extends down to the space between the legs. The chin-to-shoulder line is a half of one head length. The nipple line equals one head length, the top of the third head trunk. The belly button to the space between the legs is one head, the bottom of the third trunk head (Figure 1.8).

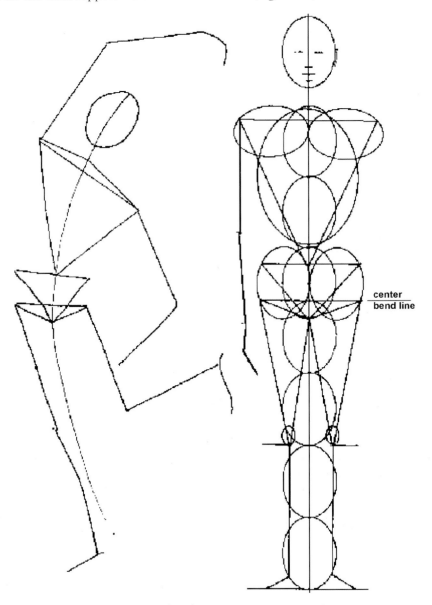

center
bend line

FIGURE 1.8: TORSO TRIANGLE

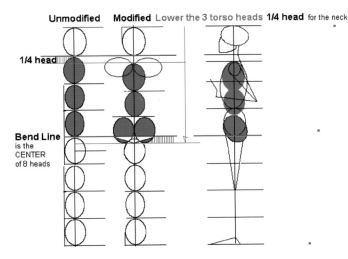

Unmodified   **Modified** Lower the 3 torso heads **1/4 head** for the neck

1/4 head

Bend Line
is the
CENTER
of 8 heads

The bend line remains the center of the body, 4 heads up.

FIGURE 1.9: FULL BODY WITH BEND LINE

The leg space is four and a quarter heads down from the top, including the quarter neck space. The center head overlaps by a quarter of a head. The width of the waist at the belly button is one head length. From the top line of the hip or trunk triangle to the space between the legs is three-quarters of one head high, and is two head widths wide. You get the idea!

The center of the body is the bend line, and can also be measured as four heads up from the base (Figure 1.9).

Bodies in Motion

In art and anatomy, the center of gravity is the point of the body that dictates where the weight is distributed. An imaginary axis used by artists determines where the weight of the body changes. When sitting, the upper body trunk and head rest on the pelvis. When someone is standing, the body is supported by the feet. In movement, such as walking, the center of gravity is pushed forward by the foot and then supported once again. Walking has several movements. Up-and-down movement of the body takes place with each step. Swinging is caused by the center of gravity being shifted from one leg to another. Twisting movements

FIGURE 1.10: ARTIST BODY, COLOR REDDISH

are caused by the shoulders and hips. When a person walks downhill, his or her center of gravity descends with each step. Makeup Artists interpret these movements on paper, sculpting, or through other artistic media.

Drawing the Body in Motion

by Dan Gheno

Begin to draw with a scribble-like gesture, moving randomly back and forth across the page, rapidly drawing the model from head to toe and from one side of the figure to the other side. Once you have a feeling for where the figure drawing is headed, start to toss in lines of action, sweeping angles that crisscross through the figure. Begin to gauge the positive and negative shapes (Figures 1.11 and 1.12).

Angles: Continue to let your hand amble, drawing seemingly random, angled lines throughout the figure, trying to find the forms that line up with or contrast with each other. In this case, for instance, note how the line of the model's right inner ankle lines up with the outside of her right hip. Observe how the complex angles of the right side of the torso

FIGURE 1.12: DRAWING BODY IN MOTION

FIGURE 1.11: DRAWING BODY IN MOTION

contrast with the figure's simpler, flatter left side. Don't limit your use of angles to the inside of the figure. Let them broadly enwrap the outside of the figure. Collectively, the outside angles are called the envelope. Use them to judge the negative space between the limbs and the torso, as well as the general relationship of the ground plane.

Positive and Negative Space: Utilize negative and positive space to help you analyze the forms of the figure (Figure 1.13). Look at the so-called empty space, or negative space, between the legs, as well as between the left arm and the head. Also look at the space between the right arm and the body. Ask yourself: How big or small are these shapes? Are they long and narrow or short and broad? Do the same for the positive shapes or body forms. For example, how wide are the model's

FIGURE 1.13: DRAWING BODY IN MOTION

FIGURE 1.14: DRAWING BODY IN MOTION

calves compared to her ankles? To keep the relative sizes of your positive shapes under control, gauge each body part against some other basic unit of measurement (see the section "Proportions for the Face and Body" by Don Jusko). For instance, how many head units does a leg measure?

The Line of Action: Look for the internal, directional movement of the forms that you are drawing. You can set them up with lines of action such as the ones drawn in the diagram. Don't be surprised if your initial sketch looks like a stick figure. Sculptors block in their figures in a similar fashion by using what is called an armature, a framework of metallic rods that will govern the thrust of their sculpted clay forms. Whether you are drawing or sculpting, you can use these very simple lines of thrust as a foundation for the outside curves and to orient the overall gesture of the figure (Figure 1.14).

1. On the paper, put a mark where you want to place the top, midpoint, and bottom of the figure. Try to stay within these boundaries when sketching the figure. Observe the center of gravity, which is represented by this vertical line that falls downward from the pit of the neck. Also observe all of the contrasting, shifting subforms of the figure. The head, neck, chest, hips, and legs are balanced back and forth over this line, one on top of the other.

2. You will usually find the midpoint of the standing figure at the hip bone.

3. The hip usually tips upward above the supporting, weight-bearing leg. Note that the shoulders usually slant in the opposite direction of the hips.

4. Where is the crescendo, or peak, of the curve? It is almost never in the middle of the curve.

5. It is important to find the ground plane of the floor under the feet.

In conclusion, there are as many ways to start a drawing of the human figure from life as there are artists. The brief outline above is a personal approach to illustrations. It was prepared for students, and has been adapted from an article in *American Artist* magazine (Gheno).

Understanding the portions of the face and body will lead you to the art of makeup. Mastering the proportions of the face will enable you to create and design any look.

> In the well-known Muller-Lyer Illusion, a straight line with flanges pointed outward seems longer than the one with them turned inward. The one tugs the attention beyond the line and seems to lengthen it, the other pulls it center and shortens it. Makeup Artists exploit this effect. For instance, by daubing shadow above the outer ends of the eyes, they draw them further apart. By applying it above the inner corners, they narrow them. (McNeill, 297)

A Makeup Artist will use this principle to compose features that are necessary for the character or beauty makeup. In all areas of makeup, you need to trick the mind as to what is being seen (Figure 1.15).

Everyone has their own unique facial features and characteristics. As in drawing, where you place a shadow or highlight represents what you are visually saying about your makeup. In anatomy, the placement of the skeletal and muscle systems in each individual highlights those unique features. Theatre is one of the strongest examples of changing shapes to create characters, although these techniques can be used in all areas of makeup application.

Face Shapes

There are five basic face shapes that are used most often. Many people have a combination of face shapes. Face shapes can be used as a guide, but would also determine where to place shadows and highlights according to what makeup look you are creating. (See Chapter 8, Design.)

Following are the five basic face shapes for you to identify and understand the differences:

Square Face: Large face, straight hairline, square chin, and cheekbones not particularly prominent (Figure 1.16)

FIGURE 1.15: MULLER-LYER ILLUSION

FIGURE 1.16: SQUARE FACE SHAPE

Diamond Face: Smaller in the chin and forehead (Figure 1.17)

FIGURE 1.17: DIAMOND FACE SHAPE

Oval Face: Evenly spaced (Figure 1.19)

FIGURE 1.19: OVAL FACE SHAPE

Heart Face: Larger on the forehead and smaller at the chin (Figure 1.18)

FIGURE 1.18: HEART FACE SHAPE

Round Face: No strong angle, widest at the cheekbones (Figure 1.20)

FIGURE 1.20: ROUND FACE SHAPE

Eye Shapes

Eyes can be categorized into six basic shapes:

Even-Set, or Balanced, Eyes: Equals one eye length apart (Figure 1.21). This is the eye shape that is considered the "perfect" one aesthetically. You can do almost anything with the even-set eye, and not be concerned with corrective makeup.

Wide-Set Eyes: Are spaced farther apart than the length of the eye (Figure 1.22). To bring the eyes closer together, place a dark color on the inside inner corner of the eye.

FIGURE 1.22: WIDE SET WITH DARK COLOR APPLIED

Deep-Set Eyes: Are recessed farther into the eye socket (Figure 1.23). To bring them out, place a lighter-colored shadow on the

upper lids. Use medium rather than dark colors in the eye crease. Less is more with this eye shape.

FIGURE 1.23: DEEP SET WITH LIGHT COLOR APPLIED

Large Eyes: Will in some cases need to look smaller (Figure 1.24). A large eye conveys surprise and/or shock, which we will cover later in our discussion of facial expression. To make the eye appear smaller, use dark colors on the eyelid and eye crease.

FIGURE 1.24: LARGE EYE WITH EXAMPLE OF MAKING IT SMALLER

Round Eyes: Can handle most colors (Figure 1.25). The eyeliner will need to be adjusted if you have to make the eye look more almond-shaped. Place eye-shadow color on the eyelid, blending up at the outside corners. You can also place a dark color on the outer top corner.

FIGURE 1.25: ROUND EYE WITH COLOR

Small Eyes: Need light-colored shadow to open them up (Figure 1.26). Dark colors will only make them smaller. To give the illusion of a larger eye, use a light color on the eyelid, and medium color in the eye crease. Again, less is more.

FIGURE 1.26: SMALL EYE WITH COLOR

Lip Shapes

Full lips are considered the perfect aesthetic. There are situations where you will have to create the illusion of smaller lips. To do this, apply lip liner just inside the natural lip line (Figure 1.27).

FIGURE 1.27: FULL LIPS MADE SMALLER

Choose a liner that is close in tone to the lip tone, or match to the lipstick. Lipstick colors should be medium to dark.

Thin lips can be made larger by applying lip pencil to just outside the natural lip line (Figure 1.28). The farther out you place the line, the larger the lip, but take care to check the symmetry of your work. This is an area in which, if things are not done properly, the illusion does not work. Choose a lip pencil that corresponds to the lipstick color or slightly darker. Powder the lip pencil before and after the application of lipstick. This will set the "new" lip line, as well as help keep the makeup from bleeding. Lipstick colors in light to medium tones are used to create larger lips, as well as all-red tones.

FIGURE 1.28: THIN LIPS MADE LARGER

To create an even lip shape on someone with a thin upper lip, apply lip pencil on or just above the top lip line (Figure 1.29). Then line the bottom lip at the lip line. Use powder to set, and then apply lip color.

FIGURE 1.29: TO CORRECT THIN UPPER LIP

To balance a thin bottom lip with the top lip, do the reverse (Figure 1.30). Line the top lip at the natural lip line. Line the bottom lip past the natural lip line to create balance and symmetry. Again powder to set your "new" lines.

What if you do not need or want to change the lip shape? In this case, apply lip liner right at the natural lip line and fill in with lip color. You do not need to powder, because you have not changed the natural line. However, if it is a kissing scene you should powder the lips to set the makeup, or use a lip stain.

Drawing Lessons

The more often you practice drawing skills, the better you'll translate that into makeup applications. Learn to see faces as planes, edges, and shadows or a living sculpture. The first lesson is a basic exercise in observation and letting go—two skills that a Makeup Artist will use often. Lessons Three and Four will train your mind to see faces and objects as shapes. When working with any of these lessons, you never want to erase.

Lesson One: Contour Drawing

This lesson should be repeated using a different part of the body each time (hand, torso, arms, and so on).

1. Choose a face or figure. (Use a live model.)

2. While staring at the model, put your pencil down onto the drawing paper at the point where you want to start.

3. Follow the edge of the form with your pencil (without lifting the pencil) onto your paper without looking down at what you are drawing.

4. After moving around the edges of the object, move your pencil inside the object. Draw the contours and planes of the inside features without lifting your pencil.

5. Now look down at your work. Add shadows or highlights to your drawing.

Lesson Two: Contour Drawing

1. Choose a few (three or four) photos of faces from a magazine.

2. Repeating the steps in Lesson One, do a contour drawing of each photo.

3. Using carbon paper, transfer each drawing that you finish onto a clean sheet of paper, overlaying each drawing on top of the other, creating your own design.

4. When you are done with step 3, fill in any shadows, highlights, or textures around and inside the drawings.

Lesson Three: Shadows

This lesson will enable you to see faces and objects in different shapes created by light and dark.

1. Find a photo of an interesting face with a lot of contrast.

2. On a clean sheet of paper, re-create the face in the photo using only the shapes of the shadows and highlights. Try not to use any lines. If this is difficult, you can work on one area of the face at a time (nose, eyes, lips, chin, and so on).

Lesson Four: Shadows

1. Take a cloth of some sort—for example, a light-colored sheet.

2. Bunch the sheet up into peaks and valleys.

3. Set a simple light source over the sheet.

4. Observe how the cloth looks under the light. Where do the shadows fall with each crease?

5. With a pencil, draw the sheet using simple outlines and only shadows, filling up the entire paper. Your design should go off the edges of the paper. At the end, your material may have a look of fluid movement or even resemble a mountaintop.

References

Barcsay, J., 2006. Anatomy for the Artist. In: The Center of Gravity. Sterling, New York.

Fehér, G., 2006. Cyclopedia Anatomicae. Black Dog and Leventhal, New York.

Gheno, D., www.dangheno.net (adapted from Starting a Figure Drawing from Life. American Artist 17).

Jusko, D., Human Proportions and Painting. www.realcolorwheel.com.

McNeill, D., 1998. Constellation of Desire, The Skin Code. Little, Brown, Boston.

2

THE BODY

Anatomy is important for the Makeup Artist. Makeup Artists who are asked to create anything that is directly related to the human body will study the vascular, muscular, and skeletal systems to correctly interpret how the makeup or appliance will be executed. The muscles that help form facial expressions, support the skeletal system, and protect internal organs are as important to the Makeup Artist as how the body moves and the center of gravity. Understanding the vascular system adds to our knowledge of how to achieve realistic trauma. There are countless books on the subject, and we highly recommend owning a collection of anatomy books as well as medical reference books.

Anatomy is the study of the human body. The skeletal system is the physical foundation of the body, with 206 bones of different sizes and shapes. The skeleton is for the most part moved by muscles acting as levers. Bones can be classified as long, short, or flat. Joints are two or more bones that fit together. Facial bones determine the high and low planes of the face—characteristics that make us all different from each other. The primary function of the skeletal system is to support the body, protect internal organs, serve as attachments for muscles, produce white and red blood cells, and store calcium. The skeletal system is divided into two different areas: axial and appendicular. The axial makes up the skull, vertebral column, sternum, and ribs. The appendicular is made up of the upper and lower extremities.

The skull of the skeleton is also divided into two parts: the cranium, which protects the brain and has 8 bones, and the facial skeleton, which is made up of 14 bones.

Figures 2.1 and 2.2 show the surface anatomy of the face, and Figure 2.3 shows the skeletal system.

FIGURE 2.1: FACIAL SURFACE ANATOMY
Photographer Darrell Peterson, copyright 2005, Elsevier, all rights reserved

FIGURE 2.2: SKULL SURFACE ANATOMY
Photographer Darrell Peterson, copyright 2005, Elsevier, all rights reserved

Anterior View

19

FIGURE 2.3: SKELETAL SYSTEM

© 2007 Wolters Kluwer Health/Lippincott, Williams & Wilkins

The Bones of the Cranium

Occipital: The hindmost bone of the skull. Forms the back of the head above the nape.

Parietal: Two bones that form the sides and crown of the cranium.

Frontal: Forms the forehead.

Temporal: Two bones that form the sides of the head by the ears.

Ethmoid: Between the eye sockets. Forms part of the nasal cavities.

Sphenoid: Joins all the cranium bones together.

The Bones of the Face

Nasal: Two bones that form the bridge of the nose.

Lacrimal: These two bones make up the eye sockets.

Zygomatic (or Malar): The two cheekbones.

Maxillae: Two bones that form the upper jaw.

Mandible: The lower jaw, the largest and strongest facial bone.

The Muscular System

There are over 600 muscles in the muscular system (Figure 2.4). Muscles are divided into three classes: cardiac, striated (skeletal), and nonstriated (smooth). We deal only with the striated or skeleton muscles that are attached to bones and controlled by will.

Ligaments (which hold the bones together) and tendons (which are connectors between the bones and the muscles) help aid muscles to execute movement. Origin is where the muscle is attached to bones that do not move. Insertion is where a muscle is attached to a movable bone.

Vascular System

The vascular system (Figure 2.3) is a set of complex veins that transport blood to and from the heart, transport oxygenated blood from the lungs to the heart, and drain blood from the intestines and the supporting organs. The cardiovascular system is made of heart and blood vessels, arteries, veins, and capillaries that together comprise the circulatory system. Pulmonary circulation sends blood on a path from the heart to the lungs and back again, and the systemic circulation sends blood from the heart to other parts of the body and back again.

Facial Muscles and Expression

Facial expressions are universal. The six basic facials codes are enjoyment, anger, fear, surprise, disgust, and sadness. Makeup Artists are often asked to reproduce these emotions with the use of makeup. The facial muscles come into play by forming these expressions. Changing or reshaping the eyebrow, adding a highlighter or shadow in the right place, can give off different emotional signals.

Facial muscles are formed in four different groups: scalp and facial muscles, eye and eye socket muscles, mouth muscles, and jaw muscles.

Six Facial Codes

Enjoyment (Figure 2.6): A smile employs two muscles. The zygomatic major curves the mouth, and the orbicularis oculi raises the cheeks. The cheeks, in turn, press the skin toward the eye, causing a squint. Eyes appear brighter.

Anger (Figure 2.7): The person appears to be in deep concentration. Eyebrows appear to have moved downward, and the lips look pursed (orbicularis oris muscle). When angry, the blood can rush to the face. A flushing of redness can occur.

Key: Muscles of Anterior Torso

1. Subclavius m.
2. External intercostal mm.
3. External intercostal membranes
4. Pectoralis minor m.
5. Serratus anterior m.
6. Pectoralis major m.
7. Rectus sheath (anterior layer)
8. Rectus abdominis m.
9. External abdominal oblique m.
10. Internal abdominal oblique m.
11. Transversus abdominis m.
12. Transversalis fascia
13. Intervoveolar m.
14. Pyramidalis m.
15. Inguinal l.
16. Linea alba
17. Aponeurosis of external abdominal oblique m.
18. Superficial fascia
19. Intercrural fibers
20. Superficial inguinal ring
21. Flexor carpi radialis m.
22. Palmaris longus m.
23. Flexor carpi ulnaris m.
24. Flexor digitorum superficialis m.

Anterior View

Galea aponeurotica
Frontalis m.
Temporalis m.
Orbicularis oculi m.:
Orbital part
Palpebral part
Levator labii superioris m.
Zygomaticus minor m.
Zygomaticus major m.
Procerus m.
Nasalis m.
Depressor septi m.
Levator anguli oris m.
Masseter m.
Thyrohyoid m.
Sternohyoid m.
Levator scapulae m.
Omohyoid m. (superior belly)
Middle scalene m.
Sternocleidomastoid m.
Trapezius m.
Omohyoid m. (inferior belly)
Subscapular m.
Biceps brachii m.:
Long head
Short head
Coracobrachialis m.
Teres major m.
Deltoid m.
Latissimus dorsi m.
Triceps brachii m.:
Long head
Medial head
Lateral head
Biceps brachii m.
Brachialis m.
Bicipital aponeurosis
Brachioradialis m. (cut)
Common flexor t.:
Pronator teres (cut)
Flexor carpi radialis (cut)
Palmaris longus (cut)
Supinator m.
Extensor carpi radialis longus m.
Flexor digitorum profundus m.
Flexor carpi ulnaris m.
Flexor digitorum superficialis m.
Flexor pollicis longus m.
Flexor retinaculum

Zygomaticus major m.
Levator labii superioris alaeque nasi m.
Orbicularis oris m.
Buccinator m.
Risorius m.
Depressor anguli oris m.
Mentalis m.
Depressor labii inferioris m.
Platysma m.

Deltoid m.

Coracobrachialis m.
Latissimus dorsi m.
Triceps brachii m.:
Long head
Medial head
Lateral head
Brachialis m.
Biceps brachii m.

Brachialis m.
Bicipital aponeurosis
Supinator m.
Biceps brachii t.
Brachioradialis m.
Pronator teres m.
Extensor carpi radialis longus m.
Flexor pollicis longus m.
Abductor pollicis longus m.
Pronator quadratus m.
Flexor retinaculum

Gluteus medius m.
Sartorius m.
Tensor fasciae latae m.
Pectineus m.
Adductor mm.:
Brevis
Longus
Magnus

Gluteus medius m.
Tensor fasciae latae m. (cut)
Gluteus minimus m. (cut)
Sartorius m. (cut)
Rectus femoris m. (cut)
Iliopsoas m.
Pectineus m.

Vastus lateralis m.
Gracilis m.
Rectus femoris m.
Vastus medialis m.

Vastus intermedius m.
Vastus lateralis m.
Rectus femoris m. (cut)
Vastus medialis m.

Iliotibial tract (cut)

Patellar l.

Tibialis anterior m.

Tibialis anterior m.

Gastrocnemius m.

Gastrocnemius m.
Soleus m.
Extensor digitorum longus m.
Peroneus longus m.
Peroneus brevis m.
Extensor hallucis longus m.
Superior extensor retinaculum
Extensor digitorum longus tt.
Peroneus tertius t.
Peroneus brevis t.

Soleus m.
Flexor digitorum longus m.
Flexor hallucis longus m.
Achilles tendon

Inferior extensor retinaculum
Extensor hallucis brevis m.
Extensor digitorum brevis m.

Key: Abbreviations
Ligament—l.
Ligaments—ll.
Muscle—m.
Muscles—mm.
Tendon—t.
Tendons—tt.
Vertebrae:
Cervical—C
Thoracic—T
Lumbar—L

FIGURE 2.4: MUSCULAR SYSTEM

THE BODY

Key: Central Figure

1. Parietal pleura
2. Right internal thoracic a. & v.
3. Right brachiocephalic v.
4. Brachiocephalic trunk
5. Left common carotid a.
6. Superior vena cava
7. Pericardium
8. Ascending aorta
9. Pulmonary trunk
10. Left pulmonary a.
11. Right lung
12. Right atrium and auricle
13. Left auricle
14. Left pulmonary vv.
15. Right coronary a.
16. Anterior interventricular a.
17. Diaphragm
18. Hepatic vv.
19. Inferior vena cava
20. Inferior phrenic aa.
21. Superior suprarenal aa.
22. Right suprarenal gland
23. Middle and inferior suprarenal aa.
24. Right kidney
25. Testicular aa. & vv.
26. 10th rib
27. Abdominal aorta
28. Inferior mesenteric a.
29. Ascending lumbar v.
30. Common iliac aa. & vv.
31. Anterior superior iliac spine
32. Iliacus muscle

Key: Central Figure (continued)

33. Iliolumbar a. & v.
34. Internal iliac a. & v.
35. Deep circumflex iliac a.
36. Superior vesicle a.
37. Urinary bladder
38. Cremasteric a.
39. Obturator a.
40. Spermatic cord
41. Esophagus
42. Spleen
43. Aortic hiatus
44. Celiac trunk
45. Superior mesenteric a.
46. Left renal a.
47. Ureter
48. Quadratus lumborum muscle
49. 4th lumbar a. & v.
50. Middle sacral a.
51. Superior gluteal a. & v.
52. External iliac a. & v.
53. Inguinal ligament
54. Inferior epigastric a.
55. Superficial circumflex iliac a. & v.
56. External pudendal aa. & vv.
57. Internal pudendal a. & v.
58. Deep dorsal v. and dorsal a. of penis
59. Pampiniform venous plexus
60. Testicle

FIGURE 2.5: VASCULAR SYSTEM

FIGURE 2.6: ENJOYMENT

FIGURE 2.7: ANGER

FIGURE 2.8: FEAR

Fear (Figure 2.8): Eyes are wide and eyebrows lifted toward each other. Lips pull back (buccinator muscle) and even tremble. Lips can be dry. In terror, nostrils dilate, pupils widen, and perspiration appears on the forehead.

FIGURE 2.9: SURPRISE

Surprise (Figure 2.9): Surprise is a lot like fear except that, for the seconds before fear takes over, the eyes and mouth open (temporalis muscle working with the masseter muscle), and the eyebrows arch (frontalis muscle). Surprise began as a protective measure. We humans raise our eyebrows.

Disgust (Figure 2.10): The mouth can open slightly. The nose can turn up slightly and wrinkle (procerus muscle), as if to acknowledge something foul.

Sadness (Figure 2.11): The face seems to sag. Wrinkles on the mid-forehead, eyebrows droop, and the corners of the mouth go down (triangularis muscle).

(From *The Face: A Natural History*, by Daniel McNeill.)

FIGURE 2.10: DISGUST

FIGURE 2.11: SADNESS

Skin

The skin (Figure 2.12) is the largest organ we have, weighing in around six pounds. The skin is made up of several layers. The outer layer is the epidermis, which protects us from disease and dehydration. The next layer is the dermis, which contains blood vessels, nerve endings, and glands. Beneath all of that, let's not forget the subcutaneous layer, which has connective tissues and fat, maintaining body heat and storing energy.

Wounds and diseases also play a big part for the Makeup Artist. It becomes clear why it is important to study the human body. Having medical books of all kinds is a valuable tool for research. Not only should you know the medical explanation of wounds or diseases, but also the scene or environment that caused the wound or disease in the first place. With that knowledge, you can then decide what products you will use and how to execute realistic makeup. The following touches on only a few examples of wounds and diseases that involve anatomy and the Makeup Artist.

Shock: A term used for tissue and organ failure. There are three forms of shock. All have three stages. Stage one symptoms include cold, pale skin, and rapid heartbeat. Stage two symptoms include weak pulse and cold, clammy skin. Stage three is unconsciousness, shallow breathing, and rapid falling of blood pressure.

Disease: Can be caused by a number of environmental conditions or behaviors (e.g., exposure to people carrying infection, smoking, drug use) or be related to inherent characteristics beyond the individual's control (e.g., age, gender). There are times when a disease has no known cause. When metabolism or cells change, symptoms can occur that, in turn, make a person aware that a disease is present. Most often a disease goes through stages, such as starting with exposure and ending with remission or full recovery.

Allergies: Can be caused by airborne irritants. Symptoms can include sneezing, watery eyes, itchy throat, headaches, sore red eyes, runny nose, and dark circles under the eyes.

Anthrax: A bacterial infection. Inhalation of anthrax symptoms are fever and nausea with flu-like symptoms. Breathing can be difficult. Intestinal anthrax symptoms are fever, nausea, decreased appetite, and abdominal pain. Cutaneous anthrax is characterized by small, elevated, itchy lesions.

Facial Skin Disorders

As a Makeup Artist, you'll need to recognize skin disorders and what is the best method for correcting or camouflaging the surface of the skin. Using an airbrush works well for many of the following situations because you will have less contact with the surface of the skin. It also reduces the amount of rubbing and blending that can irritate already sensitive skin. Skin disorders that cause the skin's surface to be dry and flaky will also benefit from less rubbing when using an airbrush. Bradley Look explains how to address selected skin disorders.

Port-Wine Stain (Nevus Flammeus): Flat, irregular red to purple patches. Starts out as a smooth surface, but can become an uneven, bumpy texture. Most often will darken with age.

Free nerve ending
Hair shaft
Epidermis
Pore of eccrine gland
Stratum corneum
Stratum lucidum
Stratum granulosum
Stratum spinosum
Stratum basale
Epidermal rete ridge
Dermal papillae
Melanocyte
Krause's and bulb
Meissner's corpuscle
Sebaceous gland
Ruffini corpuscle
Arrector pili muscle
Elastic fibers
Dermis
Outer root sheath
Inner root sheath
Matrix cells
Eccrine gland
Hair papilla

2 5

Sensory nerve fibers (myelinated)

Subcutaneous tissue
Artery
Vein
Vater-Pacini corpuscle
Muscle
Autonomic nerve fiber (unmyelinated)

FIGURE 2.12: ILLUSTRATION OF FINE DETAILS OF SKIN
© 2007 Wolters Kluwer Health/Lippincott, Williams & Wilkins

Bradley Look: To camouflage port-wine stains, mix a mint green adjuster into a base color. Lightly haze the area, letting the edge trail off. Let this dry before covering the affected area and the surrounding skin with foundation. If there is still some bleed-through of the port-wine stain, use Michael Davy's Airbrush Grade Prosthetic Cosmetic 2, which has double the amount of pigmentation.

Psoriasis: An ongoing disease with periods of remission. Dry, flaky scales, or thickened skin around lesions can be itchy and painful.

Bradley Look: To camouflage psoriasis, stipple a light layer of rubber mask grease over the affected area. Lightly powder to set. Using an airbrush, lightly cover the area with several light passes of airbrush product. Since psoriasis is notably seen only on the elbows and knees, additional body makeup might be required using the same technique if the condition is visible elsewhere on the talent.

Rosacea: Common among people with a Celtic background. Rosacea has a butterfly-like redness over the nose and cheek area. People most often mistake rosacea for acne.

Bradley Look: To camouflage rosacea, use a similar technique to the one outlined for port-wine stain.

Scars: Usually thick and pink with a smooth texture. Over time, scars should fade to a very pale white. Scars are broken down into two types: indented or protruding.

Bradley Look: For the indented scar, using a tattoo palette, apply a highlight (slightly paler than the skin tone) around the edge of the scar. Next, around the area of highlight, apply slightly darker tone than the skin color. By the creative use of highlights and shadow, you are attempting to make the scar appear less indented. Afterward, spray over with appropriate foundation color. For a protruding scar, apply tattoo palette colors in the exact opposite order as listed above. Shadow is applied to the edge of the scar and blended outward. Foundation is then airbrushed over the entire area. Note: A hypertrophy scar can be toned down using makeup; the 3-D dimension is still quite visible if not properly lit.

Vitiligo: Complete loss of pigment over time. There is often a splotchy look to the skin. In fair skin, it is often not very noticeable, but it is disfiguring to darker skin tones.

Bradley Look: To camouflage vitiligo, airbrush a medium flesh tone over the area. Next, lightly airbrush the foundation color over the affected area and the rest of the face.

Viral, Bacterial, and Other Disorders

Conjunctivitis: Bacterial infection of the eyes. Symptoms are pain, tearing, and redness with fluid discharge of the eyes.

Meningitis: Bacterial infection of the meninges, which are the delicate membranes that cover the brain and spinal cord. Symptoms can include fever, severe headache, stiff neck and shoulders, a dark red or purplish rash anywhere on the body, mental confusion, vomiting, and sensitivity to bright light.

Tuberculosis: Bacterial infection in which bacilli are deposited in the lungs. Symptoms are fatigue, weight loss, night sweats, and weakness. A cough may also be present.

Tetanus: Bacterial infection caused by open cuts and wounds having contact with infected soils, dust, and other agents that cause infection at the site of the wound. Unchecked, the infection will enter the bloodstream, causing painful, deep-muscle spasms.

Pneumonia: Bacterial infection. Pneumonia is the most dangerous to the very young and the elderly. Coughing, fever, chills, deep chest pain, wheezing, and fatigue are some of the most common symptoms.

Herpes Zoster: Viral infection. Symptoms are small, painful red skin lesions that develop along the nerve path.

HIV (Human Immunodeficiency Virus): Virus is passed by blood-to-blood and/or sexual contact.

Mumps: Viral disease characterized by swelling and tender parotid gland and salivary glands.

Leukemia: Blood disorder. No one knows the cause of this disease, although genetics, environment, and the immune system might play a part. Symptoms include paleness, high fever, abnormal bleeding, and weight loss. As the disease progresses, the symptoms become more severe, including infections, organ enlargement, and tender bones.

Rubella: Viral disease. A rash forms on the face, and then quickly spreads to the rest of the body.

Smallpox: Viral disease. A rash forms on the face, spreading to the trunk of the body. Lesions form inside the mouth and nose.

Chicken Pox: Viral disease. A small rash forms that turns into papules.

Environmental Conditions

Frostbite: Freezing of body parts, mostly nose, fingers, and toes. Frostbite has three different stages. The first stage is pain with itching, and sometimes swelling. The second stage is marked by blisters that can turn black. In the third stage, redness and deep purple colors, severe blisters, and sometimes loss of extremities in the affected area are observed.

Heat Exhaustion: Occurs after exposure to heat for long periods of time. There is also a loss of fluids. Symptoms include fatigue, nausea with vomiting, sweating, and headache.

Heatstroke: Elevated body temperature. Symptoms include red skin, no sweating, elevated body temperature, difficulty breathing, confusion, seizure, and possible coma.

Anatomy Terms

Anatomy is a complex field, but we'll concentrate on the areas that Makeup Artists most likely will use as references. The following terms outline only a few components of the skeletal, muscular, and circulatory systems.

The Skeletal System
The skeleton is divided into two different areas. The axial is made up of the skull, vertebral column, sternum, and ribs.

The appendicular skeleton is made up of the upper and lower extremities. The skull is divided into cranial bones. These bones form the cranial cavity. The cranial cavity houses the brain and facial bones, which, in turn, form the face.

The Skull
Frontal Bone: Bone located at the forehead. Helps define the orbits of the eye.

Mandible: The lower jawbone.

Maxillae: The upper jawbones.

Nasal Bones: There are two nasal bones. The vomer bone separates the nasal cavities.

Occipital Bone: Large bone that makes up the base of the cranium.

Zygomatic Arch: Bone that defines the cheekbone.

Spinal Column
The spinal column is made up of 26 bones. The bones protect the spinal cord. The spinal column is strong and flexible—allowing movement, supporting the head, and serving as the attachment for the ribs and muscles.

Upper Body
Clavicle: Collarbone.

Scapula: Along with the humerus, forms the shoulder joint.

Ribs: Curved bones connected to the thoracic vertebrae.

Sternum: Breast bone.

Humerus: Upper arm bone.

Radius: One of two lower arm bones. The radius is narrow at the end that connects with the humerus, and wider at the joints it forms with the wrist bones.

Ulna: One of two lower arm bones opposite in shape to the radius.

Carpal Bones: Wrist bones.

Metacarpals: Hand bones.

Phalanges: Finger bones.

Lower Body

Pelvic Bone: Attaches the lower body to the axial skeleton.

Femur: Thigh bone. It is the strongest bone in the body.

Patella: Kneecap.

Tibia: The larger of the two bones that form the lower leg bone.

Fibula: The smaller of the two bones that form the lower leg bone.

Tarsals: Ankle bones.

Metatarsals: Foot bones.

Phalanges: Toes.

Joints: Where two or more bones come together to either aid movement and/or keep the skeleton together.

The Muscular System

Muscles are described by size, shape, origin, and function. There are over 700 known muscles in the body. A number of facial muscle categories are mentioned here.

Jaw Muscles

Masseter: Raises the jaw and clenches the teeth.

Temporalis: Helps the masseter muscle to raise the jaw and clench the teeth.

Mouth Muscles

Buccinator: Draws the corners of the mouth backward, flattens and tightens the lips.

Caninus: Raises the corner of the mouth.

Mentalis: Raises and tightens the chin, thrusts the lower lip up and outward.

Orbicularis Oris: Circles the mouth and purses the lips.

Risorius: Pulls the corner of the mouth sideward and outward.

Triangularis: Pulls the corner of the mouth downward.

Zygomaticus Major and Minor: Muscles that raise the mouth upward and outward.

Eye Muscles

Corrugator: Assists the orbicularis muscles in compressing skin between the eyebrows. Vertical wrinkles form.

Orbicularis Oculi: Closes the eyelids and compresses the opening of the eye from above and below.

Procerus: Tightens the inner eye by wrinkling the skin on the nose.

Face Muscle

Frontalis (Frontal Part): Draws the scalp to the front, wrinkles the forehead, and pulls the eyebrows upward.

Platysma: Neck muscle that draws the lower lip downward and upward.

Circulatory System and Veins

The circulatory system is made up of two subsystems. In the pulmonary system, the right side of the heart receives deoxygenated blood from the rest of the body and pumps it to the lungs. In the vascular system, the left side of the heart receives oxygenated blood from the lungs and sends it to the rest of the body. Arteries carry blood from the heart to the tissues and organs. Veins return the blood to the heart.

Arteries

Aorta: Largest artery in the body.

Coronary Arteries: Supply blood to the heart.

Brachiocephalic Trunk, Right Carotid Artery, and Right Subclavian Artery: Provide blood to the neck, head, and upper limbs.

Left Carotid and Left Subclavian Arteries: Provide blood to the left side of the head, neck, and upper limbs.

Celiac Trunk, Superior Mesenteric Artery, and Inferior Mesenteric Artery: Supply blood to the abdominal internal organs.

Renal Arteries, Suprarenal Arteries, and Gonadal Arteries: Provide blood to internal organs at the back of the abdominal wall.

Left and Right Common Iliac Arteries: The abdominal aorta divides into left and right common iliac arteries.

Veins

Superior Vena Cava: Receives blood from the upper body by way of the internal jugular, subclavian, and brachiocephalic veins.

Internal Jugular: Receives blood from the head and neck area, including the brain.

Subclavian: Empties blood from the shoulder area.

Brachiocephalic: One of two veins that form the superior vena cava.

Inferior Vena Cava: Receives blood from the pelvis, abdomen, and lower limbs.

Portal System: A set of veins that deplete blood from the intestines and the supporting organs.

Hepatic Portal Vein: Vein that leads from the intestinal veins to the liver.

Splenic Vein: Vein leaving the spleen.

Superior Mesenteric: Blood returns to circulation through this vein by way of the small intestine.

Anatomy Lessons

It is difficult to constantly memorize and remember every bone and muscle in the body, not even counting the vascular system. But learning the basics and having those references to remind you of the correct placement of bones and muscles are important. The first two lessons are important because the more often you look at and write down a term, the faster you'll start to recognize it.

Lesson One: The Skeletal System

1. Find an unlabeled drawing, photo, or chart of the skeletal system.

2. Make a copy of the unlabeled skeletal system to write on.

3. List the bones correctly on your copy of the unlabeled chart, checking your answers from the labeled skeletal system chart in Figure 2.3. You need to list only the basic bone structures: skull, neck, shoulders, arms, chest, wrist, fingers, legs, ankles, feet, toes, and so on.

Lesson Two: The Facial Bones

1. Find an unlabeled drawing, photo, or chart of the facial bone structure.

2. Make a copy of the unlabeled facial bone structure to write on.

3. List the basic facial bone structures on your copy of the unlabeled chart, checking your answers using the labeled facial charts in Figures 2.1 and 2.2.

Lesson Three: Facial Muscles

1. Find three or four photos of interesting faces with different expressions.

2. Make copies of each of the photos.

3. List the correct facial muscle(s) on the photo that is/are causing the expression in the photo (e.g., crying, laughing, being scared, and so on).

4. Repeat step 3 for each of the photos.

Lesson Four: Body Wounds

This lesson can be done over time to get what you want. Using a camera, take pictures of several different types of wounds. You can also use photographs found in magazines or medical books.

1. Observe up close what the shapes, sizes, colors, and textures are for each wound.

2. Write down where the wound is located on the body, using the correct medical terms to describe the location (e.g., "The scratches are located on the epidermis in the torso area").

The idea of this lesson is for you to start looking at wounds or illnesses in terms of colors, shapes, and textures instead of by what you think you already know. Starting a logbook for future reference is always a good idea. At the end of one year, review your book. It may include some of the following wounds:

- Bruises (new, a few days old, a week later)
- Scratches (new and old)
- Cuts (new and old)
- Scars
- Blisters

References

(Contributors) Cheryl A. Bean, Peggy Bozarth, Yvette P. Conley, Lillian Craig, Shelba Durston, Ken W. Edmisson, William F. Galvin, Deborah A. Hanes, Joanne Konick-McMahan, Lt. Manuel D. Leal, Dawna Martich, E. Ann Myers, Sundaram V. Ramanan, Barbara L. Sauls, Janet Somlyay, Sandra M Waguespack.

Alcamo, I.E., 2003. Anatomy Coloring Workbook I, second ed. Princetonreview, New York.

Anatomical Chart Company, Springhouse, 2006. Atlas of Pathophysiology, second ed. Lippincott, Williams & Wilkins, Philadelphia.

Barcsay, J., 2006. Anatomy for the Artist. Sterling, New York.

DiMaio, V.J.M., 1998. Gunshot Wounds: Practical Aspects of Firearms, Ballistics and Forensic Techniques, second ed. CRC Press, Boca Raton, FL.

Fehér, G., 2006. Cyclopedia Anatomicae. Black Dog and Leventhal, New York.

Habif, T.P., 1996. Clinical Dermatology, third ed. Mosby, St. Louis.

Look, B., 2007. How to Cover Facial Disorders.

McNeill, D., 1998. The Face: A Natural History. Back Bay Books, Boston.

MedicineNet, 2007. Frostbite. www.medicinenet.com/frostbite/page2.html.

MedicineNet, 2007. Heat Exhaustion. www.medicinenet.com/heat_exhaustion/article.html.

MedicineNet, 2007. Heatstroke. www.medicinenet.com/heatstroke/article.html.

Moses, K.P., Banks, J.C., Nava, P.B., Peterson, D., 2005. Atlas of Clinical Gross Anatomy. Mosby, St. Louis.

3

COLOR

Color is used to create a mood, enhance skin tone, design looks or characters, and correct environmental issues such as lighting and the mixing of pigments or paint.

The basics of color theory are essential for all makeup artists to know and understand. You will be using color in every makeup job you do. All aspects of makeup use color: foundations, color-correcting skin tones, lip tones, concealing tattoos, eliminating blemishes or irregularities such as birth marks or stains, painting, and color prosthetics. There will be countless times when color issues come up that you must be able to resolve. You will not be successful at problem solving unless you understand color and its functions. The wrong color choice will change everything about what you as the artist are trying to say or create with makeup, and needless to say, will not look right.

> Coloring is one of those things that you should practice a lot and develop your own way. If you only follow what someone else does, you will never improve.
>
> —Kazu

Artists can and most often do, select many palettes to work in, whether in blue tones or earth colors; the choice will depend on the mood, design, model, or actor. Color mixing takes place when two or more colors come together to form a different color. Only three basic colors are needed to create just about any other color. For this reason, these are referred to as "primary colors." In mixing paint, inks, and dyes, the subtractive method is used, and gives you the widest range of colors. The subtractive primary colors are cyan, magenta, and yellow. For example, the subtractive primary colors are the three primary colors used in all printer cartridges. Note that the three primary colors for mixing paint, ink, and dyes are not the same three primary colors that are used when mixing light. The three basic colors used for mixing light or illumination are red, green, and blue. They are called the additive primary colors.

Color mixing works for a variety of surfaces, products, and all skin tones. PAX Paint is an example of a makeup artist's use of color theory, function, and paint mixing. PAX Paint, an industry standard, is made up of a combination of Pros-Aide (an adhesive) and acrylic paints. It is used on various surfaces where there is a need for friction proofing, waterproofing, and color that will not flake or lift off.

Professional example:

You are working with an actor who is heavily tattooed, and the character should not be tattooed or the director does not want to see the tattoos. The simplest solution is for the costume cover the tattoos, but there are several scenarios when this is not possible. If the tattoos are on the arms, legs, or neck, for example, and the costumes will expose them, you will need a friction-proof and water-proof cover (Figures 3.1 and 3.2). PAX Paint is great for this; however, you will not be successful in your application if you do not understand color and color mixing. You will need to layer several colors over each other to cancel out the tattoo inks and bring skin tone back to the covered skin.

FIGURE 3.1: REAL TATTOO(S) ON MAN'S ARM

FIGURE 3.2: TATTOO COVER ON THE SAME ARM

neutral darks. Any artist who wishes to mix dark colors without black pigments can use the RCW. You could also use this color wheel to match, darken, or lighten skin tones and to find complement colors to existing colors—for example, accents to eye shadows and lipstick colors. According to Don, "It is important for an artist to know how colors relate to one another, which opposite colors will darken the existing colors, and which colors are analogous."

In this chapter, we discuss Jusko's RCW and how it relates to the Makeup Artist.

Other examples:

Are the shades positive or negative?

How can you correct and improve skin tones?

How can you block out "port wine stains" or birth marks?

How will colors look under certain lighting conditions and environments?

How will a color register on film or high-definition (HD) digital images?

How can you "counter color" correct for film or HD?

How can you color prosthetics?

You must learn the basics of color, period. In brief, you need to study color theory in detail, as it is important to your success and will enable you to excel your artistry and applications.

Sir Isaac Newton developed the first circular diagram of colors in 1666. Since then numerous variations of this concept have been designed. Differences of opinion about the validity of one format over another continue today.

Don Jusko created the Real Color Wheel (RCW, Figure 3.3), which has modernized the way we use and relate to color. In the RCW, every color has an opposite color to be used in mixing

How to Use the Color Wheel

A color wheel in this true form gives the artist a tool to create different hues and to shade them to neutral darks. The Makeup Artist would take this one step further by considering what colors would also work under different conditions, such as lights, color corrections, color grading, and so forth. The following will give you the basic language used to decipher the blending of hues.

To begin to understand how to use the color wheel, it is important to know where to start. On the RCW, the colors on the outside of the wheel are pure hues. What you can add to alter these colors is a tint with white, a tone with white and the complement color, or a shade with just the complement color. This will determine the final outcome of that color, including the addition of analogous relationships next to each other on the wheel. Always start matching or plotting a pure color from the outside of the color wheel—this is the pure hue. Finding the correct color or area of color, you can decide where to go from there. For example, if you want to find the complement of the color that you have already plotted, go to the opposite side of the color wheel. You will know the color will work. You can then tint, tone, or shade that hue to get the desired effect.

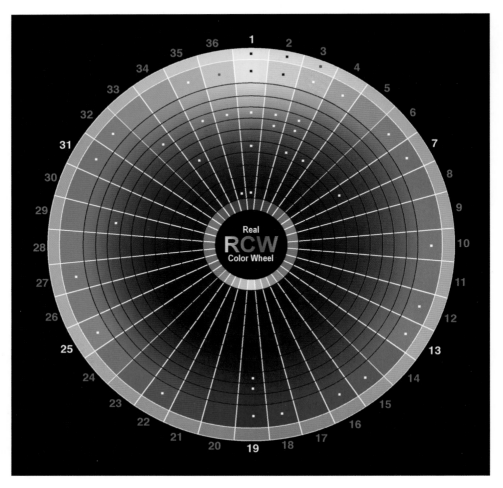

FIGURE 3.3: DON JUSKO'S RCW COLOR WHEEL

COLOR

Terms

Hue: Any color.

Primary Color (Figure 3.4): There are three primary colors. They can be mixed together to make all other colors. Transparent yellow is PY 150 or PY 153. Transparent magenta is PR 122. Transparent cyan is PB 15.

Secondary Colors (Figure 3.5): Colors that are made by mixing together two primary colors.

Red: Made by mixing yellow and magenta.

Blue: Combination of magenta and cyan.

Green: Mixture of cyan and yellow.

Tints (Figure 3.6): Made by adding white to any hue.

Dual Tone: Pigment that changes hue from mass tone to top tone. In other words, a color that changes as it gets lighter—not just in value, but in its actual color. For example, a brown color that changes to a bright yellow color is a dual tone. Purple that changes from a cool dark to a warm light is a dual tone.

FIGURE 3.4: APPLE PRIMARY COLORS

FIGURE 3.5: SECONDARY COLORS AND A WHEEL

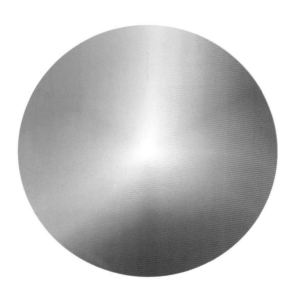

FIGURE 3.6: TINT COLOR WHEEL

Top Tone: Adding white to a color.

Mass Tone: Color right out of the tube or pure powder pigment.

Undertone: Adding clear media.

Transparent: Dyes are clear—you can see through transparent dyes.

Translucent: Milk is translucent—it can never be transparent by adding a clear medium.

Opaque: Dense, like a small rock—it cannot be seen through.

Classic color schemes will help you to decipher which way to plot a color on the color wheel.

Monochromatic (Figure 3.7): Any single color mixed with white.

Analogous (Figure 3.8): Colors next to each other on the color wheel—for example, orange and red or yellow, orange and red, or cyan and green.

Complementary (Figure 3.9): Any colors 180 degrees apart on a 360-degree wheel.

Triadic: Any three colors that are 120 degrees apart on the wheel, usually primary colors.

FIGURE 3.7: BLACK-AND-WHITE SCALE

FIGURE 3.8: DOTS OF COLOR

COLOR

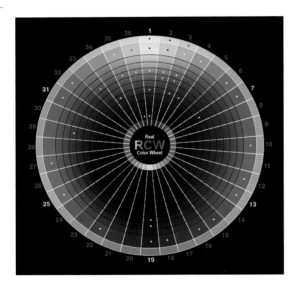

FIGURE 3.9: RCW WHEEL

Split complementary colors are formed like a Y on the color wheel—one color on each side of a complementary color. Opposition, or complementary, pigments make neutral darks. If you mix two opposite pigments, the color will result in a darker hue. This enables the Makeup Artist to work with darker pigments without using black. It is also a great way to mix pre-existing makeup when you want to form a darker

shade. Because the pigments complement each other, there will be a natural look to your work. The darker pigments will not clash against the skin tone of the person you are working on.

The following outlines the six opposition colors and the neutral darks they will generate.

- Cadmium yellow light and cadmium yellow medium are opposite ultramarine blue (Figure 3.10). Note that yellow darkens to brown. Brown and ultramarine make the neutral dark.

- Cadmium orange is opposite cobalt blue (Figure 3.11).

- Burnt sienna (Figure 3.12), which is a dark orange, is opposite cobalt blue.

- Opaque cadmium red light and red dark are opposite cyan (Figure 3.13). Cyan is also called thalo blue.

- Quinacridone magenta transparent PR122 is opposite thalo green (Figure 3.14).

- Purple is opposite yellow green (Figure 3.15). Green oxide opaque is a dark yellow green to be used as the opposition color.

The chart in Figure 3.16 illustrates how you can combine pigments to produce browns. The chart will also show you how to mix pigments that will give you cool browns or warm browns.

FIGURE 3.10: CADMIUM YELLOW LIGHT, CADMIUM YELLOW MEDIUM, ULTRAMARINE BLUE

FIGURE 3.11: CADMIUM ORANGE AND COBALT BLUE

FIGURE 3.12: BURNT SIENNA

FIGURE 3.13: OPAQUE CADMIUM RED LIGHT, CADMIUM RED DARK, AND THALO BLUE OPAQUE

FIGURE 3.14: QUINACRIDONE MAGENTA TRANSPARENT PR122 AND THALO GREEN

FIGURE 3.15: PURPLE OPPOSITE YELLOW GREEN

FIGURE 3.16: BROWN PIGMENT CHART WITH YELLOW TO BROWN NATURAL OXIDES, BOTH RAW AND BURNT

Brown neutral tones in makeup are generally complementary to most skin tones, and especially with eye shadow for a more natural look. For natural-looking makeup, a variety of neutral browns flatters and registers well for the camera. Highlighting and contouring with neutral browns has a less harsh effect. In situations where browns register darker on film, staying with neutral browns avoids having your brown registering too dark and unflattering. Remember that what you decide to use is the outcome of the problem solving for the makeup situation you have at the time. What is the skin tone? What is the lighting situation? Is this a makeup special effect? What medium is it? Are you working in theatre, film, television, HDTV, or print? Whatever the situation, knowing what pigments make brown is a plus.

Mixing Pigment for Flesh Tones

by Don Jusko

Every skin tone is unique. All the colors and ranges of colors from #1 yellow to #7 red are colors used to get skin tones. Colors from yellow to red all darken to brown, either by adding brown or by mixing brown. All skin colors have a range of 10 tints and 10 darks for each of the seven colors. To make a skin tone lighter, you will take the color already plotted and lighten it with white or yellow. To make a skin tone darker, you will take the color already plotted and darken with browns and the complement color. You can also change existing foundations or mix your own by using the color wheel.

Color Function

Usages and combinations of color greatly affect your final makeup application (Figure 3.17). You will also need to address the undertones in the skin, eyes, and lips. Color can balance, conceal, correct, or show emotion. Example: If there is too much red in the face, you can apply a green or yellow under or over the foundation to neutralize the red. You need to understand how colors function in relation to makeup artistry.

Red is one of the secondary colors. Magenta is a primary color. The complementary color to red is cyan. Red is made by mixing yellow and magenta. A cool cherry red (RCW #12.6.5) will bring life into a darker skin tone, but only if the skin tone is cool as well. Orange red will give a healthy glow to golden skin. Red is also used in makeup effects to show sun damage, alcohol abuse, windburn, crying, skin lesions and rashes, bruising and trauma to the skin, and to neutralize any gray undertones in appliances and tattoo cover-up.

Blue is a secondary color. The complement to blue is yellow. Cyan is a primary color. Blue is a combination of magenta and cyan. Blue will work with most skin tones. Blue and shades of blue should not be used for bluescreen work—it will disappear. Blue can be used in makeup to

FIGURE 3.17: TUBE PIGMENTS FOR COLOR

portray illness, death, cold, and freezing, as well as bruising of the skin.

Yellow is a primary color. The complementary color to yellow is blue. Yellow is used to add warmth to other colors. Yellow browns (gold) in eye shadows, blushers, and lipsticks flatter golden skin tones. In makeup, yellow can be use to portray illness, weakness, rotting, and bruising.

Green is a secondary color. Green is a combination of cyan and yellow. The complement color to green is magenta. Green can be cool (blue green) or warm (yellow green). In makeup, green is used to neutralize reds (for example, to tone down ruddy skin tone or broken capillaries in the face). Warm greens (with yellow added) look good on golden tones, or golden skin tones. Cool greens (with cyan or blue added) look good on cool tones, or skin with cool undertones. Green is also used in bruising and to portray illness, cold, or rotting. Green is also used to cover tattoos. Green or shades of green should not be used in greenscreen work—anything green becomes invisible.

Orange is a warm color that is between yellow and red on the RCW. The complementary color to orange is halfway between cyan and blue, called cobalt blue (RCW #22). Orange is a vibrant color that can be used as a highlighter on warm and dark skin tones. Orange is a good color to use for masking out blue, as in beard stubble and covering tattoos. Orange also will neutralize blue undertones (or blue lighting) in dark skin tones.

Violet (RCW #14) is the color between purple and magenta. Violet is a cool color. The complementary color to violet is chartreuse. Violet is used to correct too much yellow or sallowness in skin tone. Most cool skin tones look good in the color violet. In makeup, violet and combinations of violet are used for bruising, wounds, freezing, and death.

Pink is red with tint (white) added. There is a warm pink, which is a light red, and a cool pink, which is magenta. Pink is flattering to most skin tones. Magenta pink is good on cool skin tones. Warm pink (with golden tones added) looks good on warm skin tones. In makeup, pink is used in eye shadows, lipsticks, and blushers to show good health.

Black is often used to darken another color and make a shade of that color. Shading colors can also be made by mixing opposite colors together. Black mixed with white makes a neutral gray. Cool, darker skin tones tend to look good in black. In makeup, black is used in eye shadows, eyeliners, brow color, and mascara. Black can be used to add drama or depth to existing colors.

White is added to other colors to make tints. In makeup, white or off-white can be used as highlighters, or to make darker colors stand out. Cool, darker skin tones tend to look good in white.

Color Lessons

Color is one of the most important things to have a good understanding about. The more you use what you read, the easier using color becomes. Whether you use a traditional color wheel or the RCW is up to you. The lessons address using the different primary colors, but the knowledge can also be used for more traditional ways of color mixing. Just think of these color lessons as a way to mix to get even more color choices.

Lesson One: The Color Wheel

1. Using artist paper and a pencil, draw a RCW. Be sure to use the correct dimensions and straight edges. Use the RCW in Figure 3.3 for reference.

2. Paint in the correct colors on your wheel.

3. After you are done painting, number and name the wheel.

Lesson Two: Complementary Pigments Make Neutral Darks

1. Draw three simple contour drawings of an object or face.

2. Pick three of the opposition colors in Figure 3.11 to use as details, shadows, or highlights (for example, cadmium orange and cobalt blue are opposition colors).

3. Use the colors separately and mixed together to create neutral darks.

Lesson Three: Complementary Pigments Make Neutral Darks

1. Use the example from Lesson Two, but instead follow the brown pigment chart (Figure 3.16) for reference.

Lesson Four: Creating Several Skin Tones

1. On artist paper, create several skin tones by using pigments that have been tinted or darkened accordingly. Remember to use all the ranges of color from #1 yellow to #7 red.

2. Darken these colors to brown by mixing your browns.

3. When you come up with skin tones you like, write down, next to the color, the exact combination you used. This is a way to keep records for future use.

References

Jusko, D., www.realcolorwheel.com.

Jusko, D., www.realcolorwheel.com/ complementsneutral.htm.

Jusko, D., www.realcolorwheel/pigmentrcwmap. htm.

Jusko, D., www.realcolorwheel/tubecolors.htm.

4

LIGHTING

Lighting can be one of the most important tools for a Makeup Artist. It is always a good idea to know what type of lights are being applied as well as the kind of gels or filters that will be used in front of the lights or the camera lens. Makeup is often adjusted to meet those demands. Most often, if you have designed your makeup with the lighting in mind, your artistry will be enhanced by it. If you ignore the effects that lighting and color have on your makeup application, the mistakes will be obvious for all to see. It all works together and takes years to really learn, but you will get invaluable practical experience with each job. Eventually, you will recognize what colors work with the lighting situations you are in, and the more you know about lighting, filters, and gels, the better the outcome.

Before a shoot starts, ask questions of the director, the cinematographer (also known as the DP, director of photography), or the gaffer (lighting designer). If they are not available, sometimes the first AD (assistant director) can help. Of course in some jobs, you will not get the chance to ask any questions. Be observant, watch the lighting crew and camera, and ask questions when they are not busy. Most people are very happy to explain their job or situation to you. Is it a film, video, HDTV, or stage production? You should know whether you are filming indoors or outside, day or night, and what lights, filters, and gels are planned. There are so many factors, and the more you know, the better off you are. Remember, this is not a perfect world—there will be many, many times that information is not available. So know your stuff, and be ready to work out of your kit and think on your feet.

Joseph N. Tawil, president of GAMPRODUCTS, Inc., is an expert in light and color mixing. He suggests: "Often I recommend that lights be set up in the makeup room in which you can put colored gels to simulate the lighting on stage or for camera."

This is a perfect working condition, but you cannot count on it. In some productions, this will be accommodated, but it depends on the project, prep time, and—very important—the money. Lighting packages can be expensive, and so are those light bulbs.

Color Description Terms for Light

By Joseph N. Tawil, President, GAMPRODUCTS, Inc.

Hue, value, and chroma are terms from the Munsell system of color notation (published in 1905). It is a system designed for explaining color in ink and paint rather than color in light. However, the three descriptive terms are used to define the color of light, contributing more to the confusion than to the clarity of the subject. The vocabulary of color is a minefield of contradictions and confused meanings. Colorimetry is another system for describing color, and is of particular interest because it relates well to colored light. In colorimetry, the following terms are used to describe the color of light:

Dominant Wavelength (DWL): The apparent color of the light. Similar to the term "hue," meaning the apparent color (e.g., red).

Brightness: The percentage of transmission of the full spectrum of energy (similar to value). Often described as intensity.

Purity: The purity of color is similar to chroma. It describes the mixture of color of the DWL with white or the color of the source. If there is only color of the DWL, it is 100-percent pure; but if there is very little DWL in the mixture, as in a tint, the color could be as low as, say, 5-percent pure.

White: The presence of all colors in the light.

Black: Absence of all colors.

Texture: The surface properties of a color, as in shiny or matte, reflective or diffusing.

The Language of Additive and Subtractive Color Mixing

By Joseph N. Tawil, President,
GAMPRODUCTS, Inc.

Color mixing with lights is called additive color mixing (Figure 4.1). This tricolor mixing theory was proposed by Sir Thomas Young in the early 1800s, and it is the basis for all film and video color systems today. Young discovered that by mixing red, blue, and green light, he could make most of the colors in the visible spectrum. Young determined that red, green, and blue were the ideal primary colors of light because they allow for the widest variety and create a reasonable white. Red, green, and blue are three colors that are widely separated from each other. Because of this, they will combine to make many other colors, including, in the right circumstances, white.

Combining two primary colors creates a secondary color that is a complement of the third primary ("complement," as in completes). For example, by combining red and blue, you get magenta and other colors in the violet and pink range. Combining blue and green generates cyan (blue green) colors. Combing red and green creates yellow and other colors in the orange range.

Complementary colors are also called secondary colors. Violets and pinks are complementary to the primary color green because they contain red and blue. Oranges and yellows are complementary to the primary color blue because they contain red and green.

Tricolor mixing is illustrated in Figure 4.1. It is interesting to note that the complementary colors (or secondary colors) created in the additive color-mixing process—cyan, yellow, and magenta—are the primary colors of the subtractive color-mixing system. Obviously, this is not an accident, and the two theories do tie together.

Subtractive Color: Subtractive color filtering (Figure 4.2) is something all of us have experienced in elementary school, where we have mixed paints to make a variety of colors. It's possible to read art books where painters talked about mixing primaries to make different colors. The primaries are often described in these art books as red, yellow, and blue. Filmmakers, however, see the subtractive color-mixing primaries described as yellow, cyan, and magenta. Using the same language to describe primary colors in both the subtractive and additive color-mixing processes causes a great deal of confusion. Printers and filmmakers

Additive Colors (RGB)

Additive colors (RGB) create white light and the secondary colors CYM.

FIGURE 4.1: ADDITIVE COLORS

Subtractive Color Mixing

BLUE	GREEN	YELLOW	
	BLACK		
VIOLET	ORANGE		
	RED		

CYAN	GREEN	YELLOW	
	BLACK		
BLUE	RED		
	MAGENTA		

Mixing Paints   **Mixing Printers Inks**

FIGURE 4.2: SUBTRACTIVE COLOR CHART

define the subtractive primary colors more accurately as cyan, yellow, and magenta (CYM), separating them from the additive color process. In subtractive color mixing, as we mix the primary colors of paints, inks, or filter emulsion layers, the resulting color gets darker and darker, and eventually black.

Subtractive color mixing is what we do when mixing makeup pigments, as opposed to the lighting department, which will use the additive process for color mixing.

Additive Color: In the additive color-mixing process, we are adding primary colors to come to white light. In the subtractive color-mixing process, we are mixing the primary colors to come to black.

When the artist knows that the word "additive" means mixing light to get a color, and the word "subtractive" is mixing pigments (makeup), all the mystery about a light source is better understood.

Correction Filters: The primary function for correction filters is to balance to a given light source. The two points of balance most often used are 3200K (or tungsten), and daylight (usually 5600K). Most film and television is divided between the two. For example, if you are shooting in an office with sunlight coming through the window, you will want to correct for one or the other. You either warm the sunlight toward tungsten, or you raise the apparent color temperature of the incandescent to daylight. The Makeup Artist needs to understand that the light itself does not affect the makeup, but how the lights are manipulated by additive color mixing with the use of gels and filters in front of the light source does.

Fluorescent Light: This type of light is problematic because of the green spikes attributed to it. Manufacturers make two kinds of fluorescents: warm and cool. The warm leans toward tungsten, and the cool leans toward

daylight. Other problems with fluorescents are inconsistent lamp manufacturing, aging lamps that are still being used, and the fact that certain colors are always missing from the spectrum. If you find yourself on a shoot with fluorescents as a light source, and you need to match or create a specific color (let's say lipstick), take a test photo before the shoot begins.

Video Lights: Video often uses softer lights (soft boxes) for indoor interviews. Film and video usually work with HMI (hydrargyrum medium-arc iodide) if shooting outside in the daylight or with incandescent in the studio. Be prepared to make adjustments to the makeup if the actor is being moved from an interior shot to an exterior shot. There is a big difference in the visual perception of colors when incandescent lights are used inside to do your makeup, and then you go outside and shoot in daylight or with HMI lights.

If the actor is going back and forth between interior and exterior shots, and there is no time for adjustments, choose the situation that is the longest on screen, or the most important for dramatic content, for your makeup to be the best. This works for film, television, and stage.

—Gerd Mairandres, Wigmaster,
San Francisco Opera

Stage Lighting: Stage lighting uses light for different reasons. There are a wide range of colors used theatrically. When you're working in the theatre, the lighting designer is there during the technical/rehearsal period, and the color design can be discussed then.

The theatre typically uses an incandescent source unless you're looking at a xenon follow spot or HMI follow spot, which is very close to daylight, and much bluer in its energy. The makeup is decided by how bright the light will be, how large is the stage being lit, what color gels or filters are being used to light the actors or objects onstage, and how the light is used around the stage.

Photography

Still photography uses light to create greater dimension, to highlight different areas, and to reduce or magnify details. Natural light or ambient light is often used to create moods. Artificial light is used to control different shoot locations and situations. Tungsten or incandescent lighting is most common.

Whether you are shooting photographs for fashion, beauty, or editorial, the lighting, attention to detail, and understanding concepts will be very important to the final print.

Still Photography Lighting

By J.C. Cerilla

In creating an impressive photograph it is necessary that you collaborate with a great team. Photographers have a keen eye for details and an amazing photo is not created by the photographer alone. It is a group effort among different artists excelling in their own fields. I believe you are only as good as the team you work with, so I look for a makeup artist who has a keen eye for detail, is consistently conscious of the model's makeup, and always sees to it that the desired look is achieved for the photograph. Lights have different effects on makeup, so a makeup artist should always ask for and see a test photo or Polaroid. This lets you see the effect the lighting will have on your makeup and allows for any needed adjustments.

Since a key element in photography is lighting, the proper lighting is essential in achieving a great photograph and images that sell. The lighting should have a sense of balance with shadows and highlights. Facial features or objects might be highlighted to enhance the beauty of the subject or create a mood. Some photographers choose to work with a perfectly exposed image. Another lighting trick is adding reflectors or white boards on the dark side of the subject to add back some details to the shadow.

Photographers also work with different types of light modifiers, like a soft box, to change the look and feel of an image (Figures 4.3 and 4.4). The number of light strobes you use does not matter if you know how to do proper lighting. You could use all the lights that you have, but if you do not know how to properly incorporate them in your shots, they are useless.

The other key element is attention to detail. Every little detail on your image is very important for the final print. In fashion photography, the focus is mainly on the clothing, accessories, and the "look" of the model—an example would be a fashion advertising campaign (Figure 4.5). Editorial shoots are more for storytelling and are centered more on the mood of the photograph. You highlight certain features both with lighting and details to achieve a successful image.

FIGURE 4.3: SOFT BOX EXAMPLE

FIGURE 4.4: REFLECTOR BOARD

FIGURE 4.6: EDITORIAL PHOTO, J.C. CERILLA PHOTOGRAPHY

I love shooting editorials because it gives me more freedom to create (Figure 4.6). Let your imagination run wild and show your capabilities as an artist. Keep in mind that clients love a photographer with a creative vision, and the photographer loves a Makeup Artist who can contribute to that vision as part of the team.

Black-and-white photography is never outdated with its classic feel (Figure 4.7). There should be a distinguishable contrast between the shadows and the highlights in your image.

FIGURE 4.5: FASHION PHOTO, J.C. CERILLA PHOTOGRAPHY

FIGURE 4.7: BLACK-AND-WHITE PHOTO, J.C. CERILLA PHOTOGRAPHY

The main light source should be three times the power of your "fill" light: This creates more shadow on your photo, but by having a "fill" light you will still see some details on the dark areas of the image. The makeup would also require the same contrast between shadows and highlights.

Color photography on the other hand has little contrast and the lighting is more a direct source (Figure 4.8). When shooting in color, you have to know what kind of light is being used. Color temperatures differ from one light source to another. Hot lights create an orange temperature on your subject much like the sun on a clear day. Fluorescent lights tend to cast a cooler temperature like green or blue.

Remember, attitude is as important as your skill and talent! During a shoot, I need my Makeup Artist to be positive and enthusiastic. Models start their day with the Makeup Artist. If you show a bad attitude, this creates a domino effect for the rest of the day and the shoot.

Gel Filters

Gel filters (Figure 4.9) are used in front of the light source to change what the light is putting out. Lighting designers use gel filters for many different reasons. Gel filters are made of transparent plastic that is heat resistant, and they come in various translucent colors. They should not absorb

FIGURE 4.8: COLOR PHOTO, J.C. CERILLA PHOTOGRAPHY

FIGURE 4.9 FILTER COLOR WHEEL

heat, and are usually made of polyester or polycarbonate. You usually buy them in sheets or rolls. Film people tend toward rolls, theatre people toward sheets. Why gels and filters are used and what color is chosen can affect your makeup. There are also digital equivalents of lighting gels and filters created by companies such as GAMPRODUCTS, Inc. with Digital Film Tools. The following explains the color of the gels for photo cameras, film cameras, video, theatre, and digital add-ins, and what each color is most often used for, as well as how to adjust your makeup to work under these conditions.

General Breakdown of Colored Gel Filters for Light Sources

No-Color Blue: Top light for theatrical daytime. Top light in theatre tends to pale the skin tone. Areas of the face such as the eyes tend to sink or cast a shadow.

Blue Gels: Used most often to match daylight or to suggest night time. Can be used to make a light source bluer, and also used with other gels to achieve specific color temperature. If used with plus or minus green, will help correct some fluorescent or discharge sources. Used on lights and windows. Blue gels, depending on what is being shot, can have a cooling effect on the skin tone and overall makeup. Reds look like hues of violets and pinks (tints). Blues and blue greens tend to fade. Lipsticks appear darker.

Gray Gels: Used on lights where color temperature and sharp shadow or patterns must be maintained. Works as a neutralizer and will also neutralize your makeup colors.

Orange Gels: If used with appropriate amount of plus or minus green, will help correct some fluorescent or discharge sources, and can also be used to simulate sunlight. Use on light or windows. Makeup colors stay the same, but try not to layer with too many warm tones, which could create an orange face. If the person has a ruddy skin tone, add green to your makeup.

Yellow Gels: Fills for sunlight and to warm a room. Makeup stays the same, but if the person has sallow skin, use violet to add life.

Yellow Gold Gel: Warm tones, enhances skin tones. Makeup stays the same. If you have golden undertones in the skin, all the warm colors will work. If you have cool undertones, blue greens and red violets look nice.

Peach Gel: Can be used to make a light source more orange. Will enhance skin tone. Makeup stays the same. A flattering color for all skin types. Used most often for video or close-up beauty shots.

Red Gels: Used for sunsets, sunrises, fires, and to add contrast. Red fades most of your makeup. Lips appear much lighter. Greens will look darker, and violets will look black. Good to create contrast. Used most often for theatre or specialty film.

Green Gels: Used to match the green spike in fluorescent lights or discharge. Also can be used with other gels for color effect. Used on lights, windows, and to contrast. All green colors will fade. Blushers all but disappear. Lips look dark, so a lighter and brighter lipstick works. The warm tones in red orange, orange, and yellow orange look good. Blues will take on a blue green tone.

Camera Filters

By Paul Wheeler, Digital Cinematography

Camera filters are used to alter the temperature of lights, change an image, or enhance colors (Figure 4.10). The following filters can also be used in digital shooting situations:

Color-Compensating Filters (CC Filters): Come in primary colors and are used in front of the camera lens to correct light.

Color-Correction Filters: Used to correct a daylight scene when shooting with tungsten-balanced film.

FIGURE 4.10: EFFECT OF INFRARED LIGHT ON SKIN TONE
Photograph by Larry Stanley

Skin-Tone Warmers: Filters that will warm up skin tones that would appear cold otherwise.

Sepia, Coral, and Others: Filters that lend a variety of tints to a scene.

Graduated Filters: Usually come in colored or neutral density filters. These filters are used to darken or color one area of a scene without affecting the rest of the scene.

Natural-Density Filters: Used to open up the aperture at which you will shoot the scene.

Low-Contrast Filters: Reduce the overall contrast in a scene.

Ultra-Contrast Filters: Like the low-contrast filters, but work with the incident, ambient light. Ultra-contrast filters work beautifully with bringing up shadow details.

Fog Filters: Emulates fog. Images will have less definition and contrast.

Double Fog Filters: Objects near to the camera will appear less affected than those far away.

Pro Mist Filters: Give a glow around intense sources of light. Highlights become "pearlized."

Net Filters: Nets will affect the scene differently depending on the color used. A white net will diffuse highlights into shadows. Dark nets will often bleed shadows into highlights. A brown net will add richness and overall warmth.

Enhancing Filters: Bring out one color at a time without affecting any of the others. These filters affect the red and orange portions of a scene.

Fluorescent-Light (FL) Correction: The FLB filter corrects fluorescent light to type-B film or tungsten-balanced video camera. The FLD filter corrects fluorescent light to daylight camera.

Polar Screens: Screens that are used to
darken the blue portion of a sky in color
photography as well as reducing reflections in
parts of a scene.

Black-and-White Photography

Black-and-white photography with the use
of light registers color in variations of gray.
Seen this way, more attention should be given
to composition and the levels of tone that
a color will be. Tones are used with light
in black-and-white photography to portray
emotions through the lightness or darkness of
shadows. The direction of light is important
to the Makeup Artist. Front lighting will
reduce the textures and depth of the photo.
Backlighting will highlight the image and
reduce the detail. If the image is lit from the
side, it will have a greater dimension. When
shooting outdoors in direct light, shadows
will appear darker, with contrasting lights
and darks. Cloudy or misty days will soften
shadows. But this said, how the sun reacts
during a shooting day will greatly influence
your decisions. Full sun will create a harder
light, with stronger shadows and highlights.
Cloudy or partial sun has a softer look. Your
makeup could look one way in the morning
light, and another way at noon when the
sun is strongest. Be aware of this throughout
the day.

Artificial lights are used to control the brightness
of the image and for different lighting effects.
Usually tungsten or incandescent lighting is
used. These light sources can also be used in
color photography. Digital black-and-white
photography works by switching the modes
within the camera from a color liquid crystal
display (LCD) to grayscale. Pictures are
taken with color signals that are recorded by
computer-controlled display (CCD), but the
image is later processed to remove all color.
Filters are also used in all forms of black-
and-white photography. Many photographers
feel that if you have experience and expert
knowledge in black-and-white photography, you
will thrive in color photography. That is because
of the natural instincts you will develop by
working in gray tones. That theory works for the
Makeup Artist as well.

Filters Used in Black-and-White Photography

Black-and-white photography uses filters to alter
shades of gray. The following filters and their
functions will allow the Makeup Artist to adjust
makeup according to what filters are used,
whether for art's sake or for natural makeup,
when adjustments are necessary.

Red Filters: Red filters are used to add
dramatic contrast in black-and-white
photography. In color photography, red
reduces blue and green. Red filters will
enhance any red.

Yellow Filters: Will darken blues and
lighten green, yellow, orange, and red
colors.

Orange Filters: Work the same way as red
filters and yellow filters, except with less
intensity than red but more intensity than
yellow.

Green Filters: Will lighten green colors.

Blue Filters: Will lighten blues and darken
yellow, orange, and red. Works well to
enhance fog mist or haziness.

Diffusion Filters: Are used for a soft-focus
effect (as in softening wrinkles on
the face).

Optical Effect Filters: Are multi-image filters
such as star filters. These filters can bring a
soft, diffused look to the image.

Polarizing Filters: Are used in color and in black-and-white photography. Reflected sunlight is reduced, haze can be penetrated, and overall skies are darkened. Color saturation is increased. Reflections are reduced or eliminated.

Today, there is, more than ever, a growing field of technology in the world of entertainment. What a production chooses to shoot and edit with can be wide open. This technology has opened the door to new and wonderful tools to work with. One of those tools is being able to edit digitally and create the same effect that gels and filters give when used on a light source. Digital Film Lab is a unique plug-in from Digital Film Tools meant to simulate a variety of color or black-and-white photographic looks, diffusion and color-gradation camera filters, light gels, film stock, and optical lab processes. You would still apply the same principles (filter gels) on what colors to choose for makeup to better fit the digital color process it would go through later. Figures 4.11 through 4.17 show Digital Film Tools simulated color gels and filters from Digital Film Labs.

Lighting Lessons

Lighting, like color, is complex. A simple lesson in light and gels will remind the Makeup Artist why these things can affect his or her work.

Lesson One: Gel Filters

1. Take a digital camera and hold a colored gel filter up against the lens. Take a close-up picture of an object under a simple light source (for example: a plant, flower, lips, animal, or whole face).

2. Using that same object and same light source, continue to take pictures, one at a time, with the following colored gels: blue, gray, orange, yellow, red, and green.

3. Observe each picture.

4. Write down the differences that the gel filters make to the same object.

This lesson is extreme. You'll rarely have an actor pure blue or pure green because of filters. However, it does show you how your makeup should be adjusted when gel filters are being used.

FIGURE 4.11: DIGITAL PLUG FILTER, ORIGINAL
Photograph by Larry Stanley

FIGURE 4.14: COOL
Photograph by Larry Stanley

FIGURE 4.12: DIGITAL PLUG FILTER, ANTIQUE
Photograph by Larry Stanley

FIGURE 4.15: BLEACH
Photograph by Larry Stanley

FIGURE 4.13: DAY FOR NIGHT
Photograph by Larry Stanley

FIGURE 4.16: HALO
Photograph by Larry Stanley

FIGURE 4.17: (INGRY)
Photography by Larry Stanley

References

Tawil, J.N., Color Description Terms for Light. www.gamonline.com/catalog/colortheory/language.php.

Tawil, J.N., The Language of Additive and Subtractive Color Mixing. www.gamonline.com/catalog/colortheory/language.php.

Wheeler, P., 2001. Digital Cinematography. Focal Press.

Zolenski, V., 2007. Black and White Photography. www.blackboardarts.com.

Internet Resources

Cerilla, J.C., Still Photography. www.jcerilla.com.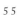

Digital Film Tools, www.digitalfilmtools.com.

GAMPRODUCTS, Inc, www.gamonline.com.

Ilford Photo, www.ilfordphoto.com.

Robin Kanta Photographic Supply, www.photofilter.com.

Stanley, L., www.montanaphotographer.com.

5

TECHNOLOGY

Makeup Artists need to be aware of what medium they are being hired to work in. Most Makeup Artists are freelance, meaning that they can work in any number of mediums in the course of a week, month, or year. Is it film, HD, TV-16 mm film, print, or theatrical? For example, a print job could be fashion, editorial, or beauty.

What are the meanings of some of the industry terms, such as digital, HD, bluescreen, greenscreen, and monitor? Our goal in this chapter is to try and help you understand the industry "tech stuff" that you will encounter as a Makeup Artist.

Today, you can and will work out of one kit for most mediums. We now share the same industry standards of products for film, print, HD, and sometimes theatre, which was not the case in the past. Technical innovations and constant product developments have greatly improved our ability to work across multiple mediums without multiple kits. It is all in the technique, skill, and application of the products. All the industry standards are multiuse products by adjusting the intensity of application and the finish. A typical week could be that your job on Monday is in HD, so you want a more matte finish for that medium. You would apply complete coverage with your foundation and powder well. On Tuesday, your job is in TV, 16-mm film, so you use the same foundation, with a sheer application and less powder. Using MAKE UP FOR EVER HD foundations as an example, you can get a wide range of coverage in multiple mediums: either full coverage with a smooth flawless finish for HD or a sheerer coverage that enhances the skin tone for film and TV, or spot painting for the most natural and undetected makeup look, with no need for powder (see Chapters 6 and 7).

Matiki Anoff uses Dr. Brandt primer Pores No More as a base when working in HD television to ensure a smooth finish and

Chanel Under Base with Shimmer over the foundations to add illumination to her HD makeup if it starts to look chalky. This is an example of using industry standards in different mediums as well as cross product use. The cross product use would be applying the Chanel over the foundation (HD use) instead of under the foundation (film use) as the product is meant to be used under foundation for retail use.

What HD Looks Like

By Paul Wheeler

High-definition (HD) images are very sharp, with long tonal ranges. Colors are lifelike and true. Whether seen on a monitor or digitally projected, there is no dirt on the pictures, no scratching, and no picture instability. Adjustments can be made with filters or within the camera menus.

With HD (Figure 5.1), one of the most obvious changes when you watch a projection by a state-of-the-art HD projector is the total lack of grain usually associated with film. However, grain can be added with filters if so desired. Images on set can be checked by real-time monitors to evaluate what your makeup looks like before the shot. A 24-inch, high-definition monitor works best.

FIGURE 5.1: DIGITAL HIGH-DEFINITION CAMERA

Makeup Department and HD

By Paul Wheeler

The relationship between a director of photography (DP), the makeup designer, and their team, I believe, has to be one of close cooperation—especially if there are prosthetics, or as so often happens in period projects, wigs. The closeness between the joint or edge of a prosthetic or lace of a hairpiece needs to be reflected in the closeness in cooperation between these two crafts.

Working on HD or film is very similar. If the HD camera utilizes ⅔-inch chips, then the DP will be restricted in the amount of diffusion that can be deployed in front of the lens in a very similar way to a Super 16-mm camera. Any form of diffusion on a ⅔-inch HD camera has to be very light. This is because diffusion has a greater effect in HD, and this makes it very difficult for the DP to find that subtle level of diffusion where the lace will disappear, but the rest of the scene will not look false. If the camera utilizes a single chip similar in size to a normal 35-mm film frame, then the ability to deploy diffusion to help with the makeup will, again, be similar—but this time the help can be greater than with the smaller-image formats.

Basically, if the makeup and hair teams are familiar with working in the 35-mm film theatrical environment, then they should have no trouble whatsoever with the HD environment. That said, a few things are easier in HD, and just a couple of things need more-careful watching.

If the production is using an HD monitor of decent quality and size on set, then the DP and makeup supervisor have a much easier task. On a well-set-up, 14-inch (or, better still, 24-inch) HD monitor, most problems can be more quickly and effectively dealt with. It's that adage of "what you see is what you get"—whereas peering down an optical viewfinder on a film camera will not tell you as much. Remember, though, neither will be quite as devastatingly critical of your work as when the image is blown up to a cinema screen. But the same has always been true of film.

Note that each frame of film has the little silver grains in slightly different places. Each pixel on an HD image is in exactly the same place on an HD image. Usually, as far as the Makeup Artist is concerned, that is not a problem—but, just occasionally, it needs watching. If the camera or the artist is moving, you can usually forget about this—but if both are static, then something like the pattern of a wig net can, very occasionally, line up with the pixel array, and the net will look awful. If spotted early on, there is no problem. Just a slight change in camera angle will usually put the aligned lines out of alignment, and all will be well.

Media Explanations

Motion Pictures in Digital: Motion pictures that are shot digitally are films in which their images are captured on digital formats. These images can be taken with any media that can use digital technology. "Digital cinematography" is a term usually used to describe when film is being substituted with digital. Cinematography digital cameras are usually progressive, high-definition formats. Cameras for digital motion pictures are becoming more and more advanced and easier to use with already-existing camera lenses for film.

Resolution in Digital: This is a little more complex than what you would assume. Each pixel of the image is partial toward red, green, or blue. The color image is taken from this pattern of colors. Film stock has a certain amount of grain in the image, which some people feel is lacking with digital pictures. However, a high-end DP knows how to light and use the correct filters to get the same images and textures of film. Color grading is often created digitally instead of using a photochemical process.

High-Definition Television: HDTV is a television broadcast using higher-resolution formats. When considering resolution, the screen and how the image is transmitted come into play. HDTV has at least twice the resolution of standard television. The picture on HDTV is clearer, with a better color spectrum.

Digital Television: DTV is a telecommunication system for broadcasting. Pictures and sound are received by digital signals. Digital television systems can carry both standard-definition and high-definition formats. Digital television can be received in different ways: aerial, pay-TV, digital cable, digital satellite, and DTV monitor.

Digital Photography: Images are captured with electronic devices that record the images in binary data. Digital photography image quality is expressed by pixel counts and the way the camera can turn data into the correct color balance.

Photographic Film: Can be polyester, nitrocellulose, or cellulose acetate. The film is coated by silver halide salts that are suspended by gelatin. When exposed to light, it forms an image. The film is put through a chemical process to expose that image.

Black-and-White Film: There is one layer of silver salts. When grains are developed, the salts are converted into metallic silver. This blocks the light and will be exposed as the black part of the negative.

Color Film: Uses three layers. Dyes are added to the silver salts, which in turn become more sensitive to color. The layers are usually blue, green, and then red. When the film is being processed, the salts turn into metallic silver, which reacts by forming colored dyes.

Print Film: Print film when processed turns into a negative. The negative can be color or black and white. Print film must be viewed by being printed on photographic paper or observed through a lens.

Bluescreen (Figure 5.2): Used often for shooting people. Skin tones (reds, yellows, and greens) are opposite of the blue background. Bluescreen works by photographing or filming an actor in front of a blue background. Shades of blue should not be used while shooting bluescreen. The blue makeup might cause a spill format in the background to appear on the surface of the face. With incorrect colors, the face can almost start to look transparent. Warm colors work best. When shooting for bluescreen, lights and gels are often used to cast off yellow, orange, and warm tones. This is all to keep the actor separated from the background.

FIGURE 5.2: BLUESCREEN
Photo by www.eefx.com Chroma Key.Screens & Supplies

FIGURE 5.3: GREENSCREEN
Photo by Bob Kertesz, www.bluescreen.com

FIGURE 5.4: MONITORS
Photo contributed by www.Marshallelectronics.net

Greenscreen (Figure 5.3): Often used in the same way as bluescreen. Greenscreen has a stronger luminance than blue and shows more detail. Because of this clarity, greenscreen is used often for special effects. Special effects can also include people in the shot. The same principle applies for makeup. Leave out colors that will blend with the background, avoiding makeup that could cause spills and transparency to your work.

Example: Superman flying through Manhattan.

Whitescreen: Used for a variety of reasons. The background is white, which adds to the contrast between screen, clothes, makeup, and hair. There are no wrong or right choices except to watch colors that are pale, clothes that are pastels or white. These colors might blend into the background.

Monitors (Figure 5.4) help the Makeup Artist to judge how the makeup looks under the lighting conditions on the set.

Monitors are set up for the director and DP first. Where they are set up and how will keep the AC (assistant camera) busy. The practice I like is for the second AC to cable from a single primary source on the camera a feed for the monitor [that] the director and DP will be using. When this is done, a second feed, totally independent from the first feed, is supplied for everyone else to tap into. The second AC can rig a single monitor for the script supervisor, makeup, hair, and costume. That is, if the DP allows it.

—Paul Wheeler

In some situations, there will be different areas for viewing, as Paul Wheeler describes. It not only depends on the DP, it also depends on the director. The director and the DP will decide where and how many monitor setups there will be. One monitor for just the director and the DP allows them to work in a quiet environment, without the distraction of others, or to work in private. It is very common to have two setups for monitors. There can also be a third setup for the clients, visiting guests, studio executives, and so on. If a monitor is not provided for you, and you need to check your work, ask the first AD if a monitor can be set up for you. Remember, every set is different. Some jobs will have monitors available for you, and some will not.

Here are a few examples of monitors to look for:

Cathode Ray Tube: CRT monitors are also available in true progressive-scan monitors.

High-Definition Monitor: A good monitor for the Makeup Artist to view. You will get a real image of what to expect, and the details will enhance any flaws. Talented DPs will actually use this monitor to light the set.

Liquid Crystal Display: LCD monitors usually found attached to the camera or on a flexible arm that allows the focus puller (First AC) to see the action being shot. This monitor is lightweight and nice to look at, but is not the right monitor to check for colors and lights and how they affect your makeup.

Plasma Screens: Available in larger screens, often between 42 and 61 inches. They have a little less quality than the CRT monitors.

PRO TIP

In filming situations, if you need to check your makeup, ask the DP or camera operator for permission to look through the lens. This way, you are seeing the image with gels, filters, and the lighting in place. Sometimes in film, using the monitor is not the best way when checking or correcting your makeup.

Script Breakdown

Script breakdown is the process of analyzing your script. Breaking down a script is not a suggestion—it is essential toward your process of analyzing, developing, and designing makeup. All departments do a breakdown of the script, starting with the producers, who need to budget

and schedule, based on the information in the script. An understanding of the script is necessary for answering the many questions that will come up during prep and filming. This allows the Makeup Artist to effectively deal with the changing conditions and concerns of a shoot. You will build lists of characters, scripted notes on the characters (how they look and dress), makeup effects, location or environments that will affect you, and any written descriptions affecting makeup. This information will influence the design and needs of the Makeup Department, including budgeting. Script breakdown is your chance to understand how the story moves, to get an understanding of everything that has to happen to the characters, the number of "script days," which scenes are daytime, which scenes are nighttime, and if there are any environmental factors (such as rain). Script breakdown will help you make decisions on how to achieve and maintain the makeup looks. There are computer programs available for script breakdown. It is recommended that you use both manual and computer breakdowns for makeup.

1. Start by reading through the script without taking notes.

2. Read through a second time, making notes on what "day" or "night" it is, per scene.

Your days/nights will need to be checked against the script supervisor's breakdown. Always defer to the script supervisor's breakdown—this is given to all departments, and is the definitive breakdown of the script.

3. Read through a third time, making character notes, and start an effects list.

4. List all characters, along with any script descriptions of their looks.

5. List all makeup effects or looks that need to play in continuous scenes. Make notes on how long an effect or look works. This is your makeup continuity.

Example: Fred is hit in SC 3. His cheek is bruised.

Question: How many scenes does the bruise work, and what is the progression or age of the bruising? When is the last time you see the bruise?

Example: Mary and Joe leave the diner. It starts to rain. They run two blocks to the car.

Question: Where do they drive to? How long do you maintain the "wet look"? Your effects list will also help you in budgeting for the department. The better you know and understand the script, the better prepared you are for conversations with the director, producers, and other department heads.

Product Update

The following products are now available for HD use:

Cargo Blu Ray HD line

Christian Dior Totale High Loose Powder

Graftobian HD line

It Cosmetics HD Finishing Powder

MAC Pro Airbrush line, use with or without airbrush, sold only to professionals, no retail

MAKE UP FOR EVER High Definition Elixor

MAKE UP FOR EVER High Definition Foundation

MAKE UP FOR EVER High Definition Powder

MAKE UP FOR EVER Rouge Artist Intense with 50% more pigment

MAKE UP FOR EVER HD Microfinish Powder

MAKE UP FOR EVER HD line

Revlon Color Stay Foundations and Powder

Smashbox HD Healthy FX Foundations and Concealer

Temptu

References

Wheeler, P., 2001. Digital Cinematography. Focal Press.

Wheeler, P., 2003. High Definition and 24P Cinematography. Focal Press.

63

Internet Resources

Bluescreen, www.bluescreen.com.

Digital photography, http://en.wikipedia.org/wiki/Digital_photography.

Digital television, http://en.wikipedia.org/wiki/digital_television.

EEFX, www.eefx.com.

HDTV, http://en.wikipedia.org/wiki/HDTV.

6

FOUNDATIONS

For every person who sits down in your chair—whether you are working on a film, designing elaborate characters for theatre, creating an image for a photo shoot, or skillfully applying a beauty makeup for television—you will need to know that person's skin tone. If you do not get this part right, your makeup will appear dull, gray, and lifeless. One of the things you'll learn as a Makeup Artist is how to be quick and to think on your feet. In many cases, we do not have the luxury of time to work on a person—everyone from the director to the crew is waiting on you. Train yourself on the steps to analyzing skin tones, and you will be a better Makeup Artist. This would also include makeup effects. Makeup effects deal in great length in the art of skin tones and color layering.

The primary function of the skin is to protect, and to regulate heat. Differences in skin color are due to the amount of melanin activated in the skin and the way it is distributed. Melanin is the pigment of the skin. Melanin protects the skin cells from ultraviolet rays by absorbing and blocking UV rays through tanning, which is a reaction to sun exposure. UV rays have the greatest impact on how skin ages. Approximately 80 to 85 percent of skin aging is caused by the sun. Melanin in the skin is nature's sunblock, and the more melanin in the skin, the darker the skin tone. Scientists have estimated that people of African descent have some 35 different hues or shades of skin. Undertones that tend to dominate dark skin tones are yellow, orange, red, olive, and blue. You have to learn and really understand how to deal with all skin undertones. Do not rely on just looking at the surface of the skin—the undertones that are present just under the surface will affect the color you apply to the skin. This takes much practical experience and exposure to the wide variety of skin tones and different combinations as well as situations that you will encounter. Ethnicity, environment, and illness all play a part in a person's individual undertones, and in

some cases are not easily recognized. Look at what happens to color when applied to the skin. Does the color enhance the skin tone, or is there a gray or dull quality? Unless the part calls for illness, your goal is a healthy tone to the skin.

Nancy Tozier, director of education and president of Take Up Makeup Cosmetics, says: "Learning color theory can help you change a good makeup application into a great one. By understanding color theory, you can take years off a face, make eyes show from across the room, create harmony, and change dull to outrageous, while always knowing exactly what you're doing."

Tozier teaches throughout the United States and internationally. She specializes in teaching the artistry of makeup, color analysis, and skin care. The following outline will show you how to incorporate the color wheel to plot skin tones. You will also learn to custom blend foundations and powders with color to enhance or correct skin tones. Again, this theory in the use of color is a basic knowledge for all Makeup Artists. Nancy will guide us with her knowledge through color theory and mixing foundation.

She explains: "The key to understanding color theory is the artist color wheel." (See Figure 6.1.) Nancy continues:

> If you divide the color wheel in half from top to bottom; the colors on your right are the cool colors—blues, and shades of blue (blue green, blue violet, and raspberry). We associate these colors with the cold. The colors to the left are the warm colors. They contain yellow. We associate these colors with fire. The color at the very top of the wheel, red, can be warmed if a little yellow is added, moving toward the orange tones on the left. That very same red can be cooled by the addition of a little violet, moving toward the blue tones on the right. In the same way, green, at the very bottom of the color wheel, can be cool if a bit of blue is

FIGURE 6.1: ARTIST COLOR WHEEL

added to it, and can be warmed by adding a bit of yellow. You can see how very similar colors can be warm or cool depending on whether blue or yellow undertones are added.

How does the color wheel apply to custom blending cosmetics? In Chapter 3, we showed you the Real Color Wheel (RCW) for mixing pigments. Nancy uses the traditional artist color wheel for custom blending of cosmetics. The traditional color wheel primaries are red, blue, and yellow. Makeup foundations have these colors in them. To custom blend a foundation to match the client's skin perfectly, you must begin by determining whether the client is warm toned (with golden undertones) or cool toned (with blue undertones). People rarely look blue, so we say cool (or blue) undertones. A variety of brown shades can be made by combining the primary colors.

To intensify a color, you add an additional amount of that same color. To neutralize a color, we look at our color wheel and choose the color directly across from the color we want to lessen. For example, if a foundation is too yellow, if we look at a color wheel, we see the opposite color is violet. We add small amounts of violet until we reach the desired tone.

Here is a guide to determine which colors intensify a color, and which colors neutralize a color.

- If the person needs more gold, add yellow.
- If the person needs less yellow, add violet.
- If the person needs less pink or has rosacea, add green.
- If the person needs less peach, first add mint, then violet.

This method can be used with translucent powders as well. Most private-label makeup companies offer the tools to custom blend, as well as empty bottles or jars, and larger-sized foundation bottles to work from. Always mix your foundations in a beaker for accurate measurements. With practice, you will learn the exact amounts to add. If you add too much color to neutralize, you can always add back in some of the opposite color. Check your color wheel.

Color Theory and Mixing Foundations

By Nancy Tozier, Director of Education and President, Take Up Makeup Cosmetics

To custom blend a foundation that matches the client's skin perfectly, you must begin by determining whether the client is warm toned or cool toned. Does the client's skin have golden undertones or cool undertones? (Cool undertones are sometimes referred to as blue undertones, but because people rarely look blue; let's say cool.) Here's what to do:

1. If you have on hand different colors of cosmetic or barber caps or drapes, these would be helpful in determining skin tones.

2. Look closely at the actor's skin tone. Do you see any gold? Don't confuse a beige or brown tone with golden. Many people with different depths of color can be cool toned.

Make sure that the actor is seated in bright daylight so that you will get the best view of the skin without interference from other sources of color.

3. If you think the actor has a warm skin tone and their skin is fair, then light golden yellow, gold, or adobe would be good colors to place next to the skin.

If you think the actor has a golden skin tone but has darker coloring, burnt orange, avocado green, or deep gold would be good colors next to the skin. What you are looking for is if their skin takes on a healthy look.

FOUNDATIONS

PRO TIP

You can use blusher or eye-shadow colors from your makeup kit that are similar to the colors suggested above for checking skin tones.

4. If a color is wrong for a person, their skin will take on a grayish cast. If the color is good for a person, they will look healthy and vibrant. Don't let your preference for a color cloud your vision. You are looking for the effect on the skin, not if you like the color. Learning to see the whole picture takes practice, so don't get discouraged if it isn't easily apparent at first. Use the chart in Figure 6.2 to help you find the colors that bring out the best for clients with different skin tones.

Foundation Mixing

By Nancy Tozier, Director of Education and President, Take Up Makeup Cosmetics

Once you have determined the shades that are best suited to the person, you will begin the process of mixing foundations to correct or enhance skin tone.

FIGURE 6.2: TAKE UP MAKEUP COSMETICS COLOR CHART

Cool Linen	Neutral Cream	Warm Vanilla	Cool Lt. Almond	Warm Almond
Cool Sand Beige	Warm Sand	Cool Porceline	Cool Pale Beige	Neutral Natural
Cool Fawn	Warm Topaz	Warm Sepia	Cool Espresso	Warm Mahogany
Add-In Lilac	Add-In Mint	Add-In Mauve	Add-In Peach	Add=In Amber

First, be sure that the client is seated in good daylight, just as you did in the color exercise. You will need to have the following on hand:

1. Several shades of foundation that are close to your client's natural coloring.

2. Several shades of corrector in mint green, pale yellow, violet, and white.

3. A glass beaker in which to mix your new foundation.

4. A skin-care spatula for mixing.

5. An empty foundation bottle in which to pour the finished foundation.

6. Clean paper towels for keeping things tidy.

Select a color of foundation similar to the level of lightness or darkness of your client's skin. At this point, you also need to try to match the client's undertones. Does her face look golden, pink, greenish, or peachy? Look for a similar foundation color. Most custom-blend foundations come with the following additives: yellow, violet, green, or white. You may have to mix two different foundations if the client's coloring falls between the shades of foundation that you are using. Place a little less than two ounces of foundation in the beaker. Remember that you will be adding some color, and you want the finished amount to fit into the bottle.

Test the color on the client's jawline. You want to match the color of the client's neck. A foundation that matches the client's neck will give the most harmonious appearance. We've all seen too many faces that appear to be a completely different color than the person's neck. A sure sign of unprofessional makeup!

Now determine whether the foundation needs correction. If, for example, the client's skin is more golden than your foundation, you would add more gold. This is called intensifying a color. If your client's skin is less golden than your foundation, you want to lessen the amount of gold in the foundation. This is called neutralizing a color. If you add too much color, you can always neutralize it by adding some of the opposite color, easily identified using the color wheel.

- If the client needs less yellow, add violet.
- If the client needs less pink or is covering rosacea, add mint green.
- If the client needs less peach, first add mint, then violet.

This method can be used with translucent powders as well. Most private-label makeup companies offer the tools to custom blend, as well as empty bottles or jars and larger-sized foundation bottles to work from.

So, in review, to intensify a color, add more of the same color; to neutralize, add the opposite.

Special Foundation Needs

Nancy explains that sometimes a person's skin color presents a special problem. For example:

- A person with rosacea needs help managing redness.

- Some clients will naturally have so much golden (yellow) tone that they look sallow.
- Some skin tones have an almost greenish hue that can actually appear unhealthy.

Here are some techniques:

If a person has very red skin, find a foundation that matches the neck (which is usually much less red), and begin by adding mint green to it. The color of the foundation will begin to look dull, but when applied to the face, it neutralizes the unwanted color and gives a calmer, less red appearance.

For someone who is overly yellow, adding violet to a foundation that matches the neck will neutralize the yellow and look beautiful. In this situation, often the neck is yellow as well, so foundation should be used to cover the neck and be well blended at the base of the neck.

Nancy gives us valuable lessons and understanding on skin color analyses and foundation mixing. In today's fast-paced industry, we work with premixed foundations, as well as concealers, tinted primers, and camouflage creams to correct if we are not mixing colors. We also mix these "premixed" foundations together on palettes to get the match needed. You will be mixing and matching on your feet, and working in environments that require you to be time sensitive. You will be doing a practical color analysis of the skin by testing the foundation on the skin at the jawline to see if it matches with the face and the neck. You will be draping your actor with a barber's drape or hairstylist's cape. They come in several colors, but most Makeup Artists use black. If the actor is wearing clothing in a color that is not suitable for the color palette designed for the project or is not good for their skin tone, the drape or cape will help you neutralize this problem and let you see how your color choices are working with the individual's skin tone.

Foundations and Primers

Makeup foundation's cosmetic purpose is to even out skin tone, hide fine lines, and provide a base on which to apply makeup. Foundations also provide added moisture to the skin, protect from the environment, and, with some products, provide a light sunscreen.

Foundation or makeup base comes in a variety of textures and consistencies: tinted moisturizers, liquid, cream, cake, stick, cream to powder, and powder. You can achieve a different level of coverage with each type of foundation. Color, consistency, and coverage will guide you in choosing what foundation to use for different skin types and situations, and if you should or should not use a primer first.

PRO TIP

Remember the three Cs of choosing what foundation to use: color, consistency, and coverage.

Ingredients are another important factor in choosing what foundation to use on the various different skin types you will encounter. Water-based, emollient-based, and mineral-based products are all industry standards and should be part of your kit. In today's industry, skin care has become very important. People pay close attention to the care and condition of their skin and the products that work best for them. You will need to stay current on the latest in skin-care treatments, products, and ingredients.

I encourage everyone to promote their own skin care at home so that we may begin with a proper surface.

—Richard Dean

Primers

Foundation primers even out the texture of the skin, keep the makeup smooth and flawless, add longevity to the makeup, and protect the skin underneath. They also prevent moisture loss. Some Makeup Artists always use a primer to prep the skin before applying foundation. Some use primers only when they decide primers are needed to achieve a certain look or when they are needed to protect the skin. Silicone-based primers are great for sensitive or allergic skin. The silicone used is nontoxic. These primers actually protect the skin from the makeup foundation by putting a barrier between the foundation and skin. This will lessen breakouts in sensitive or allergic skin. Silicone primers also fill in enlarged pores, acne scars, fine lines, and wrinkles. Primers come in violet, green, pink, and yellow tint. These are great to help even out undertones on skin that does not need heavy concealing. All primers are applied before the foundation with a sponge, brush, or hands.

Industry Standards: ColorScience, Laura Mercier Foundation Primer, LORAC, Paula Dorf, smashbox, YSL, MAKE UP FOR EVER.

Note: If you apply primers, foundations, blush, and so on with your hands, you must wash your hands thoroughly with soap and water before and after. Hand application is controversial in the film/television world; not so for print. Many Makeup Artists believe it should not be done under any circumstance, that it is unprofessional and not sanitary. Of course, just as many Makeup Artists believe that it is a valuable technique, especially when working with liquids. Actors are also split on their preference—some love it; others prefer no contact with the skin except with a sponge or brush. If you are working as an additional Makeup Artist for crowd scenes, hand application is not practical because you have too many people to make up.

Foundations

The most popular foundations in the industry are tinted moisturizers, liquids, and cream-based, water-based, emollient-based, and mineral-based foundations. You will need to have all of them in your kit, with a good selection of colors for mixing and matching. This will allow you to handle any skin tone and type. Cake and stick foundations are also used, but not as readily, although they are also found in most makeup kits.

Tinted Moisturizers: Are the sheerest or lightest of coverage, when you do not need a lot of correction. Tinted moisturizers will even out skin tone, and can add just a hint of color if needed. They are great on men, or when you need just a hint of added color on good skin.

Industry Standards: Laura Mercier Tinted Moisturizer, Stila Color Tinted Moisturizer.

Liquid Foundations: Give a sheer overall coverage that looks natural, and are easy to apply with a sponge or brush to get a smooth finish. They are good for all skin types, and are available in water-based, emollient (hydrating), and mineral-based formulas. For oily or sensitive skin, use a water-based foundation. For dry or mature skin, choose a hydrating foundation. Mineral foundations are good with all skin types. Liquids are widely used in the industry, easy to mix, and do not have to be powdered.

Industry Standards: Armani, Bobbi Brown, Chanel, Clinique, Estée Lauder, Iman, M•A•C, MAKE UP FOR EVER, MAKE UP FOR EVER HD High Definition, Revlon ColorStay, Visiora.

Mineral Foundations: Great for sensitive or acne-prone skin. There are fewer ingredients, and because the minerals are inert, they will not support bacteria. They are great for people with allergies and sensitive skin, as well as rosacea. Mineral-based makeup gives long-lasting coverage that does not settle into fine lines or irritate the skin. They should be applied with a sponge or makeup brush. They are available in liquid or powder form. They offer broad-spectrum UVA and UVB protection, are water resistant, and contain no talc or parabens. They are not tested on animals.

Industry Standards: Bare Escentuals, Glominerals, Illuminaré, Jane Iredale, ColorScience.

Cream Foundations: Usually come in a compact or stick (pan stick). They are wonderful on all skin types and provide excellent coverage. Cream foundations are widely used in all media, and are easily applied with a sponge or brush, providing overall coverage with a rich texture and deep tone. You can achieve different finishes with cream foundations: sheer, more coverage, and layering over a liquid for even more coverage. Layering over a liquid gives you a beautiful and flawless finish, but because it is more product, there could be some film and lighting situations that it would be too heavy for. It is good for all skin types, but best on dry skin. It should be set with powder.

Industry Standards: Black Opal, Bobbi Brown, Cinema Secrets, Gerda Spillmann, Iman, M•A•C, RCMA, Visiora.

Powder Foundations: Great for the two-for-one application. They give a flawless matte finish. Apply with a dry sponge or makeup brush. For more coverage, use a damp sponge to apply. These foundations are not for every skin type, and work best on oily or acne-prone skin, but also work well for normal or combination skin. They are great for quick solutions when there is no time, for on-set touch-ups, and for fast application of color. They are also good in humid conditions.

Industry Standards: Lancôme Dual Finish, M•A•C Studio Fix.

Cream-to-Powder Foundations: Are good for most skin types, but great for combination skin. They should be applied with a dry sponge.

Try: Benefit's Some Kind-a Gorgeous, Vincent Longo Water Canvas Creme-to-Powder Foundation.

Cake Makeup: Comes in the form of a "cake" and is usually applied with a damp sponge. It gives a matte finish. The sponge should not be wet, but damp to get a smooth finish. It is used extensively for stage performers for face painting, clown makeup, fantasy, and body makeup.

Industry Standards: KRYOLAN, Mehron.

Fillers and Mattifying Products: Great to use on bare skin. The fillers are clear or opaque, and fill in fine lines and scars. Fillers can be used on bare skin, under makeup, or over makeup. Mattifiers take down shine, and are great for bare skin, bald heads, and prosthetics.

Industry Standards: Make-Up International Face to Face Supermatte Antishine (comes in light, medium, and dark), Lancôme Pure Focus T-Zone.

Try: Benefit's Dr. Feelgood for smoothing and filling in under or over makeup.

Concealers

Concealers even out skin tone, and cover blemishes, scars, bruising, discoloration, and circles under the eyes. They have a thicker composition than foundation, and are available in cream, stick, tube, pots, and liquid. Sometimes a concealer is the only product a Makeup Artist needs to even out someone's skin tone (see "Spot Painting" in Chapter 7). You will also use concealers on the body to cover any unattractive marks, bruises, or scars, or to cover tattoos. For the face and body (not the eye area), concealers with a high pigment are best for camouflaging because they provide complete coverage and last longer. You need to blend the concealer well into the skin so that it disappears, especially if you are not using a makeup foundation on the skin. You can apply concealer under or over makeup foundation.

Note that concealers are designed to be applied over the foundation if you are using a liquid or cream base. If you are using a powder or dry foundation, apply the concealer underneath the base. With the exception of dry foundations, most Makeup Artists do both, under and over, when applying concealer. Your choice will become part of your working technique and style. In difficult camouflage situations, you will need to apply both under and over the foundation to get the coverage needed. Try applying concealer both under and over a foundation for effect (Figure 6.3).

Industry Standards: KRYOLAN Dermacolor, Ben Nye, Joe Blasco.

Under-eye concealers come in stick, cream, or pot, as well as liquid. Look for concealers that are creamy in texture, with light to medium pigment. Remember that the skin around the eye is delicate, so the products you use to conceal around the eye area should be, too. If the product is too thick or uses a heavy pigment, you will have to work too hard to blend, irritating the thin skin tissue. Choose a concealer one shade lighter than the foundation that you are working with, and one that has moisturizing properties. A stick concealer offers more coverage but is more difficult to blend, so it can be hard on the skin around the eyes. To avoid irritation and to keep the stick sanitary, do not apply the stick directly to the skin. Do not powder under the eyes (Figure 6.4).

Industry Standards: Paula Dorf, Iman, Kanebo, LORAC, Touche Éclat (YSL), Valorie, smashbox, AmazingConcealer.

Highlights and Contours

Throughout the makeup world, you'll get different opinions on if or when you should apply the theory of highlights and contours. As lighting and film stock have evolved, so has makeup. Back in the day, Makeup Artists would "blank out" the face to start with a blank canvas, and use the

Foundation Product Comparisons

Colors are classified according to temperature and charted below in descending values (or steps) from light to dark. Graftobian's Hi-Def Creme Foundations are used as the baseline color range for other product comparison matches because of their wide range of selection of accurate skin tone colors in each temperature.

Temperature	Graftobian	RCMA	Cinema Secrets	Visiora	MAC	Shu Uemura Nobara Cream	Black Opal	Revlon ColorStay
Warm	Graceful Swan				C15	983		
Warm	Ingénue		301S-63		NC15			Buff
Warm	Vixen		302S-65		NC35, C3			Sand
Warm	Temptress		304S-32					
Warm	Buttermilk		303S-66					
Warm	Enchantress	Shinto #1	509-62			554		True Beige
Warm	Femme Fatale	LN1						Early Tan
Warm	Desert Sand	Shinto #2				754		Rich Tan
Warm	Winter Wheat	Shinto #3	201S-67			545		Toast
Warm	Golden Sunset				NC60, NW35			
Warm	Deep Xanthe	Shinto #4						
Warm	Ginger	Shinto #5					Nutmeg	
Warm	Midnight Marigold	Shinto #6			NC50, NC65, C7			Caramel
Warm	Burnt Amber	Shinto # 7	202S-20					Cappucino
Warm	Sienna						Black Walnut	Mocha
Three shades below are unique medium to medium dark colors in warm temperature:								
Warm	Sunlit Linen						Kalahari Sand	
Warm	Caramel			CN102				
Warm	Pecan	Shinto #8					Hazelnut	
Temperature	Graftobian	RCMA	Cinema Secrets	Visiora	MAC	Shu Uemura Nobara Cream	Black Opal	Revlon ColorStay
Neutral	Bombshell							
Neutral	Prima Donna							Nude
Neutral	Leading Lady							
Neutral	Sweetheart							
Neutral	Glamour Girl					564		
Neutral	Cabaret Kitten							
Neutral	Broadway Star							
Neutral	Show Stopper							
Neutral	Screen Goddess	LN1						Natural Tan
Neutral	Diva				NC45			
Neutral	Chestnut	MB5				334	Au Chocolat	
Neutral	Warm Umber				N4, NW45 & 50		Walnut	
Neutral	Hazelnut							
Neutral	Hidden Magic		204S-27					
Neutral	Nightfall							
Five shades below are unique medium dark to dark colors in neutral temperature:								
Neutral	Evening Mist	S1						
Neutral	Olivia			MV 101	C5, C50			
Neutral	Smoke	KT4						
Neutral	Soft Wisp							
Neutral	Phantom				W55			
Temperature	Graftobian	RCMA	Cinema Secrets	Visiora	MAC	Shu Uemura Nobara Cream	Black Opal	Revlon ColorStay
Cool	Buff		501-11	MV010				
Cool	Sunrise Flush	Ivory		CN001	NC20, NW20	574		Ivory
Cool	Aurora	GENA	598-14	MV001				Tawny
Cool	Cashmere Beige	Olive #1		MV002	N1			Natural Beige
Cool	Morning Glow	Olive #2		CN002	NW25 &3 0, N2	365		Medium Beige
Cool	Afterglow	Olive #3		MV003		354		
Cool	Cedar Spice	Tan Tone		MV004				
Cool	Ceylon Cinnamon	KT2		MV005	N6			
Cool	Henna	KM5		CN005, MV006				
Cool	Auburn	RJ2		CN006				
Cool	Sable					314	Carob	
Cool	Shadow Dance						Ebony	
Three shades below are unique medium to medium dark colors in cool temperature:								
Cool	Bisque	KW4						
Cool	Butterscotch	KM2					Heaven Honey	
Cool	Sandstone	Olive #4						

Original product match collaboration by Suzanne Patterson and Mary Erickson. Chart concept design by Michelle Talley. Revised and expanded format updated with additional category and product matches by Suzanne Patterson.

FIGURE 6.3: FOUNDATION COMPARISON CHART BY MARY ERICKSON AND SUZANNE PATTERSON

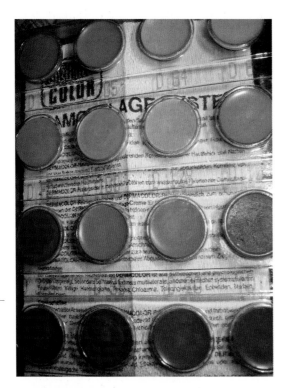

FIGURE 6.4: DERMA COLOR PALETTE

tools of highlight and contour to literally paint the preferred features back in. Today, this technique of "blanking out" the face is rarely used, but there will be a moment in your career when you will need to apply it—a drag makeup, for example. Today, Makeup Artists use highlights and contours in a subtle way, without blanking out the features of the face first. We create dimension and highlight features, but with a realistic touch or aesthetic. Sometimes a Makeup Artist is using the technique of highlight and contour without really knowing it. Examples include applying a lighter color under the eyebrow (highlight), or adding a touch of shade under the cheekbone to sculpt out more definition (contour).

What are highlights and contours, or highlights versus shading? Highlights are lighter colors that are applied to any area the Makeup Artist wants to stand out. Contours are darker colors that are applied to any area the Makeup Artist wants to

sink or set back. Although the face has shape and depth, there are certain lighting situations that can turn the face flat. The greater a three-dimensional effect achieved by the Makeup Artist, the better the makeup will be. That said, there is nothing worse than an overdone look when the director has requested a no-makeup look.

With blending, you can create beautiful, flawless makeup using highlights and contours with no one being able to see the makeup. There are many Makeup Artists who either highlight or contour, but not both. Think about it. If you apply a lighter shade, for example, on the top of the cheekbone, you will automatically create a sink or shadow right below there for your contour. The same can be said of the opposite. If you apply a contour or shade, for example, in the temple area, you will create highlights on the top cheekbone and outer upper brow bone. We'll go into more detail with the charts on what colors work well for both highlights and contours. In the long run, it is important for a Makeup Artist to learn facial structure and to recognize the importance of where light and dark fall on the features of the face.

Forward planes catch the light. Recessed planes recede.

—Gerd Mairandres, Wigmaster,
San Francisco Opera

Highlights

The correct colors to use for highlights are important. If the highlight color is too light or too heavily applied for all media (film, TV, HD, print, and theater), your work will be seen as heavy-handed. Highlights in off-whites, cream, pinks, gold, yellows, or any color that is a few degrees lighter than the skin tone that you are working on will work best—except pure white, which in most situations is too harsh. Remember what you learned in Chapter 3—that white mixed with another color is a tint, so you can be as creative as you want to be.

Contours

Shades of darker makeup from blushers to pigments can be used depending on what type of makeup you are creating. Good colors are brownish pinks, reds, grays, oranges, and again any shade that is a few degrees darker than the skin tone you are working on. You should never use pure black to contour. Remember, if you go back to Chapter 3, you'll see six examples of mixing color to get neutral darks, and color pigments to make browns.

Blending

Blending is the art of applying makeup using your tools to achieve a smooth, seamless finish with no visible line or hard edge. A skillful balance of strong or not-so-strong colors can be blended together without seams to create contrasts or dramatic effects. In painting as well as in theatrical makeup, the technique of chiaroscuro is used to create a bold contrast between light and dark. Chiaroscuro, an Italian term literally meaning "light–dark," originated as a term for a type of Renaissance drawing on colored paper. The artist worked from the base tone toward light and dark. It is also a term used in makeup to refer to blending from light to dark for a three-dimensional, seamless effect. It is very helpful for all applications of makeup to learn chiaroscuro. You use subtle gradations of color in light and dark shades to enhance the delineation of character for dramatic effect. Remember to blend to the end.

Any makeup can be bold as long as it is well blended.

—Gerd Mairandres, Wigmaster,
San Francisco Opera

Note: Chiaroscuro is also a term used in cinematography to indicate extreme low-key lighting to create distance areas of light and darkness in film, especially black-and-white film.

More about Products

Eye Shadow

Cream Shadow: Cream eye shadows are used alone or with other eye-shadow products. They can come in tubes, pots, wands, and compacts. Cream eye shadows can have a dewy, glossy, or frosty appearance, depending on the product. Some are formulated to be waterproof or water resistant.

Cream to Powder: Cream eye shadow that dries to a powder finish. Can be worn alone or layered.

Gel: Found most often in pots, gel products are used as eye shadow or eyeliner. They are quick drying, easy-glide application, and long lasting. They can be used in combination with other eye shadow products. Gels also come in glosses that dry to a shine that gives the eye shadow an appearance of being wet.

Liquid: Liquid eye shadow generally comes in a tube, usually with a wand or brush attached.

Loose Powder: Comes in jars. It can be used wet or dry. Products are highly concentrated with color. They can be used alone or layered in combination with other eye products. They are messy—the loose powder tends to "float" everywhere. If using, do the eyes first, foundation last, to prevent shadow from dropping onto the foundation.

Pencils or Pens: Are highly pigmented, frosty or sheer. Some formulas are waterproof or water resistant in small or large pencil form. You will need special sharpeners for these.

Pressed Powder: Are usually in compact or drop-in disks to customize your eye-shadow palette. It can be used wet or dry.

Waterproof Eye Shadow Products: Are usually found in jars, tubes, or pencil form. They contain a polymer ingredient. They are formulated to not crease or fade.

Eyeliner

Cake: Applied with a brush that is damp. Cake eyeliner is great for smudging. Cake products usually come in compacts or jars, and are creams or powder formulas.

Gel: Used like a liquid or cake, but is easier to apply. It is long lasting. Gel is applied with a brush and usually found in jars.

Liquid: Adds drama to your look, and a must for many "period" looks. It is applied with a brush and is quick drying, but needs a very steady hand. "Painters" work well with liquids.

Loose Powder: Highly pigmented powder that can be used wet or dry. Use a sealer on top for longer wear. Loose powder can be messy.

Pencils: Easy application and blending. They can be formulated in waterproof and water-resistant products, and come in frost, kohl, and matte, with either a fine point or thick.

Sealers: Products used to protect any eye shadow or eyeliner from smudging, smearing, or lifting. Sealers are usually found in liquid form, and can be mixed with eye shadow (or product) in the application (think watercolors).

Mascara

Cake: Is applied with an eyelash brush or small fan brush. Cake mascara and a fan brush gives you a thorough coat on the lashes, with no "clumps," and works great to get the base of the lashes, particularly on light or blonde lashes.

Clear: Comes in tubes and is applied like regular mascara. It gives a nice sheen to the lashes, and helps to show off definition and length in the "Natural Look."

Fillers: Are found alone or combined into the mascara formula. They thicken and lengthen. They are usually made out of nylon fibers.

Top Coats: Applied to the eyelashes after mascara, they are used to add sheen and vibrancy to the lashes. They can also be used as a sealer for the mascara.

Primers: Act as moisturizers for the eye, and also prepare the lashes for mascara. They are helpful in creating a longer look and in protecting the eyelashes from mascara. Remember to apply first, before mascara.

Tinted: Colored mascara, usually in tubes.

Waterproof: Smudgeproof, creaseproof, and quick drying. You must have correct mascara remover in order to take off waterproof mascara. Primers can be used first, for ease of removal.

Blushers

Cream Blush: Can be highly pigmented. It can be used alone or with other products. Formulas come in cream to powder finish. Cream blushes come in jars, compacts, sticks, and liquids.

Pressed Powder: Can be used alone or in combination with creams. It comes in a wide range of textures and formulas in compact form. It is great for "on-set" touch-ups because it is pressed and not loose.

Loose Powder: Comes in a wide range of textures and formulas. It can be used alone or in combination.

Tints and Gels: Found in creams, gels, moisturizers, and liquids. Tints and gels are sheer translucent in color. Many are made to be an "all-in-one" product for cheeks and lips. Some are water resistant and oil free. They can be used alone or combined.

Eyebrows

Cake: Powder form, pressed or loose, and come in jars, compacts, and pencil form. They are the easiest and most natural way to define a brow. Cake eyebrow definer is most often used with a stiff eye brush. It can be wet or dry.

Gels: Usually transparent, but are available in tints. Gels can be used alone or after brow color has been applied. They dry quickly, are often waterproof, and hold the brow shape in place.

Pencils: Eyebrow pencils have an extra-hard point for drawing, shaping, and filling in brows. They are very pigmented, and come in assorted colors, and can be used in combination with other brow products.

Thickening: Eyebrow thickeners are like mascaras for the eyebrows. They have hairlike fibers that are suspended in the formula to add volume and coverage to the brows.

Wax: Used to shape, enhance, or fill the brow while holding the brow shape. It comes in different colors and can be combined with other products.

Lipstick

Cream: Contains moisturizing properties and is highly pigmented. Cream lipsticks go on smooth, and some contain sun protection and vitamins. They come in matte, shine, and frost formulas.

Matte: Lipstick that is flat with no shine. It tends to be very pigmented. It is great for creating "period" looks. Matte lipsticks are long-wearing because they are so dense.

Frost: Comes in lipsticks, pots, gloss, and tints, with different levels of frost or glitter.

Gloss: Sheer formulas with high-gloss or wet look. Gloss lipsticks can be used alone or in combination as a top coat to the lips.

Treatments: Balms, conditioners, and treatment sticks for the lips. They are available with sun protection, natural plant extracts, vitamins, and moisturizing properties. They soothe dry lips and can come in tints. They may be used alone or in combination.

Lip Scrubs: Treatment products to exfoliate the lips (get rid of dry skin).

Lip Plumper: Contains ingredients for plumping the lip area. Sometimes there is a tingling sensation when applied.

Lip Wax: Wax formula used before lipstick application to fill in lines and wrinkles. Lip wax also preps the lips for lipstick.

Lip Liners: Come in pencil, pen, or stick form. They are used to reshape and enhance the lip line before lipstick application, and can be used alone with a lip moisturizer (like a tint) or in combination with all lip products.

References

Internet Resources

Frends Beauty Supply, www.frendsbeautysupply.com.

Naimies Beauty Center, www.naimies.com.

Nancy, T., Take Up Cosmetics. www.takeupmakeup.com.

Patterson, S., www.creativeartistryfx.com.

Sephora, www.sephora.com.

7

BEAUTY AND BASICS

At one time it was critical because of the nature of lighting and film technology, as well as theatrical custom, to eliminate as much detail of the actor's face as possible and to draw in, often almost cartoonishly, those features meant to be seen. As film stock and lighting became more forgiving, and "reality," rather than "theatricality," became the accepted convention, beauty makeup has, too, evolved to appreciate a more naturalistic aesthetic.

—Richard Dean

Your imagination and your knowledge of shapes, the body, color, and lighting enable you to paint with endless possibilities. In this chapter, we will start with the basic skills and makeup applications that a Makeup Artist uses every day. This is what you have been waiting for—it's time to do makeup. We wanted you to excel in the basics and principles of the previous chapters before moving on to makeup applications, advanced makeup, and makeup designs. This is why we started the book with the more technical aspects of makeup. In order to have the background needed to move forward and excel, you need to understand all the elements and aspects that affect your work. To make up the whole, you need all the parts. We will note "industry standards" throughout this chapter and the rest of the book for you to know and recognize. These are products that will be found in every makeup kit. Brand and name recognition are important to the industry. Once you know that a product works, photographs well, and does not cause skin irritation, you will rely on that product to always work for you when there is no time for discovery, experimenting, or testing. Industry standards are trusted and proven—they work. We will cover the testing of looks in Chapter 8, Design.

Within a single day, a Makeup Artist could do any number of different makeups—for example, a beauty makeup, cover an actor's tattoo, break a nose, apply a tan or sunburn, add 10 years

to a character, apply a five o'clock shadow, or give the "homeless extra" the grime needed to sell the look. An "extra" is a background actor, sometimes referred to as a "background artist"; these actors play a supportive but integral role in filmmaking, and need to have the same attention to detail as a principal actor.

We have our own slang in the makeup world. Makeup Artists often refer to "a makeup" or "the makeup" when speaking or referring to a colleague. They are referring to the specific look that is being done: a character or makeup design. Example: "The makeup looks muddy." "Muddy" is unclean, not blended well, uneven application (not good), and "the makeup" is the finished application of the artist.

It could also be a day about creating natural looks that seem organic without the assistance of makeup. You need to develop a subtle eye and hand for realistic looks. Believability to the eye is key. It is requested in all media, for all ages and genders, and is a frequent request by all directors, producers, and clients.

Understanding the many different interpretations of makeup is also important. What is natural to one person is over-made-up to another. In the beginning of your career, this is one of the more frustrating situations: unclear communication about the makeup. It is subjective and at times difficult to communicate what a look should be. With experience comes the ability to assess the situation and decipher what is being requested. There is also time during the prep phase of a job for understanding what is needed. Prep is the period prior to filming, shooting, or staging when you have initial design discussions, and may even "test the makeup looks" (see Chapter 8: Design).

Take any opportunity to hone your talents and skills for all skin tones and types. The more faces you do, the better you will be. A great opportunity is working "the line," or "bull pen," for a film or opera company. You are one of many Makeup Artists painting for the crowds, and you have little time to do it. This exposes you to many faces and corrective situations.

I take one summer job in NYC each year during my time off from the Met to hone my skills at cranking out full makeups in 10 to 15 minutes, recalling my early days on "the line" at the San Francisco Opera, where we were trained to complete a full makeup (on choristers and supers [supers are stage "extras": non-singing background artists]) in 8 to 10 minutes.

—Steven Horak

Retail cosmetic counters also offer a chance to gain experience with a wide variety of skin tones, facial structure, and vanity, but you will experience doing only "symmetrical beauty makeup," which is not always applied in film.

PRO TIP

The camera loves irregularity. It photographs well, so we do not necessarily strive for symmetry in film.

Makeup Artists use their artistry on the skin to create, but we also provide a service. We care for the person's outer look or character, and in some situations for the person himself or herself, as well as that person's skin. We care for the looks we create and the person we paint on. Maintaining the look of the character takes place over the length of the film or project, from one day to several months. Film and TV projects have long workdays—with 13 to 14 hours per day being typical, as well as the possibility of working 18 to 19 hours per day.

Makeup applied in the morning needs to be maintained and many times reapplied throughout the day. It can be grueling, but, we hope, creatively fulfilling.

With film, there is a beginning, middle, and an end to the story, with the character's movement (and makeup) throughout. In TV, there is a continuing story line, with the same character movement (and makeup)—just a much longer, and sometimes seemingly unending, story line. Print shoots have a shorter day—8 hours is the norm—creatively driven by the photographer, art director, and the client. On some exterior location shoots, they will split up the day: shoot in the morning sun, take a break from the midday sun, and start shooting again in the late-afternoon sun. Stage productions can have long hours during the rehearsal and prep time before opening the show, with 10- to 12-hour days being typical. Once a stage production has "opened," the show calls vary between three and five hours per call (or show), with one day per week as a maintenance day, where you start work earlier to do repairs and maintain the show. On a production with eight show calls per week, there will be two days per week with a matinée and an evening performance, typically on Wednesdays and Saturdays. Theatrical productions operate on a six-day week. Opera schedules are continuous throughout their season, with every opera house maintaining a different "season." Try all media available to you. It is great experience, and helpful in deciding where your talents, personality, and intuition work best.

The Skin

Opinions are divided as to the level of attention Makeup Artists should pay to skin care. There are three types of Makeup Artists. Some believe that skin care should be left up to the individual and/or his or her dermatologist to care for the skin, reasoning that it takes time to correct skin conditions and develop a proper skin-care regime, which needs to be done morning and evening. Some products need to be absorbed completely before applying makeup (and thus done at home before work), and in some cases,

81

treatment products should be used only at night before bed (retinols). It takes time and money to develop a skin-care routine that works best for the individual. Often several weeks are needed to correct a skin condition—it cannot be done in a day. This group of Makeup Artists will expect the individual to maintain their own daily routine of skin care and cleansing. They will expect the person to show up to work ready for makeup application, having already applied products at home at the proper time for absorption.

Another group of Makeup Artists are also licensed aestheticians (the study of skin care), and thus will be more involved in skin care. As the style of filmmaking, technology, and surgical procedures advances and expands, so has the trend for arming oneself with skin care knowledge. This group of Makeup Artists will recommend products and prep the skin before makeup, as well as cleanse and treat the skin at wrap. ("Wrap" is the term called by the first AD—assistant director—at completion of the day's filming.) These Makeup Artists believe in being proactive in skin care, diminishing breakouts as much as possible or correcting dull skin. Acne can be diminished by makeup, lighting, and camera filters, but with a 40-foot screen, dimensional imperfections are hard to hide. (If shooting digital, corrections can be made in "post" or the final product.) Clear skin is always the optimum, and this type of Makeup Artist has the knowledge and background to work toward the goal of correcting skin problems to achieve smooth, clear skin.

The third group of Makeup Artists falls in between the two other types. This group will have knowledge of skin care and will take the time to be current in products and treatments for the skin, although they may or may not be licensed aestheticians. They will prep, tone, moisturize, sun-block, and sometimes apply masks. They will likely do cleansing at wrap. It has become common to see a professional towel caddie on the counter in makeup trailers (towel

caddies keep wet towels warm for cleanup). All Makeup Artist groups work with sun-block. We have a responsibility to protect the skin in exterior locations. Your choice of involvement will become your working style, and should be based on your beliefs and education or knowledge of skin care. We do recommend that you take the time to keep current with skin-care trends and makeup products throughout your career. If you choose to make skin care part of your working style, please note that it adds time to your workday, and some productions will not accept overtime incurred for cleanup at wrap.

PRO TIP

Anything glued or applied to the face, neck, or body by a Makeup Artist that needs a solvent to remove must be removed by the makeup department. The time it takes to remove is "on the clock."

There are actors and individuals who will request and prefer that the makeup is removed at the end of each day. Have a supply of clean white washcloths and a nonirritating cleanser—for example, Cetaphil Gentle Skin Cleanser. Cetaphil is a gentle facial cleanser that does not strip the skin of its natural pH balance; it is an industry standard. Using bottled water, if a sink is not available (trailer water is non-potable, and is not recommended for the mouth, face, or eyes), wet the washcloth and put it in the microwave for one to two minutes. If the towel is too hot, allow it to cool before using. This is the simplest and safest way to cleanse the skin. Washcloths are a fantastic way to remove makeup and clean the skin without harm. There are also makeup-removal wipes. Choose one without alcohol

(alcohol is drying to the skin). Wash your white towels in warm or hot water with bleach to sanitize them.

Be careful with alcohol-based toners. The alcohol strips the skin of its natural oils and pH balance, causing the brain to signal the production of more oil to the surface of the skin in an attempt to bring back the balance to a "normal" pH. pH is the relative degree of acidity and alkalinity of a substance. Don't dry the skin out!

—Joel Garson, *Milady's Standard Fundamentals for Estheticians*, 9th ed.

The Setup

In order to get started, you need to "set up" your workstation with the proper products and equipment. Workstations vary by Makeup Artist, but there are industry standards for setting up your station, with station setup and products that will be consistent from one Makeup Artist to another, no matter whose station you are looking at (see Figure 7.1).

Having your station set up with the proper tools, equipment, and products, clean and ready to go, instills confidence in the individual who sits in your makeup chair. This is one of the

FIGURE 7.1: DEBRA COLEMAN'S MAKEUP STATION
Photo courtesy of Debra Coleman, Makeup Artist, and member of Local 706, Los Angeles

first moments of critique when working with new people. They will look at your station, your products, and how your kit is set up. Your makeup kit should be clean and organized for sanitary reasons and ease of movement during a makeup. Some artists keep their makeup kit on the counter next to them. You will be quickly judged on the condition of your makeup kit. Your products should be current, in good condition, with all batteries fully charged or plugged in. The strength of alcohol must be 99 percent to be effective. Makeup brushes, makeup palette, and tools should be clean and ready. Hand sanitizer (99-percent alcohol) and brush cleaner should be out and within easy reach.

Note: Alcohol is not an EPA (Environmental Protection Agency)–registered hospital-grade disinfectant.

A typical setup for a makeup station is a clean cotton terry towel (colors vary; many prefer white towels only because you can bleach them) placed on the counter in front of you with a professional prep towel on top of the cotton towel (Kimberly-Clark Professional Set Up Towels are the industry standard). This is a sanitary setup to keep your products and brushes off the counter, clean and germ-free. Your makeup palette, tools, and brushes would go on top of this two-layer setup. Clean your station, makeup brushes, tools, and hands in between each person. Make sure to have a garbage can or bag close by for disposing used materials. Also have a cloth drape or barber's cap for protecting clothing or costumes during makeup. Cloth drapes are more comfortable for the individual, but, depending on the makeup you are applying, a plastic drape should also be available. Plastic is hotter for the individual.

Sanitizing products: 99-percent alcohol in a spray and dispenser, small bowls or jars for cleaning brushes, hand wipes, gel hand sanitizer, spray water.

Industry Standards: Evian Mineral Water Spray, Glacial Spray Water, La Roche-Posay Thermal Spring Water, Jao Hand Sanitizer.

Canned spray water is preferred. It is a source of clean water for working on the face and around the eyes. There will be times when you do not have running water, and you will rely on your canned spray water for a clean water source.

Grooming equipment: shaving powder, Tend Skin (industry standard), electric shaver, sideburn trimmer (industry standards: Wahl, Panasonic), clippers for beard trimming (Wahl), small hair scissors for trimming, nose-hair trimmers (Panasonic), disposable shavers, shaving cream.

Nail care: nail clippers, cuticle trimmers, nail files and orange sticks (do not share nail files or orange sticks—buy in bulk and distribute), cuticle remover, cuticle cream, hand cream, base coat, top coat, quick-dry spray, various nail polish colors, non-acetone polish remover.

Kleenex facial tissue, cotton facial pads (cotton only, due to possible allergies to synthetics), Q-tips, cosmetic Q-tips (the tips are different, made for applying makeup), makeup brushes, makeup products, and cosmetics.

Note: This is a very basic setup. Every Makeup Artist personalizes their station, so no two look alike, but they will have some of the same products/equipment or industry standard products.

It is time for practical experience with applying makeup. For some of these makeups, you will not be given steps to follow, just text. For others, you will be given steps. It will be time to think, and paint.

> There are a million ways to do anything. Find the one that works for you.

—Randy Huston Mercer

Concealing and Corrections

Mastering the art of concealing and correcting the vast variety of all skin tones and skin types will come easier to you now that you have studied color theory and foundations.

You will use color theory to cancel out reds, blue, grays, greens, and any other unwanted color or undertones in the skin, as well as blemishes, scars, birthmarks, and tattoos. Concealing can be done under or over the makeup foundation or base, except for birthmarks, port-wine stains, and tattoos. These require full coverage, and should be done first.

> Corrective makeup is a fine convention if it is used realistically in the company of great lighting. Makeup does not generate light. Makeup only reflects existing light. Makeup cannot get rid of eye bags if they cast a shadow. Makeup cannot light an eye socket if it is in the dark. Makeup cannot disguise pockmarks in a side light.

—Richard Dean

For under-eye concealing, choose a product that is emollient and designed for the eye area. These products are lighter, more emollient, and many have reflective qualities that are great for diffusing fine lines around the eye. They glide smoothly onto the delicate skin around the eye. The least amount of tug and pull or stress from application, the better. Do not set with powder. Avoid using powder under the eyes, which can be drying and may emphasize the correction.

Industry Standards: Kanebo, YSL Touche Éclat, Iman, Laura Mercier, NARS, AmazingConcealer, smashbox.

For concealing or correction on the face, choose a product that is medium weight. Note that all types of concealers (light, medium, or dense) will work on the facial skin—it depends on what you are covering. Your style and what you have to cover will help you choose the product and application, under base or over base. The more severe the discoloration, the greater the need to use a dense product or 100-percent pigment for camouflaging.

For birthmarks, port-wine stains, and tattoos, you will need a two- to three-layer process for complete coverage. This is done before applying a makeup base. This layering of color allows you to cancel out color completely, without any bleed-through. Sometimes a color will bleed up through the cover-up, usually in a gray undertone. You will use the stipple technique to apply color over each layer. For your first color, use the opposite color on the color wheel to cancel out the discoloration. Your second color is dependent on how much coverage is needed: (a) if just two layers are needed, your second layer is a matching flesh tone, or (b) if three layers are needed, your second layer is a mauve (red) or orange tone to cancel out any gray bleed coming through from the first layer. Many times there will be a gray bleed or tone coming through the correction. You will see it with your eye and in the makeup mirror. In these situations, you need three layers of color. Your second layer will be to neutralize the gray, and your third layer is the flesh tone. This is 100 percent coverage for those situations with intense color (port-wine stain) or ink (tattoo). These products are 100-percent pigment. They are not sheer, and are designed for camouflaging.

Try: Dermacolor by KRYOLAN and Dermablend Cosmetics Concealers.

Natural Makeup

Simplicity is the ultimate sophistication.

—Leonardo da Vinci

When the character needs (or the director requests) a "natural look" for makeup, you want to show good health and appearance. You will spend most of your time enhancing the skin tone to show good health. Correct any discoloration, cover any scars or blemishes, and make the skin look healthy and vibrant. Remember to strive for realism. A tinted moisturizer works well in this look to even out the skin without looking like makeup (try Laura Mercier Tinted Moisturizers). This is also a great choice for men and children. An alternative is to mix a small amount of oil-free moisturizer (try All You Need+ from Prescriptives) with your liquid or cream base. This will give you a sheer coverage that does not look overdone. If you need a bit more coverage, use a liquid or cream without mixing moisturizer into it. In situations where the actor's skin is good and does not need a base or foundation, use the "spot paint" technique to balance out the skin tone. Spot painting is the technique of literally painting with makeup or concealer just the area or "spot" that needs it. Do not over apply or bring the makeup too far into the surrounding area of skin. You want to paint just the specific spot. KRYOLAN's Dermacolor (an industry standard) works well with spot painting. It is noncomedogenic, and gives you dense, full coverage (camouflage) that you can feather or blend the edges with your makeup brush. Set with just a hint of powder: not too much, or the area will look dry. You can forgo the powder if needed, but you will have to reapply or touch up if you do not set the makeup. Use Face to Face Supermatte Antishine by Make-Up International (an industry standard) to take down any shine on the other areas of the face. For more tips on spot painting see "Spot Painting" later in this chapter.

Remember to match the foundation or base to the skin at the jawline. This helps to balance the tone in the neck and face so you are working with as little product as possible—remember, this is the "natural look." The skin on the face is much different in tone and texture from the neck. Blend down past the jawline under the chin area. You want to avoid any lines of demarcation or "the mask" look to the face.

Once the skin is looking healthy and vibrant, you need to add color to the cheeks, and bring attention to the eyes, lips, and eyebrows. For a natural blushed effect, place cheek color in the apple of the cheeks, either cream or powder. Reds, pinks, and peaches are best.

Always put blood back into the face after completing a makeup.

Taught to Steven Horak by
Lenna Kaleva, Cincinnati

Bring it "Back to Life"

"Bring it back to life" is another makeup slang term you will hear in reference to almost all makeup applications. If something is looking dull or lifeless, you will be instructed to "bring it back to life." This can happen with concealing as well.

Next, accentuate the eyes by adding any needed definition without doing a full beauty makeup. Choose soft browns, taupes, or grays to define the lash line using pencil or powder. We do not suggest liquid liner for the "natural look"—your hand needs to be very skilled. Place the line right on the base of the eyelashes. Remember, you are defining the natural line to add definition, not doing eyeliner, so you do not want a thick line.

Trick: Use the "dot method" by placing dots of color into the lash line, both top and bottom, instead of drawing a line. By dotting in color, you create the illusion of a greater or stronger lash line without noticing the liner. This technique works excellently on men.

If you decide a bit of eye shadow is needed, use a lighter color all over the lid in creams, beiges, and pinks to even out the lid. Choose soft browns or taupes in the eye crease. Again, a very subtle hand is needed. Curling the eyelashes adds length without too much product (industry standard: shu uemura), and use mascara if needed. Clear mascara is also a great choice if the lashes are already long. If a

brown or black mascara is needed, apply a thin coat with a mascara fan. Mascara fans are great for this look—you have more control over the application and can really get beautiful lashes without too much product (we recommend Brush Up With Barbara). Remember to apply mascara to define the lashes, but not make them look coated.

PRO TIP

Dispense mascara onto artist's wax paper. Using the wand from the tube of mascara, pull off mascara onto the wax paper. This allows you plenty of product to do both eyes by using disposable wands or a mascara fan, and keeps the tube of mascara sanitary.

No double-dipping of the wand into the tube! Disposable wands come by the dozen.

Bring subtle definition to the eyebrow by grooming the eyebrows and, if needed, adding a touch of color for shape and fill. Care must be taken when adding color to the brows in the "natural look." Use short brushstrokes (or pencil strokes) in a 45-degree angle for similar hair growth. Trick: Paint the eyebrow hair instead of painting the skin in this look. Using a mascara wand, apply color directly to the hair and not the skin. This is great on men. It will not work on someone's brow that is in need of filling because of lack of hair.

Try: Roux (Tween Time) Stick by Revlon, StaColor, Reel Color. Taupe and soft browns work well and do not photograph too dark. Medium to dark browns will photograph darker than they appear to the eye. Too much color and your makeup will not look natural.

Keep the mouth looking healthy by using just enough color to blush the lip. Use lip stains, tint with a matte or sheer lipstick, or use a lip pencil with a lip moisturizer to get the color and attention needed without looking too "lipsticky." There should not be too much gloss for this look. Do not use lip gloss or heavy shine on men or children. Keep the focus on giving the individual the appearance of good health. Your technique needs to be subtle and clean without the obvious enhancement of makeup. Again, it's the "natural look" (Figure 7.2).

FIGURE 7.2: YOUNG WOMEN WITH NATURAL-LOOK MAKEUP

Spot Painting

If the actor's skin tone and condition are good, then no foundation or makeup base is needed for the "natural look." Instead, you will choose to "spot paint" the face and not apply a full application of foundation or makeup base. Spot painting is the technique of literally painting out unwanted color from the face or body. Any spots or unwanted marks are painted out with a concealer, Dermacolor, StaColor, or even foundation. The product you choose depends on what is to be covered. Spot painting is a part of concealing and correction, but in this case, we use it to replace foundation or base.

Example: You are instructed by the makeup department to "just spot paint" your actor. They do not want makeup base applied. They want you to just spot paint correction on clean skin, and only in the needed areas. This is widely used on men, children, and for all situations where you do not want to see any makeup. It has become an industry standard.

StaColor and Reel Color can be used in spot painting when the makeup needs to be waterproof, sweatproof, or friction resistant (such as for necks so color does not come off on shirt collars).

Working with the individual's clean skin, apply a sunblock first if working outdoors, concealing only where needed, and matching the concealer to the skin tone. The concealer or makeup is concentrated only on the spot or area that needs correction. Blend or feather out onto the skin, being careful not to over-paint or bring the edges too far onto the surrounding skin. You just want to paint the specific spot. Dermacolor (by KRYOLAN) works well with spot painting. It is non-comedogenic, and gives you full coverage (or camouflage) that you can feather or blend onto the surrounding skin with your brush. Choose a makeup brush that is small in size to prevent over-painting. Set the makeup with very little powder. Too much powder on bare skin is dry looking. When spot painting a face, use Face to Face Supermatte Antishine by Make-Up International (an industry standard) to reduce shine on the skin. Because the skin is basically clean, with the exception of the "spots," do not use powder to cut shine. Powder needs something to stick to, so on clean skin, use Supermatte Antishine, available in light, medium, and dark tones.

You can also use spot painting to correct broken capillaries, blemishes, birthmarks, and tattoos.

If it is obvious to the eye, it is obvious to the camera.

Steps to Spot Painting

It is recommended that you always use a sunblock as part of your prep when working outdoors. Depending on what you are covering, you have a choice of single-layer, double-layer, or triple-layer applications.

Single-color application:

1. Prep skin (if need) for all applications.
2. With a brush, apply concealer or Dermacolor to the discolored area, matching to the skin tone. Choose a makeup brush that is appropriate in size for the area you are correcting, and check to make sure it is blended. Lightly powder.

Two-color application (for stronger color correction):

1. Prep skin.
2. With a brush, apply concealer using the opposite color on the color wheel to cancel out (neutralize) the discoloration (see Chapter 3, Color).
3. Layer second matching skin tone color on top, over the neutralizing color.
4. Lightly powder.

Three-color application (for birthmarks, port-wine stains, tattoos, or gray tones):

1. Prep skin.
2. Apply first neutralizing color, the opposite color on the color wheel to the discoloration.
3. Apply second neutralizing color by layering or stippling a mauve (red) or orange over the first neutralizing color. This cuts any gray that is bleeding up from the first layer. Inks, gray undertones, and intense colors will have a tendency to "go gray." This gray tone "bleeds" up through the correction colors. You will see it with your eye and in the mirror. Cut it with a mauve, red, or orange.
4. Layer the third color in a matching skin tone over colors one and two. Check your coverage in the mirror. Is the gray gone?
5. Lightly powder.

The stipple technique is an up-and-downward motion of application using a brush, sponge, or textured sponge. This up-and-down motion prevents the removal of any layers of makeup that are being applied. It is needed in spot painting, character makeup, effects, and prosthetics, but can be applied to most applications.

We want to stress how important it is to master the art of natural makeup and spot painting before moving on to beauty makeup. Practice on your models, your friends, and family. Practice until you believe it. Take photos and critique your work.

In film, beauty makeup is character makeup. Every makeup begins with the text. Makeup is simply one of several languages used to elaborate and illustrate text. Based on the text, we make all sorts of decisions: the character's physical well-being, social and financial status, level and condition of vanity, and inclination to spend time in front of the mirror.

—Richard Dean

Beauty Makeup

Beauty makeup in film and television has many layers to it. You are accentuating the face as well as adding character and background. We discuss designing characters in greater detail in Chapter 8. Beauty does not have to mean symmetry for film or the camera. The camera and the lens love irregularity. There will be jobs where you work for symmetry, and an equal number where you do not. This does not apply to video, HD, theatre, or to the retail world. These are media that will require symmetry. You will adjust your makeup designs and application for the medium you are working in.

Unfortunately, some individuals will look in the mirror and want symmetry. If you are working on a film, sometimes a gentle reminder that the camera loves irregularity will help, but often you will have to accommodate individual insecurity and vanity. Every situation is different.

Beauty makeup should accentuate and not overwhelm. It is not a mask, or unnatural looking. Accentuate the positive, without re-creating the face. In the beginning of film, the custom was to blank out the face and to paint back in the desired features. This is no longer the custom or trend. Reality is the accepted beauty aesthetic today.

> We no longer do makeup by the pound.
>
> —Randy Huston Mercer

Beauty does not stop at the face. You also have to do necks, hands, arms, legs, and—if needed—the full body. The skin should appear healthy—in some cases, glowing. Bring attention to the eyes, define the eyebrows, and add color to the cheeks and lips. The eyes can captivate, and are generally everyone's best feature. If you cannot see the eyes, the audience loses interest, so eyes play an important role in all media.

Richard Dean's Tips on Beauty

1. Begin with a foundation primer and any eye shadow primer. Apply with a sponge. Areas of the face have uneven oil distribution, and will accept and hold foundations irregularly. A primer will have moisturizing effects in that it retards water evaporation from cells, and will create a more even surface for foundations and color cosmetics.

2. Liquid or oil foundation applied with a foundation brush. To keep a more natural look to the skin's surface, use foundation sparingly, do spot coverage (spot painting), and add pinker tones to the foundation with cream rouges as they naturally occur in the skin.

3. Cheeks are typically a bluish pink, never brown. Think blood vessels, the source of color. For a natural cheek, drag cream blusher down slightly toward the jawline and add a touch to the bridge (not tip) of the nose. This may be very subtle or quite heavy, depending on the situation. Example: Approximate the palest Irish skin with flushed cheek.

4. Powder with a yellow-based powder, then add powdered blush on the surface. The pink-yellow-red layer imparts a sense of depth, and therefore reality, to the foundation's finish. As the day progresses, try to blot before adding more powder. Remove as much natural oil as possible with blotting paper. Natural oil production plus powder creates another layer of a kind of foundation that gets heavier throughout the day if never blotted.

5. I use eyelashes for character effect.

In beauty makeup, the amount of attention brought to the eyes and eyebrows will depend on character and situation. There is a range to work from, but save the "smoky eye" for the glamour makeups that are more stylistic and dramatic.

Practice eye treatment and combinations of colors with as many models with varieties of eye color and shape as possible. Your eye and hand need the practical experience to develop your talent. You need to make mistakes as well as get it right to have the ability to deal with the uniqueness of each person.

Practice the art of eye shadow. Start with applying an eye shadow primer all over the lid. Try Paula Dorf. This preps the eyelid, helps the shadow last, and gives a smooth finish for eye shadow application. Using an eye shadow brush, apply a base color of shadow in cream, pink, beiges, all over the lid. Next, define the eye structure by applying browns or grays or blues in the eye crease. Placement is key; color choice is open to what looks good on the person. Start with browns until you have mastered placement. Have your model look in the mirror to check and correct placement. This is "working off the mirror." You will do this to correct and check your work in all situations. Does the eye look open and balanced, or drooped? Is there enough definition? Is the application smooth and consistent in color, or muddy? Is there too much color in the inside corner? Too much of a straight line in the crease? Take photos to critique placement and style (Figure 7.3).

Beauty in Print

By Daniela Eschbacher

For fashion or beauty shoots, there are no limits. It is important to ask photographers about the image they want and how they are going to work the light. Do they want contrast or sober, or luminous and mild? For example, if photographers use artificial light with an emphasis on strong contrasts, the makeup needs to reflect well in the light.

Natural colors work best in most beauty makeups, from creamy white to chocolate brown. Warm colors also work well—pink, rose, peach and oranges. In beauty makeup, you want to look for textures that could be interesting. Your goal is to have smooth, shiny, and elegant skin. Glosses on the eyes create a very fresh look. On the cheeks, eyelashes, and eye brows, glosses will attract light.

FIGURE 7.3: CLOSE-UP OF NATURAL-LOOK EYE MAKEUP (FROM SHUTTERSTOCK)

Black-and-White Photography

In fashion, you do not always know if the job is going to be in color or black and white. Sometimes during or after the shooting while the photographer is working with Photoshop, looking at both color and black-and-white images, that decision is made then. For jobs when you know in advance that you will be shooting in black and white, you need to work more with contrasts and exaggerate the intensity of colors and shades. There is a lot more "graphism" in black and white than in color photography. We concentrate on the contrasts, shadows, and lighting instead of color. Graphic lines and structure work very well for the makeup, such as strong eyebrows, eye liner, and nicely colored, matte lips. Still it's important to ask the photographer exactly how the light is going to be worked. For black-and-white photography, it's important to have a good balance between warm and cool tones to make the skin look beautiful and alive.

Prep

I start with prepping the model, cleaning the model's face with mild liquid cleanser (Crealine), and depending on the skin, applying an appropriate moisturizer. I am not a fan of heavy creams or moisturizers. Natural oils and vitamins work well without affecting foundations. Nuxe Multiusage Dry Oil hydrates very well and won't make the model sweat. Check the model's lips for dryness, as models tend to have dry lips. Take the time to prep the lips properly. Sometimes I do a soft peeling to take off the dead skin, and afterward apply Elizabeth Arden Eight Hour Cream, a must for every Makeup Artist. I also check the hands and nails. Nails should have a good shape, no old or chipped polish, and no dry skin. Apply hand cream if needed.

The Makeup

Let the oils or moisturizer absorb before applying the foundation. Use eye products that are moist and creamy in texture, with soft eye pencils to work your shape for the eyes,

blending and adding as you go. Purples and chocolate colors work well for this. To increase the contrast, use a powder shadow in gray or black only in areas that need contrast. Apply mascara and individual false eyelashes to the outside corners of the eyes to add drama and depth. Foundation is applied next. Follow with loose powder to set. I like Chanel. Use bronzer to sculpt and shape the face. Remember: Creating depth and contours is important on a shoot when the photographer wants contrast.

Shape the brows using three colors: brown, black, and gray. This mimics the different colors of the hair in the brows and you will adjust the colors depending on your model. I work with an airbrush, using Temptu products mixed with an SB solution.

On Set

Always check your makeup in the light of the studio. The makeup room is always bright and the light can be quite yellow. The studio might be completely opposite. Ask the photographer to do a test photo to see how the makeup comes across. Most photographers work in digital so the image can be downloaded right there to a computer and the results shown right away. Photographers appreciate your taking charge of knowing when it is a good time to touch-up lips, add some gloss, brush the eyebrows, and powder the skin. It is so much more interesting to participate in the entire process of making a good photo.

PRO TIP

To glue anything to the skin or eyes, use a transparent eyelash glue. When you glue anything to the skin be sure to clean the area afterward. Any glue remaining on the skin tends to shine in a photo and can be obvious in close-ups.

PRO TIP

Do not over-powder the face, especially for close-ups! This is really difficult for the photo re-toucher to correct afterward. Powder only certain areas—around the nose, forehead, and chin, and at the last minute.

Makeup Removal

For makeup removal, I normally use Crealine, which is easy to use and good for all skin types. Be prepared with makeup removal pads too; they are fast and efficient. Some models prefer to remove their own makeup, especially around the eyes and lids. Some will have their own products with them that they wish to use, preferring to avoid mixing skin-care brands. This is understandable given the amount of makeup they wear and remove.

Brow Shaping

Brow shape conveys a number of emotions and expressions, and is a focal point on the face (Chapter 1, Shapes). We use brows to draw attention to the eyes. Shaping and changing eyebrows is a great tool in character design and altering a look. The level of intensity and style of the brows will come from the character or situation. Brows should have a natural, unpainted look when doing a "beauty look" or "natural look." Glamour makeup has all the drama, with a precise shape to the eyebrow that is obviously drawn or painted on. There are several ways to shape brows using various products, including brow pencil, brow creams or shadow, eye shadow, temporary hair color, StaColor, or Reel Color.

Choose colors that are close in shade to the eyebrow or slightly lighter. Remember, browns photograph darker. For a realistic brow, use two colors, to fill in or shape.

You can use brow pencils or brushes. If choosing brushes, pick a brow brush with stiff bristles that are cut at an angle (try Cargo's brow brush).

PRO TIP

Use a combination of brow pencils to shape, and brow powders to fill in or soften the pencil work. Follow over the completed brow with a cream or light-colored eye shadow to fade your work.

Find the brow shape by taking the handle of a makeup brush and laying the handle gently on the face vertically. Starting from the inner corner of the eye at the nose, point straight up toward the brow. The general rule is to start the brow at the inner corners of the eye (or one eye length between each eye). Next, with the brush handle vertical, gently place the handle on the outside of the iris with the handle going up to the brow. This is your highest point in the arch, or where the natural arch should be, and sometimes is not. Approximately a half-inch from the arch is where the brow should end. For the beginning brow artist, take a pencil and lightly mark any area of the brow that you feel needs shaping.

Start with the inside corner of the brow and use light, short feather strokes in an upward or 45-degree angle (depending on how the hair grows). Move along the brow in this way, filling and shaping where needed. Use different colors. Remember not to fill in too much, just where needed. If you are using the brow pencil and brow powder technique, add brow powder in a lighter shade, and go over or fill in areas that are too harsh from the pencil. You can use brow pencil alone or brow powders alone, depending on your hand and eye.

Brow sealers can be used to tame unruly brows. Apply after you have shaped the brow. Sealers can darken the brows, so adjust your work accordingly. Sealers can also start to flake over time, so check your brows!

Brows also need trimming (just like the hair on the head). Makeup Artists trim brows on a regular basis, particularly on men. Have a small trimmer on hand (Panasonic), small round-tipped scissors, and a small-toothed comb (a mustache comb or brow comb works). Keep everything clean, sanitary, and running well. Follow the manufacturer's directions for the care and cleaning of the trimmer. Comb the brow hair upward, with your scissors at an angle, trimming any hair that is too long. Work a little at a time until you have the desired results. It is better to make several passes during trimming than to cut too much in one pass.

PRO TIP

Facial-hair lighteners are used to lighten naturally dark brows. This process is good for continuity and looks. Lightening is a simple process, but not something you would do on the same day as shooting. This should be done several days before, or at least one day before, shooting. Always follow the manufacturer's directions on how to use a product.

Blush the cheeks and the lips with colors that work with the skin tone, costume, and situations. Placement depends on the individual features, character portrayal, and current trends. Experiment with different colors and placement on your models to see the effects of color, placement, and shapes on the cheeks and lips. Refer to Chapter 1, Shapes.

I very much depend on the Estée Lauder Smoothing Creme Concealer, using it under the foundation of every woman's makeup that I do, and some men's. It not only works beautifully on dark circles and blemishes, but also as a successful eyebrow cover when only a small portion of the brow needs to be blocked.

—Steven Horak

Glamour Makeup

Painted perfection, beautifully sculpted—use your imagination with color, boldness in application, and dramatic placement to create a stylized look that is glamourous. Depending on the design or look you want, start with blanking out the face with a flawless foundation that has complete coverage with correction. Re-create the desired features using beautifully sculpted contour and highlight. Add drama to the eyes and eyebrows with bold shapes and color. Consider painting in the eyebrows and using false eyelashes, with eyeliner to add to the drama. Make lips luscious with a full shape using lip pencils and lipstick; top with shine or gloss. Glamour makeup should be bold in application and color, and has to be well blended. You will be working with more makeup, both in color and texture. This look is "the full slap," also known as "beat the face" (makeup slang for painted). You will need plenty of experimentation and practice in the beginning, so go for it, work it, but blend it and powder it (Figure 7.4).

False Eyelashes

Strip lashes, individual lashes, and exotic lashes are all great for bringing attention and beauty to the eyes. For subtlety in a beauty makeup, use individual lashes, which come in several lengths and styles. An alternative to individual lashes is a delicate strip lash in brown or black. For glamour, fantasy, stylistic, or theatrical productions, choose a heavier strip lash in black. Go for the flair and be as bold as the makeup design allows. Decorative or exotic lashes are wonderful in the right situations and designs.

FIGURE 7.4: GLAM EYES (FROM SHUTTERSTOCK)

Industry Standards: DUO eyelash adhesive (available in black and clear white), Andrea eyelashes, Ardell eyelashes. All are available in most drugstores.

Exotic/decorative/fantasy lashes: Elegant Lashes (www.eEyelash.com).

Before applying eyelashes, check for size. Always remove strip lashes from the tray working from the outside in to prevent damage to the strip. Without using any glue, place the strip or individual on the base of the lashes. How is the fit? Remove and trim any excess from the strip from the outside. With the individual, you are looking for length and style with the eye. This is the time to choose. After checking the fit and style, apply a thin line of glue to the strip lash. Never apply glue to the eye directly. An alternative is to put a small amount of glue onto your clean makeup palette or wax paper palette, and then apply a thin line onto the strip using a thin brush. This brush will become your glue brush. This works well with individual lashes. Always take care to avoid using too much glue, as you can glue the eye shut. Center the false-eyelash strip on the eye at the base of the lashes. With the eye closed, gently press the strip onto the base of the lashes. Have a slightly wet Q-tip ready in case you have glued the eye shut. If you do not wet the Q-tip, the cotton will stick to the glue. Application can be done with tweezers or hands, or a combination of hands, tweezers, and a soft glue brush for securing the false lashes to the base of the lashes. Successful application depends on your hands and steadiness.

Removal of false eyelashes should always be done from the outside in. Pinch the outside of the false lash with your thumb and index finger, and gently pull in toward the nose. Clean off glue by pulling off the strip, and reshape it on a tray. You can get several days on the same actor with one pair of eyelashes if they are well cared for.

PRO TIP

Curl the eyelashes and apply mascara first. Apply false eyelashes. After the glue has set (one minute), "marry" the real lashes with the false-eyelash strip by combing more mascara to combine them.

Men and Children

Script, circumstances, and skin condition will dictate your choices with makeup for men and children. In most cases, you would not want to see any makeup. Healthy skin tone, definition, and believability to the eye are key. Spot painting is recommended for both. Additional definition to the eyes and eyebrows for men is noted in the section "Natural Makeup."

Bronzers and tanning products are also recommended for men. Men's grooming should be addressed first before applying any sunblock or makeup. Check for nose hair, ear hair, unruly eyebrows that need trimming (unless the character calls for unruly), shaving mistakes, sideburns, and nails. It is always best to get all the trimming done in the makeup trailer. Use lip moisturizers that are not shiny. Try Chap Stick.

Talk about sunblock with the parent or guardian of the child. Has sunblock been applied? It is extremely rare to do a full makeup on a child. There might be spot painting of a mark, or sunblock might be needed for a child. Check for dry skin, dirty face and hands, dry lips, and scrapes and bruises. Use Chap Stick so the lips are not too shiny. Make it fun for them with flavored Chap Stick (Figure 7.5).

FIGURE 7.5: MAN AND CHILD (FROM SHUTTERSTOCK)

Body Makeup

Body makeup finishes and smoothes out the color of the skin. Even a sheer coat of body makeup will give the skin a beautiful finish that photographs better than skin would if clean. It polishes the skin for a beautiful look. Usually opaque body makeup covers veins, stretch marks, age spots, and discolorations. Sometimes you are doing just the neck and hands; other times, full leg, back, and chest, on men, women, and occasionally children. Widely used in all media, liquids are favored for their finish and are formulated for the body. Most come in water-resistant, sweat-resistant formulas.

Industry Standards: Visiora, MAKE UP FOR EVER, M•A•C.

Start with applying sunblock first, if needed, and allow time to absorb. Know the area of the skin that is not covered by clothing. Place tissue in all openings of clothes to protect from makeup. Avoid applying body makeup where clothing is covering the skin. The costume department will appreciate your protecting the clothing.

You can apply body makeup directly to the skin with a sea sponge, large foundation brush, or your hands. If sheer coverage is needed, mix with body lotion. Check for even application and no lines of demarcation. Let dry. Gently press with tissue to remove excess. Powder with a "no-color" powder or translucent powder and large powder puff. Buff off excess powder with the puff. Allow time for drying before removing tissue from clothing.

Note: Body makeup using an airbrush is covered in Chapter 10.

Covering Tattoos

Tattoos are everywhere! You will cover millions of tattoos in your career for so many reasons, such as tattoos do not work with the character, the director does not like the real tattoo and wants something more appropriate for the situation, and so on.

There are several ways to cover tattoos. We will give you two to try.

Quick and Easy

This is the fast-and-dirty method, with no prep involved, working "out of your kit" (makeup slang for using what is in your kit—and Dermacolor should be). It is for those moments of necessity and no time. This method uses KRYOLAN's Dermacolor palette, an industry standard.

1. With a synthetic precut sponge, cover the tattoo completely with Dermacolor D red B (green). Apply the Dermacolor on the tattoo itself, and not on the area around it. You do not want too much overlap, just enough to cover the artwork. This is the first color to start canceling out the ink, and therefore needs complete coverage. Note: Some tattoos have a dimensional quality from the tattooing/scarring process. You will be able to camouflage the ink, but not the dimension. You need the help of lighting to camouflage dimension.

2. Stipple Dermacolor D31 (or D32, depending on ink colors) over the first layer of Dermacolor. This color prevents gray from bleeding up through the first color, and gives complete coverage. The gray comes from the blue and black ink.

3. Stipple the third layer of the appropriate Dermacolor to match skin tone, again giving complete coverage.

4. Powder with no-color powder and a powder puff or clean sponge.

5. Lightly mist with Ben Nye's Sealer, holding the spray 12 inches away from coverage when spraying. Do not over-spray!

PRO TIP

If the coverage looks good, but a bit dull or lifeless, take a dime-size amount of body lotion rubbed into the palms of your hands, and pat onto the coverage. This "brings life" to the skin by adding moisture back without affecting the makeup. Remember to pat—not rub—and use sparingly. In some cases, red needs to be stippled over the completed coverage to bring life back to the skin. This happens with the larger designs that you have to cover. Use a textured stipple sponge with red for this, and do so sparingly to break up the color.

Tattoo Cover-up Steps

By Christien Tinsley of Tinsley Transfers, Inc.

In order to set up a tattoo cover-up, I first like to prep my workstation. Materials I have with me at all times when doing a tattoo-cover application are astringent to clean the skin, cotton pads, shavers (electric and razor), shaving cream, scissors, adhesive (Pros-Aide), latex sponges, tissue, spray bottle (water), no-color powder, powder puffs, Q-tips, 99-percent alcohol, brushes, sealer (Ben Nye's Final Seal), hand towels, isopropyl myristate, Super Solv lotion (body, hand, or face), antishine, Mac Crème Gloss Brilliance, tattoo palettes in flesh tones and primary colors; I use Skin Illustrator, Reel Color, W.M. CREATIONS, airbrush tattoo colors from Skin Illustrator, Derma Palettes, airbrush, and compressor (all items are industry standards).

No matter what approach you will take for tattoo cover-up application, you will commonly prep the skin by cleansing it with an astringent of your choice. Doing so removes dirt and oil, and slightly dries the skin for better adhesion of makeup and paint.

Depending on the size of the tattoo you are covering, you may choose to airbrush or paint it out using your makeup brushes. Either way, the colors you choose to use should remain the same. I like to think of this as though you were painting an opaque prosthetic (foam). The idea is to have a color that is not conducive to looking real, and it's attached to the skin. Your job is to make it imitate clean skin, and to blend by painting. When I say paint, I mean paint as though you have a blank canvas.

1. First, you need to start by blocking out all color of the tattoo. I like to go with a meaty red-orange color first. Paint the color solid over the whole tattoo, right to the edge, and then blend and feather it out only about a half-inch from the edge. This not only helps block out the blues and blacks used in most tattoos, but also gives you an undertone to your flesh colors.

2. Next, go in with a natural flesh tone that is about one shade lighter than the actor's own skin tone. Stipple this color over the surface—making sure it has solid coverage, but with variations of transparency.

3. Add yellows, blues, or greens to the skin to adjust the color by graying, cooling, or warming the painted area. This should give you the overall match you are looking for.

Details:

Lightly apply a hotter red to the surface already painted to bring out the effects of capillaries and natural blush colors found in the skin tones. Freckles and the occasional browning of the skin can tie the look all together.

Adjust the shade of your tattoo cover-up as you wrap around the body. Not every angle of the body has the same degree of warmth. When working on darker skin tones, you will be using reds and sometimes yellows.

4. After you are finished covering up the tattoo, a thin spray of sealer over the surface will help protect it. If your image is a little too shiny, add a little anti-shine over the surface. Try to avoid powders. Flesh-tone tattoo paints, lightly applied over the surface, can help. Use a silicone- or water-based product.

Note: Never put oils such as glycerin on top of your tattoo cover for a wet or sweaty look. This will break down the cover.

For on-set touch-ups, always have your paints and makeup colors with you in case you have to remove and reapply on set. For minor repairs, have premixed colors to match and fill in areas that have rubbed away.

For removal of tattoo cover, mix isopropyl myristate and Super Solv in a 50/50 solution. Warm the mixture to a temperature comfortable to the skin. Gently rub the remover with a powder puff in a circular motion on the area to be cleaned. Follow with a dampened hot hand towel to remove all solvent.

Five o'Clock Shadow

Painting or stippling in beard growth is done to show a "five o'clock" shadow or a few days growth without using any real hair glued onto the face. It is a basic, easy, fast technique that every Makeup Artists knows. It is sometimes requested at the last minute, on set, so always have your favorite stipple product and stipple sponges in your set bag. Skin Illustrator, StaColor, and Reel Color Products make the Makeup Artist's job a lot easier to achieve a lasting, water-resistant, beard stipple. These products are all activated by alcohol, are water and abrasion resistant, easy to use, clean off quickly, and do not rub off on clothing. They are great for doing so many different kinds of makeups that they are industry standards and invaluable for realistic effects and continuity. You should have all of their palettes in your makeup kit.

You will also be working with stipple sponges. Stipple sponges are textured sponges, available in different gauges and density for different stippling effects. Orange stipple sponges are softer to the touch and more elastic. Black stipple sponges are coarse and much firmer than the orange ones. "Stipple" is also a term used for technique as well as to describe sponges and application. It is part of the makeup industry's vocabulary. An example of this terminology: When the Makeup Artist you are assisting says, "Stipple some color into his cheeks"—she or he is asking you to use the technique of stippling to add color to the cheeks with an up-and-down motion using a sponge or brush. It is not complete coverage, but rather varied and inconsistent. The up-and-down motion is done with a light touch, using the wrist in a tapping motion. This gives a realistic look that is not masklike. It is not complete coverage of color. There is an air quality to it that gives a variation of color and intensity that is organic. This technique is essential to create real-looking beard growth. You will use it often, and for many types of makeups. If you were to apply complete coverage for beard growth it would look comical and clownish.

Stipple technique is also used to fill in real beards to make them look fuller or appear to have more growth, for long-distance shots where

FIGURE 7.6: FX SKIN ILLUSTRATOR PALETTE

you do not want to lay hair by hand, stunt doubles, and background artists who will not be shot in close up (Figure 7.6).

Let's look at the three products and how to stipple a beard growth with each.

Kenny Myers, creator of Skin Illustrator: I use a black stipple sponge with varied coarseness and sometimes by hand with round natural bristle brushes in varying sizes.

Occasionally, I've used a dye brush and thumb technique splattering the stipple for an uneven look, then going in and removing obvious blobs. Illustrator is designed to be mixed according to the complexion you are working on. But, I'll often start with a black, white, and yellow mix from the FX Palette and make variations. It's really impossible to give a specific formula or even percentages since mixing is an individual painter's eye and art. But I would always start with black as the base tone then mix in bits of yellow, blue, and white to give that blue or green cast that beard stubble can have. Adding in additional colors is for fine tuning to suit an individual. Varying opacity and building layers rather than trying to do it in one shot (always a mistake-unless you want it to look fake) is the best approach (Figure 7.7).

Matthew Mungle: Apply GBB Beard Stipple using different densities of beard stipple sponges (black beard stipple sponges) or thinned down liquid StaColors with 99% alcohol and airbrush using a splatter technique. The airbrush can be purchased

FIGURE 7.7: STACOLOR PALETTE

FIGURE 7.8: REEL CREATIONS' REEL COLOR PALETTE

through bearair.com, including Combo kit with compressor and Paache H brush with #3 nozzle (Figure 7.8).

Fred Blau, founder of Reel Creations: Using the cover-up effects palette and depending on the color, I usually use browns mixed with black. I use a coarse, plastic wire-type stipple sponge, and cut the hard edges off to make a semi round surface. The sponge should be about two inches. When stippling, don't try to cover large areas at once.

Dip sponge into the color then test on another surface. When density is good, you might get two to three hits on the face. Yes, it is time consuming but it works and it lasts.

If you have any heavy deposits, use a Q-tip dipped in Reel Developer (99% isopropyl alcohol), and touch the glitch once for a couple of seconds, and then turn over the Q-tip and touch again; this should lift the color. Do not rub! It will smear and ruin the look.

If you have any dark areas, you can use the same type of sponge and counteract the beard stipple with a flesh-tone mix (Cover-up Effects Palette). Stipple lightly on the heavy areas and the beard will lay down to match the desired shade. This is also a good technique for a salt-and-pepper look.

If you choose to use Reel Body Art instead of the palette, it is a good idea to pour the colors into a wide lid (i.e., pancake lid, one for each color). Let it thicken or dry. Then use the same technique as with the palette. Do not be afraid to lighten (density) color using some Reel Developer.

Stipple sponges are stiff sponges made in different textures used in makeup to create a variety of shapes and textures (Figure 7.9).

Stipple sponges can also be made from regular cosmetic sponges by tearing a desired number of holes into the sponge. This will create texture (Figure 7.10).

Favorite adhesive to use for chopped hair applications: Extra Hold Matte Adhesive.

Sun Protection

Everyone needs sunblock to protect their skin from the damaging effects of the sun. Makeup Artists should apply sunblock before a makeup

FIGURE 7.9: ILLUSTRATION OF TEXTURED STIPPLE SPONGE

FIGURE 7.10: MAKING A COSMETIC SPONGE INTO A STIPPLE SPONGE

as well as during the course of the day when filming outdoors. It needs to be reapplied to protect the skin through all daylight hours. You have a certain responsibility to ensure that your actor does not burn while filming or shooting outdoors. It also makes your work a lot easier if you take the time to protect the skin. Covering burned skin is a drag; it's time-consuming and painful.

The SPF (sun protection factor) can be misleading and manufacturer claims are not always accurate. Example: Waterproof sunblock has to be reapplied after getting wet or out of the water. The labels have now been changed to "water resistant," but there are still products floating around with old labels that say "waterproof." When in doubt, reapply. SPF products with a number larger than 30 have not been proven to have any more protection, experts say. Another misleading assumption is that a sunscreen or sunblock with an SPF 30 has twice the protection of a SPF 15: not so. SPF 15 blocks out 93% of the sun's rays and SPF 30 blocks out 97% of the sun's rays. Ultraviolet B rays cause damage to the surface of the skin such as burning, tanning, and other skin damage. UVA rays penetrate the surface of the skin and damage the connective tissue. UVA long-wave protection ingredients include avobenzone, zinc oxide, titanium dioxide, mexoryl sx, tensor, and helioplex (a stabilizer). Sunblocks come in creams, lotions, gels, sticks, and sprays.

A MUST HAVE: Broad-spectrum sunblock that blocks both UVB and UVA rays.

For the face, try Neutrogena Ultra Sheer Dry Touch Sunblock in SPF 55. It works great under makeup base, feels good on the skin, and it's non-greasy and water resistant.

For the body, try Neutrogena Body Mist Sunblock SPF 45. This spray goes on beautifully and is ultra-light, non-greasy, water resistant, and great for on-set touch-up or reapplying; and feels clean on the skin. You can spray it right over your makeup.

Makeup Safety Tips

Makeup and applicators should not be shared. Use certain safety standards when working. Wash your hands in between working on each person. If a sink is not available, use hand sanitizer, or hand wipes. Always remove cream products and foundations from their container with a palette knife and place onto a makeup palette or artist's paper to use for each person. Use disposable mascara wands and applicators. Cut off lipstick from the tube and place on your

palette to be used off the palette only. Clean brushes after each use. Sharpen all pencils before and after using. Clean lipstick brushes with 99% alcohol. Use sponges and puffs on one person only.

Industry Standards: Stainless steel palette, artist's paper palette, Japonesque makeup palettes, stainless steel palette knife, 99% alcohol.

Product Update

Skin Illustrator has added the following five palettes to its product line, making your creations much easier:

Dark Flesh Tone Palette: Designed as the follow-up to the original flesh tone palette, the dark colors complete the entire range of flesh tones (Figure 7.11).

Complexion Palette: This palette was created to give artists a wider range of red tones and adjusting colors that allow fine tuning of an appliance makeup or to help blend the appliance with natural skin tones (Figure 7.12).

FIGURE 7.11: SKIN ILLUSTRATOR PALETTE, DARK FLESH TONE

FIGURE 7.12: SKIN ILLUSTRATOR PALETTE, COMPLEXION

Alchemy Palette: Enhance pre-existing tattoos or create your own with these amazing colors. You've never seen such stunning metallics as these (Figure 7.13).

Zombie Palette: Every combination you need to color the dead (Figure 7.14)!

Grunge Palette: Simulates a variety of dirt, grime, and filth effects, and can be used to re-create the look of almost any dirty or soiled visage (Figure 7.15).

FIGURE 7.14: SKIN ILLUSTRATOR PALETTE, ZOMBIE

FIGURE 7.13: SKIN ILLUSTRATOR PALETTE, ALCHEMY

FIGURE 7.15: SKIN ILLUSTRATOR PALETTE, GRUNGE

References

Habif, T.P., 1996. Clinical Dermatology, third ed. Mosby, St. Louis.

Internet Resources

Blau, F., Beard stipple with Reel Colors. www.reelcreations.com.

Dean, R., Rdean1028@mac.com.

Mungle, M., Beard stipple with StaColors. www.matthewwmungle.com.

Myers, K., Beard stipple with Skin Illustrator. www.ppi.cc.

Sunscreen index. www.consumersearch.com/www/family/sunscreen/index.html.

Sun protection and suncreens. www.medicinenet.com/sun_protection_and_sunscreens/pg2.html, www.medicinenet.com/sun_protection_and_sunscreens/pg3.html.

Sunscreen review. www.comsumersearch.com/www/family/sunscreen/review.html.

Tinsley, C., Tattoo cover-up. www.tinsleytransfers.com.

8

DESIGN

Makeup Design, HD Live, Motion Capture and 3D, Inspiration and Presentation, Blocking out Eyebrows, Aging, Temporary Tattoos, Contacts, Veneers

Makeup accessorizes the character's look, mood, and style. We put the finishing touch on the actor's exterior to match the interior performance and to bring the character to life. This enables the actor to focus on the performance and not the look, and to become the character. Many times you will feel the actor start to transform before your eyes as the makeup application progresses. They are looking into the mirror and seeing the physical appearance matching the interior of their performance/character, and their body language begins to change. At this moment, both actor and artist know the makeup design (and application) is working. You know you have been successful in developing the character.

In film, every makeup begins with the text of the script. Makeup is one of several languages used to elaborate and illustrate text. Based on the text, we make all sorts of decisions: the character's physical well-being, social and financial status, level and condition of vanity, and inclination to spend time in front of the mirror. At the point the actor or actress enters our lives; his or her analysis of the same textual information meets our own. Add to this their personal needs, physical condition, areas of insecurity, and physical strengths, and we are nearly ready to put brush to skin.

—Richard Dean

We explore, examine, research, discuss, collaborate, and meet with the director, actor, costume designer, production designer, cinematographer, and the producers. From our breakdown of the script, design meetings, production meetings, and sidebar meetings, we begin to test the looks. This is the prep period of the schedule: the months, weeks, or days (for prosthetics, the prep time is much longer) before filming begins, for both film and TV.

For photography, the design is based on conversations with the photographer, art director, and client. There could be several days to create a design or look, or just one day. It is a by-project situation, with amount of time, research, and designing per job varying greatly. From exotic, very stylized fashion to natural, to designing the look and makeup for runway collections.

Personal shoots and beauty stories can be stressful; everyone is counting on the creativity of the Makeup Artist. I love the work and the preparation behind it. Before you start to design, get as much inspiration as possible. The internet is one place, but for me it is mostly books and paintings. I love to work with color, so before I think about my makeup, I think about all the colors that will be used and what atmosphere or feelings those colors will cause to come across. Once the colors are fixed, I start with the effects; shiny or matte, graphic or shady, simple or complicated. Try to prepare as much as possible, but remember that a lot of inspiration comes when you first see the model in your makeup chair.

—Daniela Eschbacher

Theatre has its own prep or rehearsal period, where designs and makeup are worked out in technical and dress rehearsals onstage with lighting and costumes. There is the same collaboration with the director, costume designer, and lighting designer—and, you hope, a chance to see your makeup "from the house" with the lighting plot and production design. This is the time to see the makeup designs from the perspective of the audience or "from the house." Viewing should be done from all areas of seating, from the front row, middle and sides of the orchestra, and back row and balcony sections to judge and gauge how the designs are "reading" to the audience. Note the sections that "read" the best, the least, and/or diminished the quality of the makeup design.

It is generally a standard in theatre or opera to work from the vantage point of the "middle of the house." With each theatre being a different size and capacity, you adjust your work accordingly.

Working for the "middle of the house" allows the maximum number of people in the audience to see the makeup. If you work for the back reaches of the house, the makeup will be too heavy for the seats in the front rows. If you work for the front of the house, your makeup will not be seen by anyone seated past the first few rows. So you split the difference and go for midway range.

> Dive into the historical aspect of the play through both text and pictures. What social status do the characters have? Where in the world (or elsewhere!) is the play set? Who is "good" and who is "evil"? Who is related to whom? Are they similar or not? Should you stylize the look or keep it normal? Is the play based on a "real" person? How does the actor's age differ from the character's? From all of these questions and many more … you will start your design.

> —Lars Carlsson

Theatre and opera also must make adjustments for HD filming during the performance. The use of live broadcasts and videotaping of the performance have altered the products and style of makeup used for stage, and has lessened the theatricality of the makeup. In most cases the filming is done only for specific performances; so the adjustment to makeup is done only at this time specific to the filming. Some companies will bring in various artists to consult and assist in the adjustments of the makeup designs, as there will be a film crew integrating with the theatrical crew.

HD Live

With Matiki Anoff

Matiki Anoff is a film Makeup Artist who adapts stage performances for filming and live broadcasts using HD cameras. This has opened up the arts and given audiences all over the world a chance to see a performance in real time. HD filming of a stage performance brings its own set of challenges. In the beginning, the performers and stage crews were uncomfortable with the invasion of the cameras, the camera crew, and the entire setup. Live broadcasts involve an entirely separate film crew and production company from the stage crew and company. As the practice has become more standard, a collaborative environment has evolved. Remember that you have been invited into an existing working relationship for your film expertise and need to work with the staff to adapt the theatrical designs for HD. The biggest challenge in adapting a theatrical design for HD filming is acclimating the performers to the look and feel of HD makeup. The products are different so the texture and feel are not the same and the broad strokes of a theatrical makeup are not there. This can be unsettling to a seasoned performer who is accustomed to the theatrical application.

Opera is the one medium that hires for vocal talent only, with no regard to ethnicity or physical appearance. The performers are so used to being theatrically made up to look younger, older, different ethnicity, or otherworldly, that they feel naked without the mask of theatrical makeup.

For both theatre and opera, the first step is seeing a "tape" of the performance. The film crew works from this first tape to become familiar with the production, including staging, lighting, and costumes. The film crew starts its design and adaptation for the cameras here. Next is meeting with the theatrical makeup department at this point to discuss what colors they used in their design and any needs or other information regarding the design of the show.

Next a "scratch taping" is done by the film crew during a dress rehearsal to check all elements and design. This "scratch tape" is used to perfect the look of the broadcast, which is particularly important in a live broadcast, making adjustments in their camera angles, lighting, makeup, and choices of shoots in preparation for filming.

The products, techniques, and approaches are different, so remember that there is also a learning curve for the performer. Many times they need to see the scratch tape to feel comfortable with how they look and how the design looks on HD.

It is very rewarding work for a film Makeup Artist to adapt a theatrical show for HD filming. The one common thread is … contour, contour, contour!

PRO TIP

Sit in all sections of the house during the rehearsal process to judge your work and gauge the "readability" of the makeup from all perspectives, including the balconies.

Motion Capture and 3D

Motion capture, motion tracking, or mocap are terms used for the process of creating a 2D or 3D representation of a live performance. Mocap records the movement of the actor and translates that movement onto a digital model. The actor wears a mocap suit and head gear with sensors to record the movement pattern that is entered into the computer through

the sensors. Facial dots are applied for facial tracking. These mocap dots need to be applied and maintained by the makeup department with consistency in placement. Each situation will be unique in terms of makeup department needs and you will need to communicate with the visual effects producer or designer regarding what is needed from the makeup department. In some cases the visual effect producer will ask for a makeup design and the application of the makeup to be done on the actor before applying the mocap dots to assist in the final look. In other situations you will apply the mocap dots on a clean face with special paint developed for mocap and 3D filming. Vauform face masks are prepared for each actor for the daily application of the mocap dots.

Mocap and Makeup

Mocap is a rapidly evolving science utilizing teams of people. Each film will have a different set of challenges and each visual effects company (VFX) will have their own style and unique needs.

Syncing LED (light-emitting diode) markers on the suits, plus testing the helmet cams (helmet cameras) is part of the process. There are also banks of manned computers and "witness" cameras that are positioned to film every possible movement of the actor/performer for future reference. The makeup department for mocap is evolving as well, and is unique to each project. At first it may seem that the department has minimal work, but the positioning of the dots is crucial to the facial cameras. The care and maintenance of the dots as well as removal of the dots is the responsibility of the makeup department. This is not always as easy as it seems since the paint used can react differently on each actor's/performer's skin. Some paints simply wipe off, while others need a prosthetic remover such as isopropyl myristate.

Before going to camera there are various stages necessary to facilitate motion capture. The principal actors/performers need facial and body scanning to follow the movement of the major muscle groups, especially the face. Technicians carefully map out the best points for facial movement and expression for the makeup department. Actors/performers are then scanned 360 degrees and photographed.

From the scans, full vacuform face masks are built for each actor/performer with the position of the dots. The positioning of the dots is critical to the facial cameras and they are a constant concern. There can be teams of Makeup Artists that maintain and track the "dot marks."

On the Job

In the film, *Caesar: Rise of the Apes*, Victoria Down found that there was a whole new technology and learning curve.

Caesar is a unique film in that mocap performers were working alongside actors in practical sets. Often the motion capture work is filmed in a totally separate, controlled studio and then integrated into the film. Taking on a project like this follows with first designs and concept meetings. Through these meetings we learned that this was not to be the usual makeup film. WETA, a New Zealand based visual effects company, was designing the apes solely by computer.

My responsibility as department head was to work closely with the mocap team, ape performers, facilitate facial and body capture, while filming live action. My first responsibility was to cast the teeth of the twelve principal ape performers. Next was designing and building ape, orangutan, and gorilla teeth that would mimic the actual animals. Each is built to appropriate scale for each actor's face. The teeth are extremely thin, and used to plump the upper and lower lips.

This will help the actors to move their mouths with fangs, aiding their performance. The teeth were also tracking markers for the VFX team to follow when they designed their own teeth for animated apes. The paint used is a special Mocap paint that was developed for *Avatar*, in specific colors depending on light levels and skin color. This paint has a fluorescent reflection, readable by the facial cameras. Paint was developed to be long wearing, because of the heat of mocap suits, and the friction of helmets with cameras attached.

On each face the Makeup Artist glued 300 tiny silver balls that had hexagonal reflective surfaces, carefully mapped out by technicians to be the best points of muscle movement and expression. Though this was a nonprosthetic makeup show, we did build twelve slip-on face masks, based on the conceptual drawings of the ape characters for use in deep background, and to help the director of photography in lighting.

—Victoria Down

There is much to think about in all areas of makeup design for all mediums, starting with: What medium is being used? What is the look (style) of the project? Is there a color palette that all departments are working with? Who are the characters (and what are their backgrounds)? What is the movement of the story? Who is the client? Is it an editorial shoot or advertising? Where are the shooting locations? What are the environmental factors; continuity issues? What are the scheduling issues? What is the director's vision or desires? What does the actor require or want? Is there an arc to the story that affects the makeup movement? What research needs to be done to create realism? What creative influences do you want to use: European fashion magazines, art books, American fashion, street or local fashion, or museums? Is it fantasy, real life, or futuristic? What is your inspiration?

Inspiration

Inspiration for design can come from just about any source. It's all around you. People watching is a great source of inspiration. Ride the subways and public transportation, visit different neighborhoods, people-watch at the airport, go to clubs and social events that appeal to the specific types of characters that you are researching. Keep current with beauty trends and fashion—think internationally with sources from Milan, Paris, London, New York. Art books, photography books, old *Life* and *Time* magazines, and old catalogues from the time period (e.g., Sears and Roebuck) are great sources. Walking down the street you see the most interesting makeup choices and characters that you never would have imagined otherwise. Inspiration is all around you (Figure 8.1).

Presentation

There are many ways to present your concepts and designs: verbally, visually, demonstrated on practical models, and of course a combination of all. Each situation and individual can require a different style of presentation. Keep in mind the need to present your designs in a way that works best for those making the decisions to clearly see the direction of the designs and that also showcases your ideas. A poorly put together presentation will take away from your designs. You should be able to discuss and show examples of your designs. Presentation books organized with illustrations, photos, sketches, story boards, magazines, and Photoshop are all standard methods for presentation. In many cases, Photoshop will be essential (Figure 8.2).

FIGURE 8.2: PHOTOSHOP
Courtesy Matthew Mungle

FIGURE 8.1: A, ETHNIC OLD MAN (ISTOCKPHOTO). B, HENNA HANDS (ISTOCKPHOTO). C, TOKYO PEDESTRIANS (ISTOCKPHOTO)

Gimp is a free, open-source software which can do almost everything that Photoshop can do for the less-experienced user. For portrait makeups (recreating a likeness from a real person), freeware morphing software will find the differences between the "real" person and the actor (Figures 8.3 and 8.4).

—Lars Carlsson

In film, there is movement to makeup and it can be necessary to work for 360 degrees.

FIGURE 8.3 MORPH IN SIX PHASES (SEE NEXT PAGE FOR LAST TWO MORPH PHASES)
Courtesy Lars Carlsson

Continued

FIGURE 8.3, CONT'D

FIGURE 8.4: MORPH COMPLETED

Our work is consistently changing with the mood or emotion, physicality, situation, and the environment of the character and the filming. It can be extremely subtle or very obvious. Attention to detail and character brings life and believability to the look. The more believable, the less focus on the fact that makeup was used to achieve a look.

Read through the text several times, making notes and breaking down the script before meeting with the director. Script breaks are done by all departments, and you must compare and defer to the script supervisor's version as the final word (Figure 8.5). The script supervisor will provide a breakdown to all department heads. Recommended reading for script breakdown is *Costuming for Film: The Art and the Craft*, by Holly Cole and Kristin Burke (Silman-James, 2005).

After meeting with the director, meet with the other departments: costume designer, production designer, and cinematographer.

Script Supervisor Breakdown
BLUE Revised Draft 6.15.10
PINK Revised Draft 6.18.10

MARGIN CALL

6.19.10
Page 1 of 7

SCENE	STORY DAY	TIME OF DAY	I/E	SET	ACTION	CAST	PAGES	EST TIME	SHOOT DAY
1	D1	4:41PM	INT	LARGE INVESTMENT BANK TRADING FLOOR	The Bloodbath begins...	Peter, Seth, Heather, Lauren Bratberg, Tom, Timothy, 3 HR	2	2:36	24-Jun
A1	D1	4:45PM	INT	ERIC DALE'S OFFICE	Heather asks Eric to follow her. That can't be good.	Eric, Heather	3/8	0:23	22-Jun
B1	D1	4:46PM	INT	TRADING FLOOR	Eric walks the plank	Eric, Heather, (Peter, Seth, Lauren, Tom, Timothy, 3 HR)	1/8	0:16	23-Jun
2	D1	4:47PM	INT	TRADING FLOOR MEETING ROOM	Eric is fired and stripped of all company goods.	Eric, Heather, Lauren Bratberg, Security Guard	2	2:18	23-Jun
3	D1	4:51PM	INT	ERIC DALE'S OFFICE	Eric & Will say goodbye. Eric learns Robertson may have had something to do with it.	Eric, Will, Security Guard	1 7/8	1:43	22-Jun
4	D1	4:53PM	INT	OUTSIDE ERIC DALE'S OFFICE	Peter & Seth say goodbye.	Eric, Peter, Seth, Security Guard	4/8	0:32	22-Jun
5	D1	4:54PM	INT	TRADING FLOOR ELEVATOR BANK	Peter walks Eric to the elevator. Eric gives him a portable hard drive and says he was onto something. But be careful.	Eric, Peter, Security Guard	6/8	0:52	23-Jun
6	D1	4:55PM	INT	SAM ROGER'S OFFICE	Sam warns Will that it'll get worse. Sam's dog is dying. And he's ready to speak to the ones who made the cut.	Sam, Will	1 1/8	0:53	25-Jun
7	D1	4:57PM	INT	TRADING FLOOR	Sam gives a helluva pep talk.	Sam, Will, Peter, Seth, traders	6/8	1:11	25-Jun
8	EVE 1	4:58PM	INT	SAM ROGER'S OFFICE	Sam doesn't believe what he says anymore.	Sam	1/8	0:12	25-Jun
9	EVE 1	4:59PM	EXT	INVESTMENT BANK BUILDING/STREET	Eric tells Sarah where to go.	Eric, Sarah	6/8	0:24	22-Jun
10	N1	5:02PM	INT	TRADING FLOOR	Seth wants Peter to go for a drink. But Peter can't get what Eric gave him off his mind.	Peter, Seth	1 2/8	0:52	23-Jun

113

Script Supervisor Breakdown
BLUE Revised Draft 6.15.10
PINK Revised Draft 6.18.10

MARGIN CALL

6.19.10
Page 2 of 7

SCENE	STORY DAY	TIME OF DAY	I/E	SET	ACTION	CAST	PAGES	EST TIME	SHOOT DAY
11	N1	8:47PM	INT	VETERINARIAN'S OFFICE	Sam and his dog stare off into space.	Sam	1/8	0:08	6-Jul
12	N1	9:32PM	INT	SOHO GRAND BAR	Seth & Will pretend to have a good time.	Seth, Will	2/8	0:22	30-Jun
13	N1	9:51PM	INT	TRADING FLOOR	Peter is starting to make sense of the numbers and they don't look good.	Peter	2/8	0:18	24-Jun
14	N1	10:10PM	INT	VETERINARIAN'S OFFICE/VISITATION ROOM	Sam and his dog wait for bad news.	Sam	1/8	0:13	6-Jul
15	N1	10:22PM	INT	TRADING FLOOR	Uh-oh. He calls Eric but the phone's been cut off.	Peter	3/8	0:19	24-Jun
16	N1	10:22PM	INT	SOHO GRAND BAR	Peter calls Seth.	Seth	3/8	0:14	30-Jun
17	N1	10:22PM	INT	SOHO GRAND BAR HALLWAY	Peter convinces Seth to come back to the office with Will.	Seth	1	0:44	30-Jun
18	N1	10:37PM	INT	TRADING FLOOR	Even through a slightly drunken haze, Will & Seth realize the severity of what Eric and Peter figured out.	Peter, Seth, Will	3 4/8	4:13	28-Jun
19	N1	10:43PM	INT	WILL EMERSON'S OFFICE	Will calls Eric's house but his wife said he wasn't home yet. He sends Peter & Seth to find him.	Peter, Seth, Will	2 2/8	1:57	28-Jun
20	N1	10:45PM	INT	SAM ROGER'S CAR	Sam gets a call. A little late, no?	Sam	2/8	0:08	3-Jul
21	N1	10:45PM	INT	WILL EMERSON'S OFFICE	Will says Sam needs to come back to the office. Sam gets something big is up.	Will	6/8	0:38	25-Jun
22	N1	11:26PM	INT	BLACK LINCOLN TOWN CAR	Peter and Seth break it down.	Peter, Seth	1 7/8	1:42	1-Jul

FIGURE 8.5A, SCRIPT SUPERVISOR'S BREAKDOWN

Continued

Script Supervisor Breakdown
BLUE Revised Draft 6.15.10
PINK Revised Draft 6.18.10

MARGIN CALL

6.19.10
Page 3 of 7

SCENE	STORY DAY	TIME OF DAY	I/E	SET	ACTION	CAST	PAGES	EST TIME	SHOOT DAY
23	N1	11:41PM	INT	TRADING FLOOR	Sam comes in and heads to Will's office	Sam	1/8	0:13	9-Jul
24	N1	11:42PM	INT	WILL EMERSON'S OFFICE	Will explains to Sam what Peter discovered.	Sam, Will	3 3/8	2:58	9-Jul
25	N1	12:52AM	INT	UPSCALE CABARET CLUB	Peter and Seth look for Eric, to no avail. Seth wonders what the ladies make.	Peter, Seth	1 2/8	1:06	3-Jul
26	N1	1:33AM	EXT	TRAFFIC	Stuck in traffic.		1/8	0:14	1-Jul
27	N1	1:39AM	INT	BLACK LINCOLN TOWN CAR	Peter and Seth discuss outrageous income.	Peter, Seth	2 1/8	1:43	1-Jul
28	N1	2:04AM	INT	TRADING FLOOR ELEVATOR BANK	Peter and Seth meet up with a freshly dressed Sam and Will on the elevator.	Peter, Seth, Sam, Will	4/8	0:48	25-Jun
29	N1	2:05AM	INT	ELEVATOR	They ride up to get a "second opinion" on Peter's discovery.	Peter, Seth, Sam, Will	4/8	0:34	6-Jul
30	N1	2:06AM	INT	HALLWAY BY JARED'S CONFERENCE ROOM	They walk the long hallway to the conference room, while Seth looks for a place to throw away his beer.	Peter, Seth, Sam, Will	2/8	0:28	7-Jul
31	N1	2:09AM	INT	JARED'S CONFERENCE ROOM	Peter is questioned by Jared & Co. Oh, and he's a rocket scientist. Everyone seems to understand that this is discovery is serious and the clock is ticking.	Peter, Seth, Sam, Will, Jared, Sarah, Ramesh, firm lawyer	7	9:46	26-Jun
32	N1	2:27AM	INT	CORNER OUTSIDE JARED'S CONF ROOM	Will tells Peter and Seth that Jared is Sam's boss	Peter, Seth, Will	7/8	0:50	28-Jun
33	N1	2:29AM	INT	JARED'S CONFERENCE ROOM	Sam tells Jared that he's overreacting. Sarah and Ramesh need more time to come to a conclusion.	Sam, Jared, Sarah, Ramesh	1 5/8	1:50	26-Jun
34	N1	2:53AM	INT	FIRE STAIRWELL	The boys argue about the best route out to smoke a cig.	Peter, Seth, Will	4/8	0:25	29-Jun

Script Supervisor Breakdown
BLUE Revised Draft 6.15.10
PINK Revised Draft 6.18.10

MARGIN CALL

6.19.10
Page 4 of 7

SCENE	STORY DAY	TIME OF DAY	I/E	SET	ACTION	CAST	PAGES	EST TIME	SHOOT DAY
35					OMIT		0		
36	N1	2:56AM	EXT	ROOFTOP	The boys takes in the view and have a cig.	Peter, Seth, Will	5/8	0:50	29-Jun
37	N1	3:08AM	INT	JARED'S FLOOR ELEVATOR BANK	Jared and sarah meet on the elevator.	Jared, Sarah	1/8	0:24	24-Jun
38	N1	3:09AM	INT	ELEVATOR	Jared and Sarah exchange few words about getting confirmation on Peter's discovery.	Jared, Sarah	3/8	0:25	24-Jun
39	N1	3:26AM	EXT	ROOFTOP	Will explains where his money goes, and it ain't charity. The cavalry arrives by helicopter.	Peter, Seth, Will	3	3:11	29-Jun
40	N1	3:32AM	INT	JARED COHEN'S CORNER OFFICE	Sarah confirms the bad news. Jared is 43. Sam chooses ignorance.	Jared, Sam, Sarah	2 2/8	1:48	26-Jun
41	N1	3:41AM	INT	OUTSIDE JARED'S OFFICE	Peter, Will, and Seth let them know the helicopter arrived. Jared calls for everyone to go meet upstairs.	Peter, Seth, Sam, Will, Jared, Sarah	5/8	0:43	7-Jul
42	N1	3:43AM	INT	JARED'S FLOOR ELEVATOR BANK	The pile into the elevator.	Peter, Seth, Sam, Will, Jared, Sarah	1/8	0:17	6-Jul
43	N1	3:44AM	INT	ELEVATOR	Jared says it could get ugly and to tell the truth. Not even the rocket scientist can outsmart this.	Peter, Seth, Sam, Will, Jared, Sarah	4/8	0:36	6-Jul
44	N1	3:45AM	INT	CEO'S TOP FLOOR ELEVATOR BANK	An assistant leads them to the boardroom.	Peter, Seth, Sam, Will, Jared, Sarah, Assistant	4/8	0:33	7-Jul
45	N1	3:49AM	INT	CEO'S EXECUTIVE BOARDROOM	Tuld gets the skinny from Peter. Jared advises to sell it all but Sam is leery.	Peter, Seth, Sam, Will, Jared, Sarah, Assistant, Ramesh, John Tuld, Carmelo	8 3/8	9:32	8-Jul
A45	N1	3:57AM	INT	CEO'S ANTEROOM	Sam and Tuld have a heart to heart. Tuld wants to "get there first". Sam thinks they're breaking the first rule of sales and accuses Tuld of panicking.	Sam, John Tuld	2 2/8	2:03	9-Jul

114

DESIGN

FIGURE 8.5A, CONT'D

Script Supervisor Breakdown
BLUE Revised Draft 6.15.10
PINK Revised Draft 6.18.10

MARGIN CALL

6.19.10
Page 5 of 7

SCENE	STORY DAY	TIME OF DAY	I/E	SET	ACTION	CAST	PAGES	EST TIME	SHOOT DAY
46	N1	4:16AM	INT	CEO'S GREETING LOUNGE	"Remember this day boys, remember this day."	Peter, Seth, Sam, Will, Jared, Sarah, Assistant, Ramesh, Carmelo	5/8	0:40	9-Jul
47	N1	4:27AM	INT	CEO'S TOP FLOOR ELEVATOR BANK	Sarah and Jared prepare for another tense ride.	Jared, Sarah	1/8	0:22	7-Jul
48	N1	4:28AM	INT	ELEVATOR	Sarah wants a strategy but Jared says he never needed one.	Jared, Sarah	4/8	0:33	24-Jun
49	N1	4:29AM	INT	JARED'S FLOOR ELEVATOR BANK	Sarah says if she goes down, he goes down. Jared says... not so much	Jared, Sarah	3/8	0:24	24-Jun
50	N1	4:44AM	INT	WILL EMERSON'S OFFICE	Seth again questions people's incomes. Will plays along. Peter needs some air. Eric's wife calls will.	Peter, Seth, Will	2 2/8	1:56	25-Jun
51	N1	4:51AM	INT	SARAH ROBERTSON'S OFFICE	John tells Sarah she's the head on a stick.	John Tuld, Sarah, Security Guard	1 7/8	1:52	6-Jul
52	N1	5:03AM	INT	PARKING GARAGE	Will and Seth get ready to pick up Eric. Jared asks Will to step up if Sam doesn't "do the right thing".	Will, Seth, Jared	1 5/8	1:40	2-Jul
53	D2 DAWN	5:24AM	INT	TRADING FLOOR	The empty floor, pre battle.		2/8	0:25	9-Jul
54	D2	5:24AM	INT	SAM ROGER'S OFFICE	Sam is asleep, with headphones on. He jolts awake.	Sam	2/8	0:18	9-Jul
A54	D2	5:25AM	INT	TRADING FLOOR HALLWAY	Sam limps to the bathroom	Sam	1/8	0:14	9-Jul
55	D2	5:26AM	INT	TRADING FLOOR MEN'S ROOM	John tells Sam he's a major piece of the puzzle and that he can't have any reservations.	Sam, John Tuld	1 5/8	2:04	7-Jul
56	D2	5:57AM	EXT	CITY STREETS	The city is waking up.		2/8	0:20	1-Jul

Script Supervisor Breakdown
BLUE Revised Draft 6.15.10
PINK Revised Draft 6.18.10

MARGIN CALL

6.19.10
Page 6 of 7

SCENE	STORY DAY	TIME OF DAY	I/E	SET	ACTION	CAST	PAGES	EST TIME	SHOOT DAY
57	D2	5:42AM	EXT	CITY STREET - STREET CART	Peter runs into Lucy. He seems lost in thought. She quips about needing investment advice. Peter says sell.	Peter, Lucy, Coffee Guy	1 4/8	1:28	2-Jul
58	D2	5:52AM	INT	SARAH ROBERTSON'S OFFICE	Sarah packs up. She tries to cry, laugh, show any emotion. Nothing.	Sarah	4/8	0:50	24-Jun
59	D2	6:02AM	I/E	WILL'S CONVERTIBLE/ERIC'S TOWNHOUSE	Will and Seth find Eric's house. Will isn't thrilled to be going in alone	Will, Seth	6/8	1:00	21-Jun
60	D2	6:03AM	EXT	ERIC DALE'S TOWNHOUSE	Eric is surprised he was right. But not willing to go back. He tells Will he built a bridge once. Oh, how life changes.	Will, Eric, Seth	4 5/8	5:12	21-Jun
61	D2	6:13AM	INT	WILL'S CONVERTIBLE	Seth finds out he'll most likely be fired. Will gives a speech about us all being necessary, even if it is necessary evil.	Will, Seth	3 2/8	3:04	21-Jun
62	D2	6:16AM	EXT	INVESTMENT BANK BUILDING/STREET LEVEL	Peter and Sam exchange awkward pleasantries. Peter asks about Sam's son.	Peter, Sam	4 5/8	4:57	10-Jul
63	D2	6:19AM	INT	LOBBY ENTRANCE	The walk to the elevator	Peter, Sam	1/8	0:18	10-Jul
64	D2	6:21AM	INT	ELEVATOR	Well, good luck...	Peter, Sam	3/8	0:22	25-Jun
65	D2	6:23AM	INT	EXECUTIVE BATHROOM STALL	Seth is distraught over getting fired. This is all he every wanted. Jared says he's sorry.	Jared, Seth	6/8	1:00	2-Jul
66	D2	6:24AM	INT	EXECUTIVE QUARANTINE ROOM	Eric and Sarah share a moment. Sarah says she passed his info on. Eric extends the olive brance	Eric, Sarah, Security	3 1/8	3:18	22-Jun
67	D2	6:30AM	INT	VIP TRADING ROOM	Sam gives his speech to sell, sell, sell.	Sam, Will, Jared, firm lawyer, 40ish traders	2 1/8	2:00	6-Jul
68	D2	8:20AM	INT	TRADING FLOOR	John Tuld shares some words of encouragement to get the traders selling.	Sam, John Tuld, 40ish traders	6/8	1:04	6-Jul

FIGURE 8.5A, CONT'D

Script Supervisor Breakdown
BLUE Revised Draft 6.15.10
PINK Revised Draft 6.18.10

MARGIN CALL

6.19.10
Page 7 of 7

SCENE	STORY DAY	TIME OF DAY	I/E	SET	ACTION	CAST	PAGES	EST TIME	SHOOT DAY
69	D2	8:22AM	INT	SAM ROGER'S OFFICE	Sam hides in his office.	Sam	2/8	0:28	6-Jul
70	D2	Varied	INT	TRADING FLOOR	Lots of sellin goin on.		1/8	1:10	6-Jul
71	D2	4:02PM	INT	SAM ROGER'S OFFICE	Jared congratulates Sam on a good day. And then "invites" him upstairs.	Sam, Jared	5/8	0:38	6-Jul
72	D2	4:03PM	INT	TRADING FLOOR HALLWAY	Sam passes the firing squad from earlier.	Sam, Heather, Lauren Bratberg	1/8	0:18	25-Jun
73	D2	4:07PM	INT	SENIOR EXECUTIVE DINING ROOM	Sam wants out but John asks him to stay on. Jared is getting promoted.	Sam, John Tuld	2 6/8	2:43	7-Jul
74	N2	11:00PM	EXT	UPSCALE SUBURBAN NYC BACKYARD	Sam buries his dog.	Sam, Mary Rogers	2	2:34	10-Jul

TOTALS:			
	78 Scenes	98	107:37

116

FIGURE 8.5A, CONT'D

ALLS FAIR: MAKEUP NEEDS

Red eyes for Scooter
Head wound for Elizabeth
Bleeding drunk lady
Rabbit w/ bloody nose

STREET FAIR:

Wig and skin tone look for Dummies
Dead People
Injured Walking
Hurt People
Killer drivers injured look
Killer Drivers Huge pupils
Mats Fractured Femur
Blood
Marion's Jugular Distension
Fair Patrons Broken arm (most likely props)
Gang banger shot 3 times
Angry Gang banger
Blood on Boone

HIGH RISE MAKEUP NEEDS:

Skate boarder kid slams into car
Nail Polish for little girl at the house
 car crashes into
Todd passed out

SHOOT OUT:

Walking wounded
Worker with thumb blown off
Cubicle girl stomach wound
Gunshot mans wound
Junior Executive wound
Interior left chest wound
Grazed skull wound
Blood
Tears
Dead and injured
Seriously wounded woman
Wounded mans leg

FIGURE 8.5B, DAILY MAKEUP DEPARTMENT BREAKDOWN

The English Patient
SCENES

Scene	Day	Set / Description / Notes
1	N1 1958	**Ex/Sahara Desert** Airplane shot down over desert: man&woman fall Stunts; man in flames

Characters	Change	Scene Notes	Background	# of Bkgd	Background Notes
1.Almasy	1		Stunt Nurses		
4.Katharine Clifton	1	Dead			

Scene	Day	Set / Description / Notes
2	N1 1944	**Int/Train** Hana kisses soldier on hospital train.

Characters	Change	Scene Notes
2.Hana	1	Fr Can Nurse-uniform
15.Mary	1	Fr Can Nurse-uniform
23.Kiss Me Soldier	1	
42.Wounded Soldier #1	1	
43.Wounded Soldier #2	1	

Scene	Day	Set / Description / Notes
3	DFB1	**Ex/Desert** Pilot rescued by Bedouin tribesmen.

Characters	Change	Scene Notes	Background	# of Bkgd	Background Notes
1.Almasy	1		Ancient Arab. Bedouin tribesmen		

Scene	Day	Set / Description / Notes
4	DuskFB1	**Ex/Desert** Pilot carried across desert

Characters	Change	Scene Notes	Background	# of Bkgd	Background Notes
1.Almasy	1		Ancient Arab. Bedouin tribesmen		

Scene	Day	Set / Description / Notes
5	Dusk2 1944	**Ex/Emergency Field Hospital** Establishing Shot
6	N2	**Int/Triage Tent / Emergency Field Hospital** Hana thinks a wounded man is dead.

Characters	Change	Scene Notes	Background	# of Bkgd	Background Notes
2.Hana	1A	on duty-uniform	Bedouin tribeswomen	39	
16.Jan	1	on duty-uniform	Expedition Arab	52	
44.Wounded Soldier #3	1		Soldiers	4	

Scene	Day	Set / Description / Notes
7	NFB1	**Ex/An Oasis** Merchant Doctor attends pilot.

Characters	Change	Scene Notes
1.Almasy	1	
35.Bedouin Doctor	1	

Scene	Day	Set / Description / Notes
8	N3	**Int/Triage Tent** Hana,giving blood, hears her boyfriend has died

Characters	Change	Scene Notes
2.Hana	1B	on duty-uniform
14.Oliver	1	
16.Jan	1A	on duty-uniform
45.Canadian Soldier		

Scene	Day	Set / Description / Notes
9	D4 1944	**Ex/Beach Front , Italy** Wounded soldiers, nurses walk along beach.

Background	# of Bkgd	Background Notes
Nurses	30	
Walking wounded		

FIGURE 8.5C, COSTUMER SUPERVISOR BREAKDOWN

This is the time of discovery and aesthetic decisions. It is also a time for research. Once you feel you have done your due diligence, talk to the AD (assistant director) about meeting with the actors. The AD handles all scheduling. Your first meeting could just be a meet-and-greet (no makeup applied). If that is the case, you and the actor will discuss looks, products, and ideas. If the schedule allows, then there would be a makeup day to test or work out the looks. If there are makeup designs that are still in the experimental phase, work out the design on a model first, perfect the design or products to use, and then apply this to the actor. If you are not experimenting, work out your designs with the actor. Makeup Artists also use Photoshop to design looks and to use for a show-and-tell. Prep time and money in the budget will dictate how much makeup testing there will be. In some cases, you will not have access to an actor. Normally, there is at least one day of makeup testing done on-camera, called a "test day." This gives everyone a chance to put the work on film, look at it on-screen, and make decisions based on what was tested. When the tests are screened at "dailies," everyone involved is present. Discussion on the looks and problem-solving happens during the screening and additional tests may be requested. Many feel that prep is the most difficult time in the production schedule. This time of collaboration can become a time of too many cooks in the kitchen!

For photography, you will develop your makeup design from directions and concepts given to you by the photographer and client. On the day of shooting, test photos will be taken (or Polaroids) and, after reviewing and consulting on the photo, any adjustments or requests that are needed will be made. In theatre, your designs will start with the text and meetings, and develop during the technical and dress rehearsals in the schedule.

In all situations, remember to stay flexible in mind and hand. This is part of the process of problem-solving and collaboration that go into designing looks and characters. There will be times when you will be asked to change or correct something. Do not be put off, but understand that you will not always get it right the first time. Ideally, you will have the opportunity to start out with small projects, independent films, industrial projects, and small print jobs to hone your skills, creativity, and intuition. These small projects help to develop and perfect your problem-solving ability in design. Knowing how to achieve a look with very little money or resources, or how to create a look when the environmental issues at hand will cause problems (like humidity) is an asset. You will struggle to achieve and maintain your makeup if you do not look at the whole picture. It is foolish to not consider all elements to each design situation.

You now have some idea what the makeup department head (HOD) or makeup designer

goes through. In the beginning of your career, you will not be privy to all the meetings, discussions, and decisions regarding design. The bigger the budget and show, the more this is true. This is why we remind you often to follow instructions given by those members of the department who are supervising the makeup crew. This is true for all mediums, as much has gone into the design and choices for a project long before you arrive for your first day of work. If you are a daily hire, the larger the show, the more likely it is that you will have very little interaction with the HOD. The HOD will be relying on their crew to instruct and manage a large staff. There is a temptation in a large work situation to "grandstand," or stand out from the group. Resist the urge! When you are new and wanting to impress, all you have to do is your job! The HOD might not have the time to chat with you, but they know who is getting the work done. This is what will impress those you work for: doing the makeup asked for, paying attention, being professional on and off set, and not trying to over-step your position to get attention.

> Meetings are an important time for meeting the team… [I]t makes the whole process interesting, fun and human to take the time to sit down and discuss the project.
>
> —Daniela Eschbacher

Character Design

Character design can be thought of as all makeup designs; even a beauty makeup is a form of character design. When referring to character makeup, some people do not realize this point. They think of an old age makeup or an obvious physical alteration to the actor to show character and not beauty. All projects begin with text or concept; there is your character. Working subtly is just as challenging as painting with broad strokes when creating a character. Nicotine stains on the teeth and fingers of a character who smokes is an example of conveying the subtlety of a character. Many times the audience does not consciously notice these design details because the look is so authentic to the physical portrayal. Richard Dean is one of the top Makeup Artists in the film industry. His work gives Makeup Artists inspiration, and for the beginning Makeup Artist he will illustrate some of the thought processes for designing a makeup:

In designing the makeup for *Fatal Attraction*, the female character Alex Forrest (Glenn Close) is clearly attractive and sensual, but with an underlying layer of terrible disturbance and ill function. Symmetry and balance could not tell this story. Instead, I made an effort to suggest that something was always hidden by emphasizing the natural lack of symmetry in the human face, by lining the eyes to stress that one was slightly smaller and by tossing a shaft of hair over one eye to create a kind of three-quarter (rather than honest full face) gaze. The lady had her secrets and her "beauty makeup" contributed to her mystery. In the retail world, balance and symmetry are more useful than they are in film.

The movie camera seems to adore the less-than-perfect if it exists within the confines of perfect reproductive health and heat. Just examine the specific features of today's biggest stars. I struggle to learn what each face wants to say about itself. Unless there is a particular demand made upon one feature's emphasis over another, my habit is to let the face of the actor tell me. Or their voice if they are so inclined.

—Richard Dean

We use every trick available to tell the story and sell the look. We change eyes, teeth, eyebrows, noses, nails, skin color, and hair color. We reverse age, add age, add tattoos, change facial features, and, of course, alter with prosthetics. Your designs can be sketched, done with Photoshop, tested on models/actors, or verbalized. The better your prep and research of a project, the better your work will be. There will be times that you have no prep or research time, such as last-minute jobs, on-the-spot requests because of a new inspiration by the director or actor, or accidents that require fast problem solving. Remember that attention to detail gives your makeup designs life and so does the ability to think on your feet.

It can be daunting to execute a makeup on a leading lady when she is the second or third soprano to sing the role during the run of an opera, and there is no chance to observe her in a rehearsal and make any necessary corrections. This is where one's instincts and experience must guide one's hand.

—Steven Horak

Patty York, a film Makeup Artist with a passion for perfection, and a background as a commercial artist, prefers to illustrate her designs for film. Patty also prefers illustrating her makeup continuity charts (or face chart) as well. She meticulously shows a painted illustration and includes written details of her makeup designs, including a photo of the completed makeup on the actor or actress.

One of my job requirements is makeup continuity for the film project at hand. This means reproducing the makeup designs I've created for the film on paper, a face chart, if you will, with painted illustrations and written details. I love doing them. I get a sort of Zen buzz from the process.

—Patty York

Many times you will have to re-create looks for continuity reasons on a project. Scheduling, story line, and cost affect how often one look will be recreated throughout a shooting schedule. You need to remember what you did, how you did it, and what you used.

119

These face charts or makeup charts go into a makeup continuity book that is kept by the makeup department and turned into the studio on completion of the film. If there are re-shoots or additional photography requested by the studio to finish or change the film, the looks can be re-created by referencing the makeup continuity book—regardless of whether the original makeup department is available. These decisions are made "in post" on a project; the powers-that-be decide to change, redo, or add to a scene for many reasons, one of which is a testing audience who do not respond well to the movie. All departments in film and television keep continuity books. Everyone puts their own stamp on how the book is done. Digital photos, notes illustrated with photos, sticky notes that attach to the back of the photo, makeup charts (face charts), labeling of the cosmetics used with the scene and actor on the label, and combinations of all of the above, are some of the tools used to document continuity. Patty's face chart gives you all the detail and description to recreate her makeup design for this character (Figure 8.6A).

Kim Felix-Burke gives us another example of a makeup chart. Kim was requested to duplicate a makeup based on an ad. This shows how a photo from fashion or advertising can inspire a makeup design. The photo is from a Sephora makeup ad (Figure 8.6B).

For fashion and beauty photography, Daniela Eschbacher gives her experience with design.

> In a city like Paris, it is hard to break into the business. When I started out in the fashion industry, I contacted as many photographers and stylists as possible to do "test shooting" to build my portfolio and contacts. It is a lot of work contacting everybody and running after magazines but all that hard work pays off. After working for magazines and commercials, people get to know you and pass your name along.

In fashion, sending out your newest editorials to photographers and magazines will keep them updated on your work.

For commercial shoots, it's important to have all the information necessary from the client or photographer. The client normally knows exactly what they want, and they expect the makeup artist to realize it. When the call is for a commercial shoot I ask the theme of the shoot, the makeup look wanted, if it is an interior or exterior shoot, and how many models they are using. For beauty it is important to ask the photographer the reference of the model. The photographer can either email her portfolio to you or you can look at the agency's website for the model's book. Once you have all the information, it is time to start thinking about the makeup, products, and to double check that you have everything you need for the shoot.

If the photographer or client cannot express the type of makeup and colors they want, it is up to me to find the right look. Working in fashion is different than cinema, it can be more spontaneous. Even if you have agreed on a certain look before shooting, it could all change on the actual workday.

On larger, more complicated shoots there are meetings before the job. It is really helpful working with the art director or stylist, as they know the overall image. The stylist knows the clothing, so they can give more direction and the theme of the shoot. Sometimes a simple makeup works better than one too sophisticated or creative.

—Daniela Eschbacher

Eyebrow Blocking

Changing eyebrow shape is a wonderful and powerful tool to developing and designing a character. The eyebrows frame the eyes, the windows to the soul, making them very

FIGURE 8.6: A, PATTY YORK FACE CHART. B, KIM FELIX BURKE FACE CHART

influential on the focus of the facial features. Block out the eyebrows to completely alter a face or show "period" (for example, Victorian England). As with all makeup, it can be a very subtle or extreme block.

Three Techniques

Adhesive Block: To block out the brows, choose an adhesive that is easy to remove (see adhesives under product information). Spirit gum or resin-based adhesive works well. It is easy to remove, dries fairly quickly, and comes in different grades of matte formulas.

1. Apply the spirit gum, brushing into the brows to lay flat and smooth against the skin.

2. Using a soft cloth or powder puff wrapped in nylon, gently press and roll the brows until the adhesive looks matte. (Leather shammies or nylon or silk fabric works best with spirit gum, because they do not stick to the adhesive.)

3. When the adhesive is dry, apply a sealer over the top of it.

4. Apply foundation, choosing one that fits the character's skin tone, with full coverage and staying power.

Removal: Use alcohol or spirit gum remover.

Wax Out: Eyebrow wax comes in several degrees of hardness and many brands to choose from. We use KRYOLAN's eyebrow wax.

1. Apply wax over the eyebrow with a spatula, blending the edges into the skin.

2. Cover the brow with a sealer. Dry.

3. Finish with the correct foundation color.

Combination: Combine the spirit gum and wax for more hold and block.

1. Apply spirit gum, brushing into the hair against the skin.

2. Let dry, and follow with an application of eyebrow wax.

3. Apply sealer.

4. Apply foundation.

Appliance Block

Eyebrow appliances will give you a total block, but you must be able to blend the edges for successful application. They are applied directly over the eyebrows. Plastic-based products are easier to work with. Here we use KRYOLAN's eyebrow plastic.

Making the appliance using KRYOLAN's plastic, take a round object (such as an orange or grapefruit—they both give a nice texture) to simulate the pores of the skin.

1. Apply on the fruit a thin layer of plastic that is slightly larger than the eyebrow area and shape. Let dry.

2. Reapply a second layer. Let dry.

3. Powder with no-color powder. Lift off the fruit.

4. Apply eyebrow wax to brows to flatten.

5. Press with clean powder puff; there should be no powder or talc on the puff.

6. Apply spirit gum around the edges of the brow.

7. Lay the plastic appliance on top of the brow, being careful not to fold or crease the edges.

8. Secure and glue down the plastic. Go around the edges with alcohol to blend the edges.

9. Apply foundation of choice, and then powder it.

PRO TIP

To prevent the eyebrow hair from "bleeding" up though the plastic, lighten the hair with tattoo paints or Roux 'Tween Time Color Stick, by Revlon.

The complete removal or shaving off the eyebrows sometimes is the best and only choice in certain situations. This is a design choice that affects not only the overall design but the budget, casting requirements, and the actor's personal life. There can be additional compensation to the actor for shaving off their brows, the costs of lace brows to wear when not filming, and the added burden to the casting directors to cast actors who will agree to remove their brows. This choice does not come lightly; there is much discussion and testing before making this kind of decision among the director, producers, casting agents, and actors.

Lift Off

The "Traynor Lift" is a beauty device used by Makeup Artists for stage, film, and TV to give a youthful look to the face. Mark Traynor Face and Neck Lifts and Isometric Beauty Bands are used on both women and men for beauty, glamour, to reverse aging, and in character makeups (think *Tootsie*, drag queens, transvestites).

The "lifts" eliminate lines around the eyes and mouth, and help give a smooth, firm look to the jawline and neck. They tighten the skin and lift the eyebrows. Many times you will use them in tandem with a wig, but lifts can also be used without a wig. The hairstylist will work with you to incorporate the lifts into the hair style or wig. They are fantastic for projects where the same person goes through several decades of aging. You would use "reverse age," current age, and old age to show the passage of time (Figure 8.7).

Mark Traynor's lift package consists of two pieces of hypoallergenic surgical tape attached to two elastics, one of which has eyelets on it for adjusting the tension. To apply the lifts, the pull is very important. Start with a clean face, and decide on placement of lifts before doing any

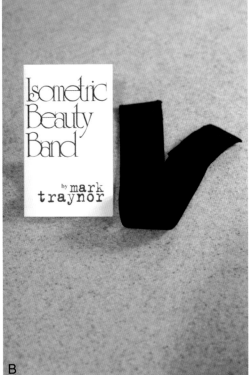

FIGURE 8.7: A, TRAYNOR LIFTS. B, TRAYNOR BEAUTY BANDS

makeup. At some point nearing the completion of the makeup application, you will stop doing makeup and attach the lifts. This ensures that your placement of makeup is correct. Once the lifts have been attached and the skin is tight and smooth, complete your makeup. The eyebrows should be done last, when the lifts are in place, to get the proper shape.

1. With the person sitting (clean face), looking straight into the makeup mirror, stand directly behind your subject. Placing your fingers at the hairline, pull to see where the lifts should be placed. You must work off the mirror image. Check the pull by adjusting your finger placement. See where it looks too tight or just right.

2. Clean the area with alcohol to remove natural oils. Let dry.

3. Apply the tape to the prep area. In some climates, you can also add a medical adhesive to the tape for extra holding power.

4. Gently place the elastics to the side or back of the head, with a clip to get them out of the way for makeup application. You are not attaching the elastic yet.

5. When your makeup application is almost complete, attach the elastic. You should work with the hairstylist at this point, to coordinate elastic with hair style.

6. Finish the makeup, and check for any adjustments that are needed. Always follow all manufacturers' instructions.

Old Age

Your knowledge from previous chapters on shapes (Chapter 1), the body (Chapter 2), and highlights and contours (Chapter 6) are needed to guide you in aging a character. We can add age to a character by painting in lines, age spots, broken capillaries, graying the eyebrows and hair, hollowing out the features by using highlights and shadows, adding fine lines, and giving an old-age texture to the skin. Texturing the skin is the finishing touch to complete your aging. Otherwise you will have painted wrinkles on smooth skin not selling the effect of the wrinkles. Each face will tell you how and where to create the look of aging. Using family genetics is a great trick in creating aging. Ask your actor for a photo of a parent at the

FIGURE 8.8: A, ASIAN FATHER AND SON. B, CAUCASIAN MOTHER AND DAUGHTER. C, CAUCASIAN FATHER AND SON

age you are re-creating; doing so will give you a blueprint on aging specific to their genetics (Figure 8.8).

Have your model raise and lower each section of the face that you are painting to find the lines (see Chapter 2). Using a medium brown with a fine-tipped makeup brush, paint in the line where the wrinkle forms. For very subtle aging, use a taupe brown. If a heavier line is needed, blend the top edge out and leave the lower edge of your line hard (unblended); this hard edge will recede the wrinkle further. Practice and work out your aging on as many models as you can at various ages. Review Chapters 1 and 2 before starting your aging exercise; we will not be giving you step-by-step instruction on aging since each aging makeup will be unique to the individual.

How We Age

Age 20

At twenty the facial appearance is lean with a deeper nose bridge. There is less softness in the cheek area, jaw line is firm, neck muscles are stronger and skin texture is thicker (Figure 8.9).

Age 30

At thirty the eyes become deeper set. Early wrinkles start to appear around the outside corner of the eyes and forehead. The jaw line becomes a little fleshier (Figure 8.10).

FIGURE 8.10: FACE CHART, AGE 30

FIGURE 8.9: FACE CHART, AGE 20

Age 40

At forty the wrinkles become more pronounced. The chin and jaw line begin to sag with flesh developing around the neck. Hair becomes thinner (Figure 8.11).

Age 50

At fifty the front hairline thins. The upper lid begins to sag and the cheek bones protrude. Wrinkles become deeper and the flesh under the jaw line drops towards the neck. Neck wrinkles become apparent (Figure 8.12).

Age 65

At sixty-five the eyebrow hairs become more untamed. Features on the face such as the nose and ears seem to become enlarged. You can see tiredness in the face. Folds of the face are deepening with the skull becoming more apparent (Figure 8.13).

FIGURE 8.11: FACE CHART, AGE 40

FIGURE 8.13: FACE CHART, AGE 65

FIGURE 8.12: FACE CHART, AGE 50

Age 80

From the age of eighty on the face ages considerably. There is considerable sag to the upper eyelids with deep wrinkles. The skin is thin and fragile looking with the lips receding into the mouth. Bone loss or teeth missing gives a bony look to the face. The hair is super-fine and receding (Figure 8.14).

Painting Old Age in Theatre

Gerd Mairandres first considers what is to be communicated about the character when designing an age makeup. For example, the sex, age, health, ethnicity, and social standing all influence the character's appearance. Is the time now or in the past? Two elements should be considered: choice of foundation, as complexion goes to all the previously mentioned points; and the character's hair, as gray or degrees of gray can contribute greatly to the appearance of age.

FIGURE 8.14: FACE CHART, AGE 80

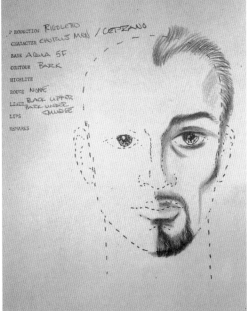

FIGURE 8.15: THEATRE AGE DRAWING. COURTESY, GERD MAIRANDRES

If the character is male and if it's appropriate for the time and place, the character may have facial hair. This can often help break up the smooth skin appearance whether it's applied facial hair or stipple.

It's vital to consider the actor's physiognomy. The makeup has to move with the actors facial expressions. Shading should follow the natural planes of the face and should follow the laws of gravity. When a face ages, the muscle structure relaxes and sags set in. Features to emphasize with "sags" may include eyes (a droop in the lid, the corner of the brow, the under-eye), the cheek area near the bottom of the nose (nasal labial folds), the corners of the mouth, and the jaw line, as well as a general deepening of the hollows created by the bone structure. Sometimes it's effective to stipple over the makeup to help create the illusion of skin that is not smooth (Figure 8.15).

When applying lace facial hair pieces for an age makeup, it is sometimes effective to deepen the shading that is to be covered by the appliance, especially if the facial hair is sparse, still allowing the facial anatomy to show through (Figure 8.16).

FIGURE 8.16: OLD GREEK WOMAN, CHART

Aging Using Stretch and Stipple

Many times the painted technique of aging is not enough to achieve the age needed. In this situation, the professional Makeup Artist should know how to do aging using the stretch and stipple technique. This is a very simple technique using three-dimensional appliances to achieve wrinkling and aging of the skin. We are going to tell you how to do stretch and stipple with two different products. Basically, the technique of stretching is the same with both products. The key to stretch and stipple is how you stretch the skin to get realistic-looking wrinkles. There will be times that you will be asked to do this without any preparation, so having the skills and products for stretch and stipple will allow you to work directly out of your kit, at a moment's notice.

Note: The information contained in the following sections is presented in good faith. The responsibility for the use of any material in special makeup effects rests solely with the user. The authors assume no responsibility for the use, or misuse, of any material, technique, or the informational content discussed here.

Green Marble SeLr Aging Technique

By Richard Snell and Kenny Myers, reprinted from Premiere Products Inc. (www.ppi.cc)

Green Marble SeLr is often used as an aging product. The results are subtle and effective. A technique called stretch and stipple (or stretch and brush) is used in the aging process. These procedures were refined by Douglas Noe during a particularly brutal summer while filming in Atlanta. To mix Green Marble into an ager, you must use Green Marble SeLr concentrate and Attagel (clay powder used in facial masks).

Very important: Do not use this technique with the spray Green Marble SeLr.

Recipe

One ounce of Attagel to six ounces of Green Marble concentrate still works well as a fine line wrinkler when used lightly. This formula also works for lighter applications or where texture change is all that is needed. You might want to custom blend the recipe to get a desired effect for different areas of the face.

- 1 to 3 oz.—Heavy ager on most skin types
- 1 to 4 oz.—Medium heavy
- 1 to 5 oz.—Medium light
- 1 to 6 oz.—Light ager on most skin types

Your makeup kit for stretch and stipple with Green Marble Concentrate:

- Kleenex
- Puffs
- Sponges
- Towels
- Hair dryer
- AF thinner (RCMA)
- Assorted makeup brushes
- Cups, Q-tips
- Cotton pads
- Kiehl's blue astringent

- Flat white synthetic brushes (3/8, 1/2, 5/8, 7/8, 1 inch)
- Cape
- Skin Illustrator Color Palettes
- Makeup remover
- Eyewash drops
- Moisturizer
- Hand sanitizer
- Powders
- Hand fan
- Green Marble SeLr Concentrate
- Chubs
- 99-percent alcohol
- Telesis 5 Thinner

Prep the Actor

Remove any fine hairs from the actor, and lightly wipe the face with Kiehl's blue astringent (product of choice) or witch hazel. To prevent lashes from sticking while you work, apply AF thinner to lashes with a mascara wand before you begin. Recline the actor in a chair for easier working conditions. An upright position is perfectly fine also. You might find yourself doing both throughout the process.

The Methods

Use a flat white synthetic bristle brush (between 3/8 and 1 inch in width), depending on the area being aged. The application changes only with the tools you use to put the SeLr to the skin. Have your brushstrokes complement the directions of the wrinkles. One to four layers, and up to as many as nine layers, can be used to get the desired effect. Stretch the area being stippled. While still stretched, apply SeLr concentrate ager with a brush, complementing the directions of the natural wrinkle. While the skin is still stretched, powder the area just done. Now release your stretch. Repeat the process until you have the number of layers desired.

If possible, for multiple layers and if you can hold the skin that long, try not to powder in between layers. This will enhance the finished look. But whatever you do, don't let go of the skin before your final stipple and powder are applied. Use a hand fan while working to keep the fumes away from the actor and to encourage the drying process of each layer. A hair dryer can also be used on a cool low setting. When aging an actor, don't get too close to the mouth or nasolabial area. Too much buildup of product will only cause you to have constant repairs because this is a very mobile area. Remember to keep your fingertips powdered at all times.

Where to Stretch

Furrow lines: Area between brows is pulled upward and outward (Figure 8.17).

FIGURE 8.17: FURROW LINES

Forehead: Subject scowls to lower brow line, and hairline is pulled away from face (Figure 8.18).

FIGURE 8.18: FOREHEAD WRINKLES

Crow's feet: Pull away from outer corners of both eyes (Figure 8.19).

Eyelids: Pull up at eyebrows, both eyes (Figure 8.20).

FIGURE 8.20: EYELID WRINKLES

Under-eye area: Pull down and toward center of face, both eyes (Figure 8.21).

FIGURE 8.21: UNDER-EYE AREA LINES

Option one: Lift area away from center of face.

Option two: Puff the area to be aged.

Nasal labial fold: (Figure 8.22).

FIGURE 8.22: NASAL LABIAL FOLD

Upper lip: Puff entire area to be aged (Figure 8.23). (Puff means having the person fill the upper lip with air and hold it until application is dry.)

FIGURE 8.23: UPPER LIP PUFFED

Chin: With neck arched, pull both sides of chin away from the center of the subject's face (Figure 8.24).

FIGURE 8.24: CHIN STRETCH

Cheek: Using the subject's index finger, reach deep into the cheek and push out. This is a perfect opportunity to tie the nasolabials, under-eye area, and crow's feet together. Do both sides (Figure 8.25).

FIGURE 8.25: CHEEK STRETCH

Neck: Begin with the head back. Do the throat first. Then, with head turned, do both sides (Figure 8.26).

FIGURE 8.26: NECK STRETCH

Repairs

Depending on how many layers you have applied, areas around the mouth may crack or flake. You'll most often notice this damage around lunchtime and near wrap. Repairs are easy and quick:

1. Paint 99-percent alcohol in the direction of the wrinkles.

2. Apply Telesis 4 Thinner and/or acetone (faster) with a brush. Then apply Green Marble SeLr with a brush, sponge, or spray.

3. Apply the original ager material.

Removal

Massage isopropyl myristate or IPM Gel with your fingertips into the skin that has been aged. Take your time. The material will dissolve—slowly, and then faster and faster. When the product has loosened, follow with a hot towel for thorough removal.

Stretch and Stipple

W.M. Creations, Inc. has old-age stipple available in four formulas: A, B, C, and Crusty. Neutral and dark skin formulas are available by special order.

A: Used in a perspiration-free environment. Will give slight wrinkling effect when applied to un-stretched skin.

B: Perspiration resistant. Under normal use, gives heavy wrinkling effect even if the skin is not stretched. This is the most widely used stipple.

C: Heaviest wrinkling effect possible. Good for use on hands.

Crusty: Gives the illusion of deeply weathered skin. Great for use on hands. Apply a thin layer of Pros-Aide or Beta Bond before stippling hands for maximum adhesion.

1. Prep the skin with 70- or 99-percent alcohol.

2. Decant stipple into a small container, and heat in the microwave for two seconds.

3. Be careful not to overheat, or the stipple will coagulate.

4. Stretch and stipple skin area with a light coat of old-age stipple.

5. Powder and release.

Castor oil makeup base or Stacolors may be used as translucent washes over or under stipples for a natural look. A wash of castor oil and 70-percent alcohol may be used to remove the powdery look of latex over the stretch and stipple area.

Removal

1. Massage liquid hand soap into stippled area, and let soak for at least one minute.

2. Apply a warm, wet towel to the area for one minute and repeat the process.

3. Stipple may be rolled off the skin.

Aging Hands with Crusty Old-Age Stipple

1. Clean top of hands and fingers with 99% alcohol.

2. Airbrush or paint on veins and age spots with W.M. Creations, Inc. Stacolors Old Age Spot and Black/Green.

3. Stretch skin and curl fingers while stippling Crusty Stipple onto skin. Dry each layer before applying another layer. Make sure each additional layer is stippled within the perimeter of the previous layer; otherwise, thick edges will be produced.

4. Powder with RCMA No Color powder after four to five layers have been applied and dried. If additional layers are needed, wipe off the powder and reapply more stipple. Dry and powder again (Figure 8.27).

DESIGN

FIGURE 8.27: A, CLEAN HAND. B, PAINTED HAND. C, STIPPLED HAND. D, FINAL OLD HAND
Courtesy Matthew Mungle

Contact Lenses

Custom contact lenses are a great way to complete a makeup design, and are sometimes necessary to sell the look of the makeup. Examples of contact lenses being necessary to complete a makeup are a badly beaten face, illness, death, or portrait makeup (look-alike). With a badly beaten face, if there is bruising/ wounds to the eye area, there would be broken blood vessels in the whites of the eye. In illness, you would show yellowness and broken vessels. In death, you would use a death lens that is cloudy. In portrait makeup, you would change the eye color of the actor to match the person they are portraying. In all of these situations, having lenses to remove the "life" in the whites of the eye, or to change the color of the iris, completes and sells your artistry. Contact lenses are a fabulous tool for the Makeup Artist.

There are many ways to order contact lenses. Cristina Patterson, contact lens technician and special effects coordinator, takes orders from all over the world. The most common method for her is via email. Christina says:

> Depending on the production, sometimes I am asked to actually create the designs for the contacts, or the Makeup Artist requests their designs to be painted. It's tricky when a Makeup Artist creates their own. A lot of times, they will design something that takes the lens all the way to the edge. People forget that lenses are round, so if you stretch a lens out one way, they also have to go the other way to complete the circle. It also depends on the size and curve of the actor's measurements. For instance, if the actor's measurements permit only a smaller size of the sclera lenses, it's definitely not going to the edge. Makeup Artists should also be aware of adding any light reflection flares to the design. Although it looks nice, the reflection can be confusing to interpret during the painting process. At times, it becomes a collaboration between the Makeup Artist and myself. The Makeup Artist will give me a design that I will alter in Photoshop to better fit the contacts to be worn. This would be the easiest way to see what the Makeup Artist wants and how the design can be executed. Most designs are created in Photoshop beforehand, and then e-mailed to me. After discussing what is doable, I'll sit down to paint. A mock-up is painted first, and, if time permits, a picture is taken to be sent off for approval.

The most commonly used contact lenses are kept in stock with different curves. Television shows tend to need contacts at the last minute. Actors would be fitted for contacts right away to be used in same-day or next-day situations. Sometimes the contact lenses are not in stock.

The Makeup Artist must have the actor fitted by a professionally licensed doctor. When wearing contacts, you can get tunnel vision— just like looking through a straw. Everyone is different in terms of comfort level when wearing contacts. A properly fitting lens should be reasonably comfortable. There is no definite wearing time. It is completely dependent on the actor's comfort level. Environmental conditions will have an impact as well. Artificial environments are all irritants to the eye, which affects contact lens comfort. Artificial snow, smoke, wind, lots of splashing water, and the occasional sand can make all lens wearers unhappy campers.

Lens colors can be adjusted or used in such a way to accommodate media such as bluescreen and greenscreen. Effects can be included with this. For example, green or blue lenses have been used to make an actor disappear on-screen, or to project an effect onto the sclera lens that is being worn.

Contact lenses should be the last thing to go on the actor, and the first to come off. Most lenses stay with the Makeup Artist after the shoot. He or she will bring them in to be sterilized and sealed for long-term storage. If the lenses are to be used again after they have been stored for a year or so, the Makeup Artist should take them to an eye-care specialist to be checked out for imperfections, bacteria, and so on. Also, the artwork on the lenses should be checked for fading or opacity. If the lenses are in good shape, they can be sterilized for use.

All Lenses Are Unique

There is no such thing as a generic contact lens. Every person has a slightly different eye curvature and eyelid tension. Only a licensed eye-care professional can fit a contact lens. You are putting your eyes at risk by purchasing special-effects lenses from online auction sites, flea markets, convenience stores, or shops, for example. Soft lenses are currently the standard of the industry. Almost anything can be painted, printed, or laminated on a soft lens. Rigid lenses are used for a variety of effects—although the wearing time is much less than for a soft lens, and rigid lenses take longer for the actor to get used to (Figures 8.28 to 8.30).

FIGURE 8.28: CONTACTS/SINGLE EYE, DILATED PUPIL
Courtesy Professional Vision Care

FIGURE 8.29: BLOODSHOT CONTACTS
Courtesy Professional Vision Care

FIGURE 8.30: BROWN EYE, OLD AGE
Courtesy Professional Vision Care

Scleral Lenses

Scleral lenses cover the sclera, or white part of the eye. They are larger in diameter (18 to 24 millimeters) than traditional lenses, which generally cover only the iris (colored part of the eye, usually 14 to 15 millimeters). Scleral lenses work great for bloodshot eyes, hemorrhage effect, jaundice, full black, demon eyes, and other monster effects, where the entire inside surface of the eye needs to be covered to avoid seeing the edge of the lens (Figure 8.31).

Contact Lens Information

Cost: The cost of a lens is related to the difficulty and type of special-effects lens design.

FIGURE 8.31: SCLERAL LENSES
Courtesy Professional Vision Care

Fitting and Exams: All exams include internal and external eye-health evaluation to determine if the actor can in fact wear contact lenses, plus refraction for prescription.

Getting Fitted by Another Doctor: To purchase lenses without being able to bring the actor in for fittings to your favorite special-effects lens maker, forward the information directly to the shop. This is what you'll need to submit:

1. Current refraction.

2. Keratometric (K) readings.

3. Visible iris diameter (millimeters).

4. Pupil size (millimeters).

5. Normal iris color (photo if possible).

6. An exact color rendering of effect to be created.

7. If scleral contact lenses are the desired lenses, the actor must be fitted by a doctor who has the compatible fitting set. Scleral lenses must be fitted physically; they cannot be determined solely by corneal curvature measurements.

Teeth

As with contact lens, changing a person's teeth to go with the makeup design is an essential tool to create realistic effects. It is also a wonderful choice for character design and comedy. As with contact lenses, teeth that don't go with the makeup design will take away from your makeup job. For example, assume that you have aged an actor from 40 to 80 years old, and the actor's teeth are too white. This will detract from all of the aging work that has been done.

It is important to use a qualified professional in both areas when designing characters involving eyes and teeth. The professional's technological and medical background protects the actor that you are making the changes on.

Gary Archer of G.A. Enterprises, a specialist in dental prosthetics for the film and television industries, explains the process and current reasons for tooth transformation:

One of the main reasons for tooth transformation is that in today's Hollywood society, a perfect smile is essential. Unfortunately, with the latest in porcelain veneers, implants, and cosmetic bonding, we have beautiful smiles in life—but under the lights and in front of the camera, it is entirely too dazzling and therefore unrealistic. We have had requests to darken actors' teeth to make them less perfect. We can give them gaps where no gap exists, and stains to represent neglect and poor dental care; have them missing teeth, or have them fall out on camera. We also make "grills," ranging from single teeth with faux diamonds to full arches with designs and styles on them. We make perfect teeth bad, and bad teeth good! We have also developed a range of fake braces and retainers that will fool the most critical eye. In addition, we have copied smiles of famous celebrities and influential figures of the past to transform the actor's teeth into whoever it is they are portraying (Figures 8.32 through 8.34). Plumpers are another specialty to help swell out or fatten a character's mouth, and are another unique product.

PRO TIP

Plumpers are a great makeup tool for changing facial shape, such as for aging or swelling from a fight or accident.

FIGURE 8.32: BRACES VEENERS
Courtesy Gary Archer

FIGURE 8.33: BROKEN TEETH
Courtesy Gary Archer

FIGURE 8.34: VAMPIRE TEETH
Courtesy Gary Archer

Safety Tip from Gary Archer

The mouth is a very delicate place. Be careful what you plan to put on an actor's own teeth. All the new technology available to dentists in the advancement of "tooth beautification" means that it is very easy to damage a veneer or to stain cosmetic bonding. Stay away from "paint-on stains and colors." They can permanently stain delicate bonding and unsealed margins on veneers.

Obtain accurate dental casts of the actor. It is recommended that you use a dental professional when transforming teeth for a character. Do not use old molds that the actor may have from previous projects. They are usually older than the actor remembers them to be, have been used for a previous prosthetic appliance, and may be damaged or inaccurate.

Gary takes us through the steps of dental casting and dental molds:

1. First, an alginate impression is taken with a metal tray. Plastic trays are not rigid enough and can cause distortion.

2. Second, a cast is made in a hard yellow or blue stone.

3. Be careful loading the impression tray. Using too much material can gag or choke the *patient* (actor), which causes stress in the artist-actor relationship, to say the least. Not using enough material can lead to a shortened or under-extended impression that doesn't capture the areas that you need.

PRO TIP

If you are not sure of the procedure, call for help.

Once the positive dental casts have been done, the design process starts. A diagnostic wax-up can be made to show the Makeup Artist and director exactly what the teeth will look like. This helps to eliminate surprises on the set, and will enable all parties to be on the same page. It helps to bring it all (the design) together.

After the designs have been approved, a last wax pattern is cast to fabricate the acrylic veneers. Heat-cured acrylic is used to give the most accurate, color-stable, and realistic look for the veneers. Self-curing plastics tend to have a very monochromatic and dull appearance, so they should be avoided.

Once fabricated, the veneers are quite thin and delicate. Given time, the actor can actually forget they have teeth in, and care must be taken to ensure that the actor does not forget they have veneers in, and go to lunch wearing them. This has happened, much to everyone's amusement.

PRO TIP

Remind the actor that a pocket is not recommended for storing their veneers, as they will break!

Normal process time from design to fabrication and completion of a set of veneers is usually one week. In some cases, GA Enterprises can turn them around faster, but there are certain rules to using dental acrylics, and attempting to rush or speed up the process usually produces low-quality results.

Care of Acrylic Veneers

Gently rinse under cool tap water, and store in the case provided for each set. Add a small amount of mouthwash in the case to keep them fresh tasting.

Things to know as a Makeup Artist working with veneers:

- You will need to work wearing latex or non-latex gloves.

- Ask if the person has an allergy to latex, and what flavor preference they have for mouthwash. Mouthwash helps to keep the veneers fresh, as well as being great for a fast rinse on-set if needed.

- You will be putting in, as well as taking out, the veneers. Always wear gloves. This is also necessary on-set. Sometimes the actor will want to do this, but there are always moments when the Makeup Artist must be prepared to do this.

- To help the actor adjust to something on their teeth, they need to get the feel of them. Have them wear the veneers well before going on-camera to give them time to forget them. This also helps with their speech. At first, they might sound a bit different, but this goes away when they forget that the veneers are on. You will need to do this only for the first few days of use. The actor will quickly get used to them, and not need to put them in early. Soon you will be popping the veneers in on-set!

On-Set Touch-Ups

On-set, you will need to bring with you:

- A dental case: the veneer case for each pair of veneers working

- Latex gloves

- Non-latex gloves

- Bottle of mouthwash

- Bottled water

- Paper towels

If you need to remove veneers on-set, put gloves on and remove the veneers, placing them in a paper towel or directly into their case. Sometimes you have to be the one to actually remove the veneers from the actor's mouth.

The actor can't do it. Regardless of who takes them out, they will need to be rinsed and stored properly. Ask the actor to please not drink hot coffee or tea while wearing veneers.

Bald Caps

Bald caps are used in character design to show old age, illness, receding hair lines, aliens, creatures, fantasy, and photo or stunt double for a bald actor. You could go years without the need for a bald cap, but you should know how to apply one. You will need several practical applications to be proficient at applying a bald cap. Head prep, where and how you place your edges, gluing and blending of edges and final coloring of the bald cap are key to a successful bald cap.

Michelel Mulkey on Bald Caps

When it comes to bald caps, the question most Makeup Artists face is what kind of bald cap to use. The choice between vinyl and latex both have their pro and cons, so the decision should be made based more on what the actor or model will be required to do while wearing the bald cap.

If the actor will be doing little movement throughout the day, such as a photo shoot or lying in a hospital bed, then a vinyl cap is probably the best choice. Vinyl caps will often appear seamless with very little work from the Makeup Artist due to the fact that the edge of a vinyl cap can be melted into the skin with a small amount of acetone. This will often save time on set since little to no Bondo-ing will be required for the edge of the cap. Another benefit to using vinyl bald caps is that you can use any type of makeup to color the cap without jeopardizing the bald cap's integrity. If the talent will be required to do a lot of movement or acting in the bald cap throughout the day, then a vinyl cap may not be the best choice. The downside of a vinyl cap is that it is basically a thin piece of plastic. If you stretch out a piece of plastic then let it go, the plastic will stay stretched. This is also true of a vinyl bald cap as the actor moves around. As the cap stretches, it

will start to form buckles in the material around the base of the neck, back of the head and the edges. This can quickly kill the illusion you have just created by applying the bald cap.

If the actor is required to do a lot of movement throughout the day, then a better choice in this situation is a latex bald cap. Latex caps are made out of rubber; it has both elasticity and memory. If you stretch out a rubber band and then let it go, the rubber band will return to its original shape. Latex bald caps work in much the same way. As the actor moves, despite the stretching of the latex, the cap will return to its original shape with little or no buckling around the back of the cap or the edges. The down side to using a latex cap is that, to date, there is no product strong enough to melt the edges, yet safe enough to use on the skin without causing irritation or burning; therefore you must Bondo the edge of the latex cap to blend it seamlessly into the skin. Bondo-ing the edges will take more time, so the Makeup Artist must plan accordingly for this added step when estimating the application time for production.

Another downside to using latex caps is that you must use a latex-friendly makeup, Rubber Mask Grease Paint (RMGP) to color the cap. Some ingredients in regular makeup, as well as certain hair products, can compromise the integrity of latex, causing the cap itself to split or rip during application or filming.

Bald Cap Prep

Prepping the actor for the application of a bald cap is the same regardless of what type of bald cap you are using. You need access to the entire neckline and face, so it is best to request in advance that the actor wear an article of clothing that allows for full access to the neck and buttons down the front. Remove all jewelry. In some situations you will need to shave the skin at the nape of the neck; check the nape hairline for this.

1. Unfold the cap and remove any residual powder with a small amount of water or 99% alcohol.

2. Clean skin around the hairline with a small amount of 99% alcohol on a cotton pad.

3. Wet the hair with water and comb hair flat to the head. You can also use hair products like Hair Slick or Gafquat in the hair to smooth the hair flat to the scalp. Note that these products will dry hard and can give a texture or ridge to the hair under the cap which will make the cap appear "not smooth." For long hair, you will need to place the hair in a pony tail or wrap the hair in a circular direction around the head to flatten it. The hair prep is very important; you want the hair as flat to the head as possible without distorting the actor's head shape (Figure 8.35).

4. Place the cap over the head, starting at the forehead and pulling down to the nape, making sure the cap lies flat against the nape of the neck. With vinyl caps, there is usually a lot of excess cap material over the face area. Trim excess portions of the cap, making sure that the face and the eyebrows are exposed. If you have determined that you will be attaching the cap over the eyebrows, you would trim the cap below the eyebrows at the upper eyelid (Figure 8.36).

5. Create an anchor point for the front of the cap by pulling up the cap at the center of the forehead and applying Pros-Aide.

6. Create a second anchor point at the back of the cap by pulling up the cap at the back center of the nape and applying Pros-Aide. Place Pros-Aide on both sides of the pony tail (if one was used) or across the base of the neck for short hair (Figure 8.37).

FIGURE 8.35: BALD CAP PREP

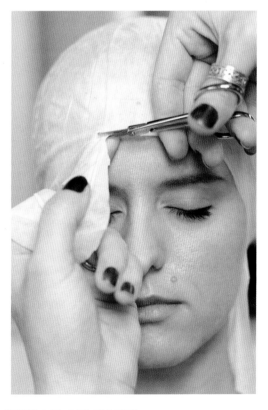

FIGURE 8.36: BALD CAP TRIM

FIGURE 8.37: A, BALD CAP ANCHOR. B, BALD CAP ANCHOR.

A

B

7. Cut around the ears using a makeup pencil, and round-tip scissors. Start at the top of the ear and mark a circle on the cap with the top of the circle starting about one-fourth inch from the top of the ear. The circle should be about the size of a quarter. Then draw a line straight down from the bottom of the circle to the edge of the cap. Use the round-tip scissors to cut straight up the line and cut out the circle. Additional trimming may be needed to ensure that there are no wrinkles in the cap around the area (Figure 8.38).

8. Starting at the back anchor point, apply Pros-Aide from back anchor to just behind the ears on both sides. Then, apply Pros-Aide from the front of the ears to the front anchor point on both sides.

9. Once the bald cap is glued down the entire way around the cap, gently lift the cap out of the glue and trim the edge of the cap to within approximately one-fourth inch from the hair line. As you trim off the excess cap, press the remaining edge into the glue (Figure 8.39).

10. Blend the cap edge using a small amount of acetone on a cotton-tip applicator; when working around the eye area you must protect the eyes by covering them with a powder puff or cotton round at all times. Note: If there is still an "edge" after using the acetone, use a small amount of Bondo to fill in the remaining edge (Figure 8.40).

11. Apply a thin layer over the entire edge of the bald cap to the blend and ensure that there is no lifting on the edges (Figure 8.41).

FIGURE 8.38: CUT AND DRAW EAR

FIGURE 8.39: A, REMOVE. B, PRESS

FIGURE 8.40: PROTECT EYES

FIGURE 8.42: FINAL BALD CAP

FIGURE 8.41: BLEND EDGES

12. Once the Pros-Aide is completely dry, powder.

13. Stipple a thin layer of fixer spray or sealer over the edge of the cap with a textured white sponge.

14. Color the cap. For vinyl, you can use any type of makeup or foundation. For latex caps you need to use Rubber Mask Grease Paint (RMGP) or a latex-friendly makeup to ensure the integrity of the cap (Figure 8.42).

For additional information with DVD instruction, see Edward French's instructional DVD (www.edwardfrench.com). It's an excellent source for the demonstration and application of bald caps. Ed gives great information and instruction, and it is fun to watch. We feel you will greatly benefit from a visual lesson as well as the text lesson in this area.

References

Corson, R., Glavan, J., 2001. Stage Makeup, ninth ed. Allyn and Bacon, Needham Heights, MA.

Cole, H., Burke, K., 2005. Costuming for Film: The Art and The Craft. Silman-James Press.

Internet Resources

Archer, G., Dental prosthetics specialist for film, dental/teeth information. G.A. Enterprises. www.gaenterprises.net.

Carlsson, L., Makeup-FX Company. www.makeup-fx.com.

Dean, R., 1028@mac.com.

French, Ed. BALD CAP, The Instructional Video. www.edwardfrench.com.

Mark Traynor Lifts and Beauty Bands. Huston Mercer. tracterproject@aol.com.

Myers, K., Green Marble Stretch and Stipple. Premiere Products, Inc. www.ppi.cc.

Mungle, M. www.matthewmungle.com.

Patterson, C., Professional VisionCare Associates, contact lens information. www.fx4eyes.com.

143

9

HAIR

In the film and television industries, the Makeup Artist is responsible for anything that is applied to or glued onto the face, including facial hair and sideburns.

> IATSE Local 706's general definition of Makeup Artists: "Makeup Artists perform the art of makeup, which includes:
>
> Application of all moustaches, chin pieces, side burns, beards, false eyebrows and lashes."

There are many professionals who do not feel that hair experience is necessary in today's market, because Hollywood has become so specialized. We disagree, and feel that in order to be a professional Makeup Artist working in film and television, you need to learn the skills for working with facial hair. If, at some point in your career, you choose to not polish these skills or to not use them, and prefer to "hire out" or not accept jobs requiring these skills, that will be your option. Not learning to work with facial hair will limit you. Until you have the working experience to know what your forte is, you will need experience and exposure to all areas of makeup artistry. So, learn all the skills that are required to be a professional Makeup Artist before deciding what suits you. Having a working knowledge of all aspects of your field not only makes you a well-rounded professional, but is extremely beneficial during conversations with producers and directors on how to create certain looks. It is not uncommon today to "hire out" jobs that require a high level of skill and expertise; it saves time and money to have the best. Early in your career, you will be hired for jobs in which there is no available budget to "hire out" specialists, so the producers will hire a makeup department that

can handle all the makeup needs. This is an example of what can happen if you do not have all the skills required to be a professional, especially at the beginning of your career. You most likely will be working on projects that have small budgets and cannot "hire out."

Remember, Makeup Artists who specialize have done so after achieving a level of experience in all areas, prior to specializing in an area of makeup design that is their forte or passion. It is in your best interest to learn all of the skills required to become a well-rounded Makeup Artist before deciding if you want to specialize in a given area, or that a particular area of makeup design is not for you. Doing so will give you a more complete education, and the essential background experience that you will need in the film and/or television industries.

Most department heads will hire a Makeup Artist who is skilled in everything, so they do not have to worry about the makeup designs that you are assigned. For example, there will be moments when an actor shows up in the morning and has accidentally shaved off his moustache or has changed the shape of his sideburns. In this instance, your film continuity will not be affected because you are able to fix the problem by laying hair or applying a lace piece. As a well-rounded Makeup Artist, you will have the skills and resources to take care of the situation—not to mention that the actor will be relieved and pleased by your ability to fix the problem. Accidents do happen.

Erwin H. Kupitz is a Makeup Artist and wig maker. He trained in a classic German apprenticeship, which included a unisex hairstylist license, makeup artistry, and wig making for five years, with three examinations and one final examination. Unfortunately, there is no longer an apprenticeship program of this magnitude in the United States. This is a wonderful method of training because the learning period is long, and the practical experience is invaluable. Erwin specialized when he emigrated to the United States, after seeing the need for wig making and facial hair experience, and recognizing that Hollywood had evolved into an industry with specialization in each area of makeup.

Erwin will guide us through facial hair design, the laying of facial hair and lace facial hair pieces, and where to start the design process. Things to think about beforehand follow:

- What is the period of the project (current, past, future)?
- Who will wear it, and what medium are you working in?
- How many shooting days?
- Interior or exterior, rain or snow? What is the climate?

PRO TIP

The questions affect how many pieces are made, and how much hair you need.

- If it is a reshoot, and you are matching something that was shot a year ago, what are you going to match to as far as shape and color? Is a good photo available for reference?

Once all the script information is collected, the design process starts. You will need:

- A template or live cast of the actor
- A hair sample from the actor
- Reference of the final look to be created
- Approval of the design
- Approval from production on cost, and a purchase order issued with instructions for billing

PRO TIP

When ordering anything, you need a purchase order number to give to the vendor. This gives the vendor permission to start work, and constitutes a guarantee of the agreed-upon price and payment.

Template

When possible, it is best to have the wig maker do their own fitting, using a template or face cast. If this is not possible, knowing how to do a template or head cast will save you time and money.

Making a Full-Beard Template
By Erwin H. Kupitz

Materials and Tools

- Eyebrow pencil
- Plastic wrap
- Clear tape or matte tape
- Permanent markers
- Scissors
- Baby oil or makeup remover
- Tissue or cotton pads
- Camera (digital or instant) (Figure 9.1)

Procedure

1. Cover the actor with a cape (Figure 9.2).
2. Using the eyebrow pencil, follow the beard shadow of the actor, and mark it on his skin (Figures 9.3 and 9.4).
3. Cover the beard area (and disregard the moustache for now) with a single layer of plastic wrap, and secure with tape on the

FIGURE 9.1: ERWIN H. KUPTIZ'S WORKSTATION

FIGURE 9.2: ACTOR COVERED WITH CAPE

FIGURE 9.3: EYEBROW PENCIL MARKING OF BEARD SHADOW ON ACTOR'S FACE

FIGURE 9.4: CHIN VIEW OF EYEBROW-PENCIL MARKING

top of the actor's head. Make sure that your eyebrow pencil notes (markings) are all covered with plastic wrap (Figure 9.5).

4. Start using clear tape, and tape over the plastic wrap. Make sure that the tape is tight around the chin. This is very important for a proper fitting of the lace beard around the chin (Figure 9.6).

FIGURE 9.5: BEARD COVERED WITH SINGLE LAYER OF PLASTIC WRAP

5. Take special care below the chin and around the neck, making sure that the taped plastic wrap is tight. Two to three layers would be appropriate (Figures 9.7 and 9.8).

6. Now proceed to the sides of the beard, and cover again with two layers of tape. Use a permanent marker to trace the eyebrow pencil markings onto the tape (Figures 9.9 and 9.10).

7. After the full beard is done, do the same to the moustache, lip piece, and two connector pieces between moustache and chin (Figures 9.11 and 9.12).

8. Now cut out the beard template above the permanent marker lines about two to three millimeters, and try the entire template again. Take special care around the chin. The template should lay tight around the chin and below the chin, and should lay flat onto the actor's hair at the sideburns (Figures 9.13 and 9.14).

FIGURE 9.6: USING CLEAR TAPE OVER PLASTIC WRAP

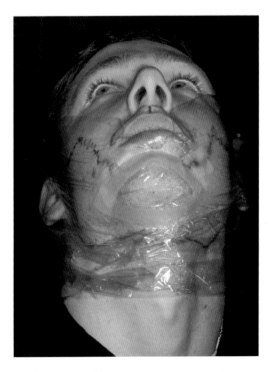

FIGURE 9.7: TAKE SPECIAL CARE AROUND CHIN FOR TIGHT FIT

FIGURE 9.8: CHIN FULLY TAPED

FIGURE 9.10: SIDE VIEW FULL-BEARD TAPE

FIGURE 9.9: FULL-BEARD WRAP

FIGURE 9.11: MUSTACHE LIP TAPE

FIGURE 9.12: LIP DETAIL

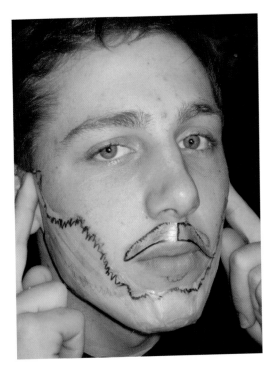

FIGURE 9.14: TEMPLATE CUT AND CHECKS

FIGURE 9.13: FINISHED TEMPLATE

9. After the beard template is checked and finished, while the eyebrow pencil markings are still on the skin, take photos from all sides. Clean up the actor's face (Figure 9.15).

10. Cut out a hair sample from the actor's own hair. If the actor's hair is too short, refer to a swatch ring or hair color swatch book

FIGURE 9.15: CLEANING MODEL

for reference. Sometimes sending hair from another source, such as a wig or someone else's hair, is an alternative. Try to make a base that matches the desired skin tone of the actor, or a final skin tone of a character, and spread it onto a clean white paper or in between two layers of plastic wrap. This sample is needed as a guide to color the lace.

11. Double-check to make sure that you have all of the items needed by the wig maker before you release the actor. (The approximate time to make a full beard is about four working days in backup or doubles.)

Masking Tape Technique

Use a lip or eyebrow pencil and masking tape to transfer markings from the face into the tape. This technique is very good for small or partial facial-hair additions. It also works well on a clean-shaven face.

Material and Tools

- Masking tape
- Eyebrow or lip pencils
- Scissors
- Loose powder and powder brush
- Towel

Procedure

1. Using the lip or eyebrow pencil, mark all facial-hair additions or trace the natural growth pattern and shape of the model's facial hair. If needed, different colors help to design new shapes or mark special patterns (Figures 9.16 and 9.17).

2. After all markings are done, use small pieces of masking tape, and apply one or two layers over the marked areas. Try not to use more than two layers because this would be too much of a build-up. In this demonstration, sideburn and chin-beard extensions and the addition of a lip piece are created (Figure 9.18).

FIGURE 9.16: MODEL WITH MARKINGS USING BROWN EYEBROW PENCIL

FIGURE 9.17: MARKINGS FOR SIDEBURN EXTENSIONS USING BROWN EYEBROW PENCIL

FIGURE 9.18: SIDEBURN, CHIN-BEARD EXTENSION, AND LIP PIECE WITH TAPED AREAS

FIGURE 9.19: WARM TOWEL AGAINST CHIN TAPE

FIGURE 9.20: REMOVING TAPE CAREFULLY FROM FACE

3. Using a warm towel (warmed for 10 minutes in a wig dryer), the areas are wrapped and pressed down tight with your hand. The heat of the towel as well as the pressure from your hands will transfer the grease in the eyebrow or lip pencil into the adhesive. A combination of gentle rubbing and pressing for about two to three minutes is recommended (Figure 9.19).

4. If doing a full-beard or chin-beard pattern, special care has to be taken around the curves of the chin to make sure the tape is pressed tight against the chin curve. This will ensure the proper shaping of the pattern and a tight fit of the final lace beard.

5. After the pressing and rubbing is done, carefully start to remove the tape from the face. The markings are transferred into the tape.

6. Carefully remove the tape from the face (Figure 9.20).

7. The removed tape pieces are organized on a towel and are ready to powder. Using loose face powder, powder the tape pieces to prevent them from sticking together or getting messed up (Figure 9.21).

FIGURE 9.21: USING LOOSE FACE POWDER AND POWDER BRUSH ON REMOVED TAPE PIECES

PRO TIP

Use a loose face powder and powder brush to powder removed tape pieces.

The beard template can now be cut out and applied to a beard block. After the lace pieces are completed, it is recommended to store them together with pictures of the actor, as well as hair color and lace color swatches, in a plastic bag or box for future reference.

FIGURE 9.22: ERWIN'S WORKSTATION: TOOLS AND
PRODUCTS TO CUT AND STYLE FACIAL PIECES

FIGURE 9.23: CHARACTER LACE BEARD PRIOR TO CUTTING
AND STYLING

Tools in the photo of Erwin's workstation (see Figure 9.22):

- Cutting comb for combing hair during cut

- Rat-tail comb for separating and sectioning

- Small hair clips to secure separations

- Lifting comb for detangling and lifting permed hair

- Hair-cutting and thinning shears as well as razor for cutting hair

- Tweezers for eventual plugging and finishing of hair line

- Ceramic iron heater

- Flat curling iron for lifting and shaping

- Small marcel iron for texturizing and curling

- Natural bristle brushes for wax and tattoo color

- Pinking shears for precutting excess lace

Products in the photo of Erwin's workstation:

- Moustache wax or stronger hair wax

- Plastic sealer in pump bottle or a strong, fast-drying hair lacquer

- Tattoo color for detail work on finished beard (Figure 9.23)

- 99-percent alcohol

- Lace pieces

Construction of a Ventilated Beard

Ventilating is the technique used by wig makers to knot hair (either human or synthetic) into wig lace. It is similar to tying a rug, and has been used since King Louis XVI of France. There is single knotting and double knotting, and many versions of lace and qualities of hair. Most lace pieces in film do not use synthetic hair—it does not look real. The quality of lace and hair and the blending of colors are extremely important.

The medium of the lace piece, as well as the design of the facial hair, will dictate what materials and hair are used. The hairline or beard line is always the finest quality of knots to create the illusion of the hair coming out of the follicle.

The Base
The base is made of one layer of custom-dyed nylon lace using a blend of layers of fabric dye following the manufacturer's directions. Match the actor's skin color or the foundation makeup used on the actor as closely as possible.

Construction includes seven separate pieces: chin, two side pieces, one lip piece, two connections, and one moustache. A light coat of acrylic spray is applied before hair ventilation to the finish base. This adds durability.

The Hair

Use human hair from different origins (Asian, Indian, European), as well as yak tail and belly hair. Blends of thicker and coarser hair are used at the bottom of the beard for body. Thinner, finer hair is used closer to the edges.

All hair is custom color blended using darker colors at the bottom and lighter colors at the edges, and then permed using a mild alkaline perm. The diameter of the perm rod will determine the curling result. In this case, a medium to small perm rod is chosen for a frizzy, "ungroomed" result. This will ensure that the beard keeps the shape, and restyling will be minimized.

Ventilating Hair

Knotting the preblended and permed hair into the lace base is done hair by hair (single-hair knotting), using the various color blends to design natural shading and highlighting. Lighter colors are always used around the edges of the beard (front shade), building up more volume at the bottom and in areas where denser beard growth appears, and decreasing the amount closer to the edges for a natural appearance (Figure 9.24).

How to Cut Facial Hairpieces

A good haircut can eliminate half of the styling and maintenance later on. Because perming is done on the hair, it needs to be treated like curly hair, which means caution is needed during cutting. Texturizing and cutting with razor and thinning shears (cutting different lengths into the hair) will give a more natural appearance to "beard hair." Blunt cutting a straight line, especially on the moustache, will result in an unnatural "fresh-cut look" that is very "eye-catching" for the camera. The proper cut for a beard is as important as the proper cut for a hairstyle. If the cutting and texturizing are finished and the permed hair is reactivated with water, let it dry naturally.

The beard shape and style should be almost completed after proper cutting. Finishing can be achieved with curling irons.

Elevating your hand while you razor the hair will give a layered-hair effect. All hair except for the sides of the beard is cut to this guideline. The sides of the beard are blended in length into the sideburn length of the design (Figures 9.25 and 9.26).

Cutting a guideline to the desired length with the tip of the razor cuts the moustache in the same manner. Make sure that both sides are

FIGURE 9.24: BEARD SEPARATED IN SECTIONS READY TO CUT INTO SHAPE

FIGURE 9.25: CUTTING LENGTH GUIDELINE BY USING RAZOR

FIGURE 9.28: USING RAZOR FOR CUTTING LIP PIECE TO
DESIRED LENGTH AND SHAPE

even in length and shape. All of the hair is then
cut to the length of that guideline with the tip of
the razor (Figures 9.27 through 9.30).

Mist the precut beard with water, and lift hair
using a lifting comb, so the curl can go back
into its permed style. The beard is then dried
in a wig dryer on a low setting: 100 °F, or 45°C
(Figure 9.31).

FIGURE 9.29: SEPARATIONS FOR CUTTING MUSTACHE
GUIDELINE AND CONNECTING PIECES BELOW MUSTACHE

FIGURE 9.27: FINISHED CUTTING AND BASIC TEXTURIZING
OF FULL BEARD

FIGURE 9.30: CUTTING GUIDELINE TO DESIRED LENGTH
WITH RAZOR TIP

FIGURE 9.31: MISTING PRECUT BEARD WITH WATER AND LIFTING HAIR USING LIFTING COMB

FIGURE 9.33: SHAPING FACIAL HAIR AND BEARD WITH MARCEL CURLING IRON

After the hair and the base (lace) are truly dry, the hair is then lightly waxed using moustache wax and a bristle brush. The wax will protect the hair from the heat of the curling irons and from moisture (Figure 9.32). The facial hair is now ready for final styling with the curling irons and tongs.

To bring the permed texture into shape, a small marcel curling iron and waving technique is used. Caution is to be taken that the texture does not appear like finger or marcel waves similar to the waves in hairstyles. Using artistic input as well as practice, this technique is useful for all longer beards and facial hairpieces for building texture, movement, and style (Figures 9.33 and 9.34).

FIGURE 9.34: SHAPING FACIAL HAIR AND BEARD WITH MARCEL CURLING IRON

FIGURE 9.32: LIGHTLY WAXING DRIED HAIR WITH MUSTACHE WAX AND BRISTLE BRUSH

Final touches are done on the texture of the beard prior to styling the moustache (Figure 9.35).

A flatiron, or tongs, is used to shape the moustache and the lip piece (Figure 9.36). Because of the use of perm-textured hair, the moustache hardly needs curling. Only the ends at the bottom of the beard are blended under. A root lift is applied to the edges by lifting and sliding a warm flatiron to the hair.

Final color touch-ups are done using tattoo color and 99-percent alcohol (Figures 9.37 and 9.38).

FIGURE 9.35: FINAL TOUCHES ON TEXTURE OF BEARD
PRIOR TO STYLING MUSTACHE

FIGURE 9.38: APPLYING TATTOO COLOR WASH TO BEARD
WITH EYEBROW BRUSH

FIGURE 9.36: USING FLATIRON OR TONGS TO SHAPE
MUSTACHE AND LIP PIECE

Using an eyebrow brush with a lash comb attached, a tattoo color wash (more alcohol than color, like an aquarelle color drawing) similar to the beard's color is then brushed over the lighter shades around the edge (front shade). Brushing and immediate combing of the hair will make blending easy. It is important to keep the knots light, while softly blending the ends of the lighter hair into the beard color. Be careful not to make it too opaque or even too dark. The beard line should still be lighter than the beard for a natural effect. This technique will keep the edges soft, and knots will blend more easily around the edges with the skin color. After coloring is done, a light coat of matte clear acrylic spray is applied to the finished beard.

Figure 9.39 is a photo of the finished, styled beard before removing it from the beard block.

Sample Application of a Beard with Stubble

Materials Needed:

- Chin lace piece

- Lower lip piece

- Sideburns

- Chopped curly hair matching beard color

- Scissors, thinning shears

FIGURE 9.37: USING TATTOO COLOR AND 99% ALCOHOL
FOR COLOR TOUCH-UPS

- Metal tail comb
- Adhesive (W.M. Creations Adhesive)
- Tattoo color (e.g., Reel Hair Palette)
- Hair spray
- Makeup sponges
- Brushes
- Alcohol, 99 percent
- Cotton swabs
- Makeup cape
- Concealer pencil in skin tone matching actor

Steps for Application:

1. Start with a clean face.

2. Start applying the chin beard. Check its placement, and use the concealer pencil to mark dots where the edges of the piece belong.

3. Brush a thin layer of adhesive onto the skin, staying about one centimeter below the markings of the lace piece edge.

4. Stipple adhesive with your finger until tacky. Apply a thin second layer and repeat. Be careful not to get adhesive over the concealer marks.

5. Glue the lace piece in place using your rattail comb. It is important that you press with the tail in between the hair at the base of the lace. Make sure you do not glue down the beard hair flat against the skin. This will take a few minutes, and a bit of practice.

6. Use a cotton swab dampened with alcohol to carefully remove your concealer markings.

7. Use a new cotton swab or a finer brush to apply a very thin layer of adhesive to the skin. Tack it with your finger or a brush until flat and tacky.

8. Press lace piece gently into place using your clean rat-tail comb. Continue pressing all edges until they are smoothly glued down to the skin.

9. Apply the lip piece in the same manner. Because it is very small, you probably don't need to use the concealer pencil. Placement of a lip piece should be easier than the placement of a larger beard piece.

10. Apply the sideburns in the same manner. It is important that you position them directly at the bottom of the actor's own sideburns, without a gap in between.

11. Cut the sideburn hair to match the actor's own sideburn hair at the same length, using thinning shears.

12. Brush in a little tattoo color to blend possible color differences between the actor's hair and the false sideburns.

PRO TIP

Lace facial hairpieces for high definition (HD) are much more difficult because the HD shows every detail so crisply and sharply. The lace pieces have to be designed in sections that puzzle together onto the face, with a lower hairline edge that has to be overlaid with hair by hand to finish off the edge of the facial-hair design. The glue must be totally matte.

13. After all of your lace pieces are applied, you can start using chopped hair to create a patchy, shorter beard stubble.

Lace facial hairpieces require an investment of time and money that pays off in the long run. The work and materials used are expensive, but the result is a more natural, consistent look, with easy maintenance.

Beard Stubble

As with everything else in makeup, there are several ways to create beard growth that looks like more than several days of growth. There are different products and techniques to use, depending on the situation you are working in. As with all areas of makeup, you will need to be able to answer critical questions before designing or choosing what to use. The hardest beard growth to simulate is between five and 10 days, too long to be painted in, and not long enough to use lace pieces. You will need to use one of several techniques to create the look and length needed. The length of hair for beard stubble will depend on how much time has passed, or how scruffy the look is designed to be, or how many "story days" in the script that the actor has not shaved. The actor's own beard growth and density will also affect your decisions.

What is the growth pattern like, what color is the hair, how old is the beard growth, and how many days will you have to re-create the look? These are the questions to which you will need to have answers. Look at the growth pattern of the actor—this is your guide for placement of hair stubble. This is very important in creating realistic beard stubble. If you do not follow the natural growth pattern and beard line of the person, it will not look real.

In some cases, the actor's own beard growth and growth pattern are minimal or sparse. You will still need to follow the person's own beard as a guide. If you choose to add more to make the stubble read better on camera, be careful—your

stubble will look unnatural if you add or fill too much on an actor with sparse growth.

Hair color for beard stubble needs to be a blend of colors, with highlights and lowlights—and in some cases, a bit of auburn or red added. Use caution with adding too much red to your blend—this can look too artificial, even if the actor has a lot of red in his own beard.

Careful hair color blending with proper placement will sell the look. We will look at creating beard stubble by using a hair ball, a lace net, and a makeup brush.

Erwin Kupitz's Hair Ball Method

The chopped hair should be no longer than 0.5 centimeter; otherwise it will be very hard to apply. Prepare the chopped hair by making little hair balls of about the size of a walnut. The chopped hair is placed in the palm of your hand and then rubbed in a circular motion between your two palms until a ball is formed. This can also be done in advance to save time. If you do so, spray the prepared hair balls lightly with hair spray, and store them in a plastic box until you are ready to use them.

Hair Ball Application

1. Apply only one layer of adhesive, starting close to the chin lace piece.

2. Stipple adhesive with a makeup sponge until flat and tacky.

3. Quickly pull one of the hair balls apart, and you will notice that the short hair is sticking out of the ball where it has been separated.

4. Lightly touch the adhesive with the *standing hair,* and pull the hair quickly away from the face. The short hair will adhere to the face, and it will stand out like real beard hair. **Do not press hair flat to the face. If you do, it will look very unnatural.**

5. Continue this process until you have finished your design.

6. After all of the hair has been laid, spray a light mist of hair spray over the beard. Be careful not to point the bottle straight into the actor's face. Have the actor hold his breath and close his eyes while you are spraying the beard. Make sure that you mist only the hair and not the skin, because this could create a sheen effect, and it is very uncomfortable on the skin.

For actors and beards with a curlier texture, you can use chopped permed hair, and you don't have to build a hair ball out of it. Chop the hair to about 0.5-centimeter length, and apply it directly to the skin. Because of the curly texture, it cannot lay flat.

Your character's beard application using lace pieces in combination with chopped hair is now complete (Figures 9.40 and 9.41).

Matthew Mungle's Net Lace Method

1. Apply spirit gum adhesive to the surface of the beard area to be stippled.

2. Press down with a soft cloth to take out or matte the shine of the adhesive.

3. Lay down a piece of hair lace into the adhesive.

4. While the chopped hair is still wet, press it into the lace using a stiff makeup brush, sponge, or atomizer.

FIGURE 9.40: MODEL/ACTOR BEFORE BEARD

FIGURE 9.41: MODEL/ACTOR IN CHARACTER (AFTER BEARD)

5. Before the adhesive dries, pull the lace up and away from the face, leaving the cut hair behind, standing straight up or at the angle the lace net is pulled off the skin.

Beard Stubble with Brush

For stubble looks by hand, you can choose to use a medium-sized makeup brush or a small atomizer, with a matte spirit-gum adhesive or beard stipple wax by KRYOLAN. We will show you this technique using the makeup brush and stipple wax. The wax is clear on the skin no matter what the skin tone, and has no shine whatsoever. This is a huge advantage for HD and close-up work. If you use spirit gum, we recommend W.M. Creations, Extra Hold Matte Adhesive. Blend and prep your hair using at least two colors of hair.

1. Lay white facial tissue on your workstation or counter.

2. Wet your hair with a small amount in your hand. Hold over the tissue, making uniform cuts to the hair, so that the chopped hair drops onto the tissue.

3. Let the chopped hair dry on the tissue.

4. Remember, it is best to cut the hair when wet, and to take care making each cut the same size.

161

5. There is a tendency to make your cuts too long. Look at your first cut of hair to check length.

6. Hair needs to be completely dry before being applied to the face.

7. Apply beard stipple wax over the beard area of the face where you want to apply hair.

8. With a clean, medium-sized makeup brush, pick up the desired amount of chopped hair from the tissue by dipping the brush into the hair on the tissue.

9. Using a quick, light motion with the end of the brush, apply at a slant to the beard area. The quick hand motion, or stipple, needs to barely touch the skin to create a raised beard area. If you hit the brush with too much pressure, the hair will stick flat. It helps to have a bit of static electricity in the makeup brush. You can get static in your brush by rubbing the brush quickly back and forth over a towel.

10. Go back with a small, stiff brush or tweezers, and lift any hair that is not sticking out straight. You do not want any hairs to be lying flat against the skin.

11. Sometimes there can be clumps or patterns that you will need to thin out.

12. Be gentle. This application is fragile, but easily touched up.

Remember, as with all hair applications, you need to stand back and really look at your work, as well as getting up close to the skin and checking. Check your work in the makeup mirror from all angles, by rotating the actor around.

If you believe it up close, so will the camera.

Glues and Adhesives

In film, television, and HD, use only matte adhesive. The application is very important because any shine or glow from the adhesive under the lace piece will register. This will cause the viewer to realize it is not real facial hair.

W.M. Creations Adhesive is lightweight but strong. It is greenish in color during application, but dries clear.

K.D. Spirit Gum is a processed spirit gum, and works very well with lace pieces.

Alternate Adhesives

Telesis comes with its own thinner, and the application is slightly different from spirit gum. The brush usually has to be dipped into the thinner, then into the adhesive. All of the adhesives dry very fast, and are not recommended for use by the beginner.

Adhesives to Avoid

Any kind of latex-based adhesive should be avoided. It is impossible to clean it from the lace without the danger of destroying the lace piece and its edges.

Exception: If you have a new lace piece for each day, for all of the shooting days, using a latex-based adhesive for facial hair works—in other words, the lace pieces are not reused the next day. If it is a small piece, Pros-Aide usually works better than latex adhesives.

Cleaning the Lace

Once the lace pieces have been removed from the actor, you will need to clean the lace and re-dress the pieces. With classic spirit gum or lightweight adhesives, the actual removal of the lace from the skin also removes some adhesive from the lace. Any adhesive left on the lace can be removed by the following steps:

1. In a saucer or plate filled with the cleaning agent about one-half inch deep, lay the pieces in the solution with the lace facing down (hair up). Try not to have the hair

covered entirely by the cleaning solution. Let it set for one to two minutes. The heavier the adhesive, the longer it needs in the cleaning bath.

2. Lay the piece on a towel, but try to avoid pressing the hair flat.

3. Dip the brush into the cleaning agent, and brush out any leftover adhesive from the lace.

4. *Important:* Always follow the direction of the knotting on the lace. Example: On a moustache, brush from the nostrils down to the upper lip.

Very important: Never brush against the knotting. This results in opening the knotted hair, and the knots will appear larger and eventually fall out.

5. After all the adhesive is removed, place the pieces on a clean towel and let evaporate for 10 to 20 minutes.

The pieces are ready for blocking and any re-dressing.

The cleaning agent varies according to the glue and/or adhesive being used:

Classic spirit gum: Easy cleaning with a mix of 99-percent alcohol and acetone (1:1 ratio).

Matte adhesives: 99-percent alcohol.

Silicone-based adhesives: Use special cleaner that often has a slight oil base in it. Lay the facial hair in alcohol after using these cleaners, and let soak for a few minutes to dissolve the oil. Remove, do not comb, and let dry without stretching the lace, on a clean towel. After the facial hair is completely dry, it can be re-dressed.

Latex-based adhesives: Need a heavy oil and alcohol mix. Try a mix of baby oil and alcohol (1:1 ratio). A stiff bristle brush is used to brush off the residue of the latex—this is labor-intensive.

Beard stubble wax: Cannot be used with lace pieces as an adhesive. It is a tacky wax paste, and the lace hairpiece would not successfully stay on.

Hair Texture

All facial hair needs to be texturized before applying it to the face. The texture varies from kinky straight (Asians, Indians), to slightly wavy (European), to kinky curly (African). All hair used for knotting into wig lace is custom permed before ventilating into the lace, and therefore will not turn straight if it gets wet or during cleaning.

Quality facial hair takes all kinds of hair origins into consideration, and the texturizing creates the look of real facial hair. The color design enhances the simulation of the facial hair, again creating the illusion of a real beard.

Hair Laying Using Bald-Cap Material (Plastic Cap)

By Christien Tinsley

One of the greatest challenges Makeup Artists face is the ability to hand-lay a believable beard. Successfully accomplishing this technique will require you to recognize the problems of traditional methods.

The laying of human hair down with spirit gum is one of the oldest and most widely used techniques by veteran artists. This same method of application has been slightly modified and updated throughout the years and is, at present, commonly being employed with the use of Pros-Aide. Both approaches to laying down the hair start with applying a thin layer of the adhesive to the skin and gently pressing the tips of the hair into the glue allowing for realistic-looking growth. The glue is often treated with a matting agent or powdered during the process to keep the natural glossy sheen of the glue minimized. After the hair has been applied, it is commonly cut, curled, and dressed.

Common problems with this technique follow:

- The glue is always too shiny, giving an unnatural look to the skin under the hair.

- The glue remains or becomes tacky, which the hair eventually lays flat on and sticks to. Often in the case of doing beard stubble this becomes an absolute disaster when the hair lies flat rather than sticking on end.

It is almost impossible to color the area of skin under the laid hair because:

- Alcohol colors will reactivate the glue.

- Common makeup contains grease and oils that will eventually loosen the hair and act as a remover.

On the Job

I was faced with the challenge of applying a half-face prosthetic. The actor's face was partially shaven to apply the prosthetic and I had to match the prosthetic side to the actor's own one-quarter-inch length beard stubble. Two weeks into shooting I had exhausted the flocking, hair-through-lace, and hand-laying approaches. Being unsatisfied with the results of traditional techniques, I decided to experiment. When my actor came in one morning, I told him that I wanted to try a new concept and that it could fail miserably. Fortunately, he obliged with no resistance.

My idea was simple: Use plastic cap material as the adhesive and synthetic hair for the stubble. Plastic cap material has been around for decades and has been used most often for making plastic bald caps. It is a plasticized plastic bead that is dissolved in acetone until it turns into liquid. You can thin it to the point of spraying through an airbrush. When the acetone dries, the solution becomes a flexible plastic skin that can be adhered with glue and re-melted with acetone. This has made it useful for not only bald caps but also prosthetics and over the last decade has been used as the barrier for GFAs

(silicone gel–filled appliances). The process is very simple and is as follows:

1. Assemble your hair by blending the colors you wish to use. (Human hair works just fine, and for longer beards to be dressed it is the best choice. However, for stubble, synthetic is cheaper and because it is an acrylic it holds much stronger in the "plastic glue.")

2. Cut the hair into short lengths that are more manageable and not wasteful. Remember, you will be cutting this to a short length after application.

3. Formulate your plastic cap by thinning it with acetone to a thin syrup-like consistency.

4. Prepare the actor's skin by cleaning with alcohol and/or astringent.

5. After the skin is cleaned I recommend laying down a very fine layer of thinned-down Telesis. This is not necessary but it acts as a primer for the plastic. Cap plastic likes this surface more than skin. It should be unnoticeable to the eye and touch. If it is glossy or thick, you have put too much on.

6. When applying the plastic cap, you must work fast. The acetone dries almost instantly and gives you very little time to react. So prepare your hair in one hand and your plastic applicator in the other. (It is important to note that your hair should be slightly fanned between your fingertips. You will be laying directly into place, so you don't want the hair to be in clumps resulting in an unnatural growth pattern.)

7. Work in small areas from the top going up and lay down (in a small area) the wet plastic and then quickly stick the roots of the hair into place. Hold this for a moment (5 to 10 seconds) and then let go.

8. Repeat until you have the required area(s) covered. After the application is complete you have no need to powder and/or to be concerned with the hair laying flat and sticking because the plastic does not remain tacky.

9. Grab your electric trimmers with the spacers. That's right: ELECTRIC TRIMMERS!! Shave as though it was the actor's own hair. (Of course you can use scissors if you prefer.)

10. You can, at this point, paint the area if necessary with any form of makeup or inks. They should not affect the plastic in any way.

PRO TIP

If you find areas need to be filled and you have clumps of hair, simply fill in using the same technique and/or take a Q-tip with a touch of acetone and gently dot the area you wish to remove hair from. Use tweezers and quickly pull the hair from the area. The acetone dissolves the plastic, allowing the hairs to loosen and be removed easily. Once the acetone evaporates the glue dries and re-connects the hair.

The end result is a tack-free, clean (no dirt sticking to tacky areas), matte, paintable surface with believable rooted hair. If at any time during the day the hair wants to lift, simply glue down with adhesive under the lifted plastic and/or re-melt to the skin with a touch of acetone.

To detach the beard, you can use any remover you normally would use for adhesive or prosthetics. (Isopropyl myristate works great and is gentle on the skin.)

1. Take a powder puff and dip into the remover.

2. Apply to the skin and use gentle strokes in a circular motion until the hair is removed and the skin is no longer tacky.

I found the results to be exceptional and with a little practice I hope you do as well.

Reference

Cimuha, Inc, Kupitz, E.H., wig maker design, laying of facial hair and lace facial pieces. Tel: 818-769-6465.

Mungle, M. www.matthewmungle.com.

Tinsley, C. www.tinsleytransfers.com.

10

AIRBRUSH

Airbrush makeup is a tool in creating certain looks, especially a flawless finish to the skin. Airbrush makeup has also found a niche in the retail cosmetic world. It is used in all areas of makeup: beauty, body makeup, body art, tattoo cover, bruising, effects, and fantasy. Airbrush is used in all media—print, film, television, and theatre—and is a mainstay in HD and HDTV. The airbrush machine is a tool that is going to be a personal preference for the artist and the actor/talent you are working with. In some situations, or in makeup design, you will have to airbrush to create the look that is needed. In other situations, the department head will require you to airbrush. You will be at an extreme disadvantage if you do not learn how to airbrush and care for the equipment.

What is an airbrush? An airbrush is a small, air-operated tool that sprays various media, including ink and dye, but most often paint, by a process of atomization. An airbrush works by passing a stream of fast-moving (compressed) air through a venturi, which creates a local reduction in air pressure (suction) that allows paint to be pulled up from an interconnected reservoir at normal atmospheric pressure. The operator controls the amount of paint by using a trigger that opens a fine tapered needle.

Understanding Your Airbrush

By Badger

Airbrushes have three usual characteristics:

1. Action performed by the user triggering the paint flow.

2. The mechanism for feeding the paint into the airbrush.

3. The point in which the pressure (PSI) and air mix. (PSI means measurement of air pressure, i.e., pounds per square inch.)

There are two different ways that an airbrush mixes air with paint, allowing you to airbrush:

Internal Mix: The paint and the air mix together inside the head assembly to produce a thoroughly atomized fine-dot spray pattern.

External Mix: Indicates that air and paint mix outside the airbrush. Air and paint come together outside the head, or fluid assembly. External-mix airbrushes produce a larger-dot spray pattern than internal-mix airbrushes.

Airbrush Triggers

Single Action: Refers to airbrushes on which the trigger controls only the airflow. When the trigger is depressed, a preset amount of fluid is sprayed. The amount of fluid is regulated by turning the needle adjustment screw at the back of the handle, or, in the case of an external-mix airbrush, by turning the fluid cap on the paint tip at the front of the airbrush.

Dual Action: Refers to airbrushes on which the trigger controls both air and color (down for air, back for color). This simple maneuver allows the artist to change the width of the line, the range of value, and the opacity of paint without stopping hand motion.

Feeds

Gravity Feed: Refers to airbrushes with top-mounted color cups in which gravity draws paint into the airbrush. Less air pressure is required, enabling slower hand movement, which creates excellent control for fine detail.

Bottom Feed: Refers to airbrushes on which paint enters through a siphon tube or color cup attached to the bottom of the airbrush. Removable jars or various-sized color cups can be connected to and utilized with bottom-feed airbrushes. This configuration is generally more versatile and enables the user to change colors quickly. This is important when working with several colors at once. This enables the artist to move quickly when changing colors, as well as for storing colors during use.

Side Feed: Refers to airbrushes on which a small color cup fits into the side of the airbrush. The side-feed color cup rotates, enabling the user to work on either a horizontal or vertical surface. The side-feed configuration also permits the user to achieve fine detail without the possible sight obstruction of a top-mounted color cup.

Hybrid Airbrush: Airbrushes that have a combination of gravity and bottom feed.

Airbrushes

Badger Model 100 G: Gravity-feed airbrush with 1/16-ounce color cup (Figure 10.1).

Badger Model 100MU: Airbrush with 1/3-ounce color cup and makeup-specific head assembly (Figure 10.2).

Badger 360 Universal: Airbrush is capable of performing in a gravity-feed as well as a bottom-feed mode (Figure 10.3).

Badger Model Omni 5000: Gravity-feed airbrush with 1/8-ounce color cup (Figure 10.4).

Paasche VJR#2: Gravity feed, double action, internal mix. Airbrush used to create a wider range of tinting, shading, and details. Color cup is on top for easy color changes. Good for both right- and left-handed users (Figure 10.5).

FIGURE 10.1: BADGER AIR-BRUSH MODEL 100G

FIGURE 10.2: BADGER AIR-BRUSH MODEL 100MU

FIGURE 10.3: BADGER AIR-BRUSH 360 UNIVERSAL

FIGURE 10.4: BADGER AIR-BRUSH MODEL OMNI 5000

FIGURE 10.5: PAASCHE AIRBRUSH VJR#2

FIGURE 10.6: PAASCHE AIRBRUSH DOUBLE ACTION GRAVITY

Paasche H#3 Single Action: External mix airbrush.

Paasche Talon Double: Double-action, gravity-feed airbrush (Figure 10.6).

Iwata HP-C Plus: Large gravity-feed cup with a large needle-nozzle configuration. Fine-spray output, and entire range of stippling effects. Airbrush has a short paint passageway.

Iwata HP-CH: Designed for artists who need control for detail work. Airbrush uses new Micro air-control-valve technology.

Iwata HP-CS: Gravity feed with 0.35-millimeter needle and nozzle combination for fine-detail spraying. Generous-sized cup and funnel shape.

Iwata HP-CR: Gravity feed designed for quick change of custom-mixed colors. Internal-mix airbrush, ergonomic handle design, fine-detail work, and easier spraying.

Eye shadow is best applied via an airbrush with a very fine needle/ nozzle ratio like the Iwata High Performance HP-B, which is 0.2 millimeter. Although much too light to apply foundation, it gives you the ability to keep your colors focused. Fine-needle/nozzles are popular for lining eyes, and with effects artists for veining. An appropriate needle/nozzle range for most airbrush makeup, both face and body, is 8 millimeters + 5 millimeters, with the wider apertures leaning toward the body makeup end of things. The smaller the nozzle, the more control you have. When the nozzle is too small, the application will take longer than necessary unless you need to focus the range of space you are working on.

—David Klasfeld, CEO/Creative Director, Obsessive Compulsive Cosmetics, Inc.

Compressors
Terminology

CFM: Measurement of airflow.

Moisture Filter: Removes water from air.

Oil Filter: Removes oil from air.

PSI: Measurement of air pressure (pounds per square inch).

Air Regulator: Adjusts air pressure.

Listing

Iwata Smart Jet Pro: Compressor shuts off automatically when not in use. It has an oil-less piston air compressor with built-in airbrush holder; moisture filters (removing water from air) with an air regulator (adjusts air pressure); and bleed-valve adjustment to release moisture.

Iwata Power Jet: Compressor has oil-less dual-piston air with a 3.5-liter air-storage tank. It has zero pulsation, moisture filter, and a mounted pressure gauge with air regulator for precise air-pressure adjustment.

Iwata Power Jet Pro: A compressor with a 2-liter air-storage tank with zero pulsation and an air reserve for spraying at higher air pressures. It has dual-adjustable pressure regulators plus dual-moisture filters and dual-mounted pressure gauges. The compressor also has dual quick-disconnect ports and dual built-in airbrush holders.

Iwata Power Jet Lite: Adjustable pressure regulator, moisture filter, and built-in airbrush holder.

Iwata Silver Jet: Compact and quiet single-person use with working pressure adjustable from 10 to 18 PSI. The compressor has a coiled air hose, pressure-adjustable knob, handle, airbrush holder, and pressure gauge.

Iwata Sprint Jet: A mounted air-pressure gauge with a bleed-valve airflow adjustment to lower air pressure. Pressure works from 1 to 35 PSI. Zero maintenance with an oil-less piston air compressor.

PRO TIP

In general, use compressors with a lower PSI or compressors that allow you to adjust the settings for direct airbrushing on the face. The higher the PSI, the more kickback you'll get from the product.

PRO TIP

Makeup companies (such as Mac Pro and Obsessive Compulsive Cosmetics), which offer small portable compressors, often use the Iwata Series.

171

Paasche D100: ⅛-horsepower compressor delivers 15 to 25 PSI with most model airbrushes (Figure 10.7).

Paasche D500SR: ⅛-horsepower with switch and regulator, which is capable of delivering 20 to 40 psi. With an oil-less piston.

Paasche D3000R: Oil-less diaphragm compressor that is tank mounted. The compressor is compact and portable with a maximum of 40 PSI (Figure 10.8).

Badger Model 80–3 Mini Compressor: Produces 3 to 5 PSI (Figure 10.9).

Badger Model 80-7xaIR Compressor: Produces 10 to 12 PSI (Figure 10.10).

Badger Model 80-8x Air Compressor: Produces 10 to 12 PSI with built-in regulator (Figure 10.11).

FIGURE 10.7: PAASCHE AIRBRUSH D100

FIGURE 10.8: PAASCHE AIRBRUSH D3000

FIGURE 10.9: BADGER MODEL 80–3 MINI COMPRESSOR

All-in-One Airbrush Systems

Small all-in-one airbrush systems have fantastic overall weight. Traveling with these compressors is a snap, and using one in small spaces is a breeze. This size goes anywhere, a great advantage for the professional. There are no fancy pressure gauges or moisture meters that make airbrushing intimidating. Air Pro, Temptu, and Dinair are a few of the portable-airbrush companies on the market today (Figure 10.12).

AIRBRUSH

FIGURE 10.10: BADGER MODEL 80-7X AIR COMPRESSOR

PRO TIP

Small compressors with an output of 6 to 8 PSI are perfect for the face and small areas of the body, such as covering tattoos.

FIGURE 10.11: BADGER MODEL 80-8X AIR COMPRESSOR

FIGURE 10.12: TEMPTU COMPRESSOR AND GUN

Battery Compressors: Runs on a battery pack. Great to take your airbrush on set or in any situation where you need to be mobile.

Ninja Jet: Compact size, airbrush holder, carry handle, low-maintenance oil-less piston motor. Obsessive Compulsive Cosmetics (OCC) sells starter kits.

Temptu: AIRbrush Makeup System.

Dinair Mini-System Beauty Kit: Compressor weighs less than a pound. The system comes with a travel adapter (100 to 240 volts), and has a PSI of 0 to 7. The airbrush is a Dinair 400CA. Also included are stencils, instructions, and makeup (Figure 10.13).

Airbrush Product Lines

By Bradley Look

People ask me all the time about the dangers of airbrushing. There is an unfounded fear about the airbrush. What I usually find is that airbrushing is not being properly used in some of those cases, which leads to many of those problems. As a Makeup Artist, it is your responsibility to stay on top of the most current information and how products interact with each other. Manufacturers of airbrushes, compressors, and airbrush makeup all have instructions, plus suggestions on how to use their products so that you'll get the most from airbrushing with success. Before you start using that airbrush,

FIGURE 10.13: DINAIR MINI SYSTEM BEAUTY KIT

know what makeup is available and, more important, what kind of makeup you are buying. What is in airbrush makeup?

Here are the six formula breakdowns of airbrush makeup available:

Water Based: This type of makeup is not unlike the standard liquid variety: finely ground, cosmetic-grade approved pigments dispersed in water. Water is the most common solvent found in cosmetics, and is usually referred to as aqueous dispersion.

PRO TIP

Water-based makeup makes cleaning your airbrush equipment easy. Just clean after each use with water.

173

Polymer Water Based: This cosmetic formulation is one of the more commonly used for airbrush makeups. Once the makeup is airbrushed, the polymer vehicle upon drying produces a continuous film on the skin.

Polymer SD40-Alcohol Based: This is just like the polymer water-based formulas (listed above), with one major difference. SD40 alcohol is used as the solvent in place of water. The alcohol assists in the drying of the product on the skin.

Alcohol Based: This type of airbrush makeup is normally known within the makeup industry as the "temporary airbrush inks" associated with the production of faux flesh art (tattoos).

Silicone Based: This is the newest formula of all the airbrush makeups currently available. This brand of cosmetic claims that it stays looking "just applied" all day without fading or wearing away.

PRO TIP

To alter coverage of silicone-based products, you can thin them only with formulas that work with silicone. (Example: Mac Pro has an airbrush cleanser that also works as a thinner for their silicone-based airbrush makeup.)

DHA Based: Although technically not really considered an airbrush makeup, DHA (dihydroxyacetone) based products constitute the sunless-tanning systems. The use of the airbrush in spraying cosmetics gave the sunless-tanning manufacturers an idea: Why not produce a formula that can be atomized?

Now let's talk about makeup and what is on the market today. Products are listed by their brand name and/or by the manufacturer's name. All of the products listed are pre-reduced to a consistency for spraying straight from the bottle. However, if you should desire to thin the product further, check with the manufacturer first. Also, these products have been formulated to be atomized at a low PSI, usually between 3 and 6. Using the right product for the right job means a good makeup.

Airbrush Bodyart: Airbrush product available in both water and alcohol formulations. DHA tanning system offered as well.

Airmakeup Cosmetics: Polymer water-based product.

AirPro Airbrush Makeup: A water-based formula. The company also has a sunless-tanning solution. Airbrush cleaner is available for the line.

Bodyair: Polymer water-based line of products.

DCK Airbrush Cosmetics: Polymer water-based product line.

Dinair: There are three product lines available through this company: polymer water based, polymer SD40-alcohol based, and DHA. Dinair also manufactures an airbrush cleaner.

Duratat: Water-based tattoo ink containing no alcohol.

Fantasy Faces: Polymer SD40-alcohol–based formulation. Thinner for product also available.

Fashion Aire Foundation: Polymer water-based and sunless DHA formulation. An airbrush cleaner is available.

Graftobian: Polymer water based as well as polymer SD40-alcohol based. Both thinner and airbrush cleaner are available.

JanTana: DHA sunless tanner.

Jomo: SD40 alcohol based.

Kett Cosmetics: Water based and polymer SD40 alcohol based. An airbrush cleaner is also available.

KRYOLAN: Currently, KRYOLAN has a polymer water-based and an SD40-alcohol–based product line.

MAC Airbrush: Polymer water based and silicone SD40 alcohol based.

Make Up For Ever: Water and alcohol based.

Mancini Airbrush Makeup: Water based and offers an airbrush cleaner.

Marvaldi Makeup: Water-based formulation.

Michael Davy Airbrush Makeup: Polymer SD40-alcohol based.

Mist Mirage: Silicone SD40-alcohol based, as well as DHA sunless formula. An airbrush cleaner is also available.

O2 Cosmetics: Water-based formula. Also available in a DHA sunless tanner.

Obsessive Compulsive Cosmetics: Water based and SD40 alcohol based.

Reel Creations Body Art Inks: SD40-alcohol–based line.

Safari Airbrush Makeup: Polymer alcohol-based formula. DHA sunless tanner is also in the line.

Skin Illustrator Colors: SD40-alcohol–based formula line.

Stacolors: SD40-alcohol–based product line.

Su-do Body Art: Polymer water based, SD40 alcohol based, and DHA in product line. Airbrush cleaner is available.

Temptu: Water based, polymer water based, polymer SD40 alcohol based, and silicone SD40 based. An airbrush cleaner is also available in the line.

Totally Tattoo Party Body Paints: Polymer water based.

Trendy Tribals: Polymer water based.

Uslu Airlines: Polymer water based.

Remember to keep in mind that not all brands interact well with each other. So don't try mixing together two different manufacturers' product lines—their chemistry may not be compatible. A classic example is thinners. A Makeup Artist wrote to me to say she was having a hard time applying a certain makeup brand that would not adhere or cover well when thinned with the product she was using. It turns out the makeup is silicone based, which has a chemical reaction to the product she was using as a thinner. Some silicone-based makeup products do have thinners to go with their product line. The same can be said of all of the abovementioned makeup brands. Here are a few airbrush makeup tips that I have found to work over the years.

1. Less is more when airbrushing. The makeup should not feel like a mask.

2. Use a PSI of 3 to 6 when airbrushing the face. If you airbrush with a stronger PSI, there will be a larger quantity of "bounce back" of the product into the air.

3. Hold the airbrush at a downward 45-degree angle when airbrushing the eye area on the talent (Figure 10.14). Of course, have the actor close their eyes!

4. If you are going to airbrush on the eyelid, use a PSI of 3 or less.

5. Using stencils when airbrushing works well for eyebrows. (Note: Freehand actually works better and looks more natural if the person airbrushing is quite skilled.)

6. When airbrushing the face, spray in small, circular motions (Figure 10.15). This keeps the makeup even.

FIGURE 10.14: AIRBRUSHING AT AN ANGLE

FIGURE 10.15: AIRBRUSHING IN A CIRCULAR MOTION

FIGURE 10.16 TISSUE OR SHIELD

so popular, there is nothing better than the airbrush. Many of my clients also do red-carpet events that are mostly shot in HD. HD can be very harsh, so it is imperative that the makeup be flawless. I really believe you must use the correct color in the foundation for the look to be natural. Easy touch-ups are also essential. On set, I usually use a makeup brush for touch-ups.

7. Have a folded tissue or shield to protect the hairline from overspray of makeup (Figure 10.16). Do not add tap water to a water-based makeup to thin. Use distilled water. Tap water contains minerals that can contaminate or compromise the chemistry of the makeup.

PRO TIP

Read the ingredients of products you buy. Many of the cosmetic and airbrush companies have products that work well with each other. Know what you are buying. You'll have the best results possible when airbrushing.

PRO TIP

What's in Kris Evans's makeup kit (demonstrated in Figure 10.17)?
Primer
Foundation
Pressed powders
Lipstick, lip stain, and/or lip gloss
Eyebrow pencil
Mascara
Eye shadow
Excellent makeup brushes
Tweezerman tweezers
Eyelash curler
Cleanser
Moisturizer

PRO TIP

It's very important to clean your airbrush immediately after each use. You want to prevent the makeup from drying inside the airbrush. If not cleaned properly, your airbrush will not give the proper spray.

Airbrush Lesson for Natural Beauty Makeup

By Kris Evans

[Kris Evans's vast experience in film, television, theatre, HD, and print editorials helped her to develop an airbrush system and products for the professional Makeup Artist.]

I use the airbrush on everything and find it much faster and easier. With HD becoming

FIGURE 10.17: PHOTOGRAPHER, GREGORY CANNON;
MODEL, NICOLE MALGARINI; BEAUTY MAKEUP, KRIS EVANS

staying power for your airbrush. Squeeze six to seven drops of makeup into the airbrush cup. For a more translucent effect, add one to two drops of water. Remember to replace the cap on your airbrush to avoid spills.

3. Start the compressor. Position your hand on the airbrush lever as if you were holding a pencil.

4. Have your actor close his eyes. Airbrush horizontally 3 to 4 inches from the face, pulling back the airbrush lever with your fingertip. You'll see a fine mist start to adhere onto the surface of the skin. Keep moving around the face in a circular motion without stopping in one place. It's this constant movement that keeps the makeup even. Application should take about 15 seconds. If any areas need more coverage you can lightly airbrush a second coat of foundation to those areas.

177

How to Start

1. Set up your station with everything you need to airbrush. Be sure you are familiar with the airbrush makeup you will be using.

PRO TIP

Keep on hand a small squeeze bottle of distilled water or spring water or suggested product by the manufacturer for thinning airbrush makeup.

PRO TIP

The first time you airbrush, put only water into the cup, and spray onto your hand or a tissue. This will give you a feel for the airbrush and how it works.

2. Apply the moisturizer or primer of choice to the skin first. Apply the primer with a sponge and not through the airbrush. A primer ensures a smooth surface with

5. Corrective spot covering is easy. For under the eyes, you can use a shade lighter than the foundation first. Then airbrush the entire face with the color you chose. For problem spots on the face, you can lightly spray a second layer of the foundation color.

6. Adding color for blusher or highlighters is easy. Blow out any leftover makeup color through the airbrush with a few drops of

water. Add your next color choice to the cup. Blusher should be a soft blush color applied by hand or an airbrush. Lightly spray a highlighter color along the cheekbone, brow bone, under the eye, or anywhere a highlight is needed.

7. Set your makeup with a setting powder. You are now ready to finish the rest of your makeup application. Sweep an eye color over the lid—and, if needed, a subtle eyeliner. Don't forget the eyebrows. Top your makeup off with a flattering lip stain, lipstick, and/or lip gloss.

8. When all the makeup has been fully blown through the airbrush, detach the gun from the hose, and place the cup under running water. Connect your gun to the compressor. Turn it back on and run through with the appropriate cleaner for the airbrush makeup you are using. Many makeup lines need very specific cleaners.

    Maintenance: After every few applications, pull the needle out and wipe clean. Be careful not to bend the top of the needle.

Airbrushing with Stencils

By Dina Ousley, Founder, Dinair

Stencils are used in beauty airbrush makeup to achieve a cleaner, softer, less made-up look. With HDTV and digital HD cameras, every detail is visible. Feature or flaw, it shows. Airbrushing an entire makeup is perfect for these technologies. Shields and stencils are used to protect areas of the face or body where you don't want colors to go, while allowing you to define perfect natural eyebrow shapes, lip shapes, and to feather and blend existing colors. At Dinair, we use shields (stencils) for beauty makeup, fantasy, glamour, and tattoos. The following sections explain how to work with and apply the use of shields in a natural beauty makeup.

Foundation

Start with a clean face, and make sure that the spot where you choose to spray the airbrush makeup is free of any moisturizers or oils. Apply a primer before the foundation. Choose a color that is in the shade range of the skin tone you are working on. The liquid must be shaken before use to correct pigment. If you want to create a custom color match, you can always mix your foundation colors using the airbrush with a technique called back bubbling.

If you were to look at airbrush makeup under a magnifying glass, you would see that the makeup consists of light, medium, dark, and blush-colored dots. Look at the actor's skin tone. If there is anything dark around the face—such as hyper-pigmentation, birthmarks, or age spots—lighten with one or two shades lighter than the person's natural color before applying the natural shade. You need only five to eight drops of makeup to spray an entire face, neck, and ears. Spray the natural shade over the concealer. Spray sparingly so you don't lose your highlights.

Work in passes. A pass is every time you go over the same area, the dots fill in, and the coverage becomes more opaque. Make sure to use one pass at a time—one pass, two pass, three pass, and so on, until you have the right coverage. Dots are the ultimate in camouflaging.

Leave enough open coverage. Open coverage is the space around the dots of color (your skin) that you have sprayed. This allows you to fill in with some blush color or use the natural redness of the skin to become the blush. We call this the window of opportunity. Spraying sparsely is the key to success. Keep the distance of your airbrush about six inches away from the skin while spraying foundation, using circular motions with back-and-forth movements. This is key to an even application.

3. Keep the eye area clean and free from moisturizers or oils. Moisturizers can cause eye shadow colors to crease.

4. Set the airflow to 3 or 4 PSI.

5. Hold up a shield (stencil) that follows the contours of the eye, and gently pull back the airbrush lever.

6. In a small, continuous motion, spray the shadow color by making several passes until you reach the level of color desired. Note: If you hold the stencil flat against the skin, your edge will be more defined. Holding the stencil slightly above the skin will give a softer feathered edge (Figure 10.18).

Eyeliner

1. Change out any color you desire for eyeliner.

2. Set the airflow on a low PSI of about 3 to 4.

3. In the same way as for the eye shadow, follow the natural lash line in a back-and-forth motion, building the color with each pass. Note: An eye shadow stencil held directly on the lid close to the eyelashes will give you defined eyeliner. A stencil held just off the lid while airbrushing eyeliner color will appear feathered.

Eye Shadow

1. Put two to three drops of liquid eye shadow into the airbrush cup.

2. To create a custom color, mix them by creating back bubbles with your airbrush.

Eyebrows

1. You will want to put a total of two to three drops of eyebrow coloring in the cup.

2. Hold the stencil up to your eyebrow, and bring it flush against your skin for a sharp edge.

$$\triangle \quad + \quad \triangle \quad = \quad \triangle$$

yellow   blue   green
new color

Mixing and Matching. When we mix, We mix only a couple of drops of this, with a couple of drops of that, and then suddenly, we have a endless amount of color combinations. Create your own custom colors, get creative and see what happens.

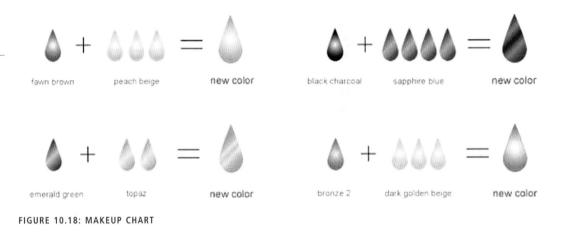

fawn brown   peach beige   **new color**   black charcoal   sapphire blue   **new color**

emerald green   topaz   new color   bronze 2   dark golden beige   new color

FIGURE 10.18: MAKEUP CHART

3. Distance the stencil, allowing the overspray to cover and define the brows, giving them a soft, naturally feathered look. Note: You can use the stencil to spray the entire brow, or just fill in the brow where needed. You may also want to use the front of one brow stencil and the tail of another, creating the perfect eyebrow look for you.

Dinair has hair stencils to fill in sparse areas. Each stencil has a selection of hair shapes that can be tailored for your needs. This is a particularly good way for women who have lost some of their eyebrows to again have naturally beautiful brows.

Lip Color

1. Change out your eyeliner color for a lip color of choice.

2. Take a lip edge and lay it flat against the lips.

3. Work on small sections at a time. Note: Laying the stencil flat against the lips will give you a defined lip line. Work closer to the lips for a narrower line.

4. Work farther away from the lips to finish the rest of the lips.

5. Apply lip gloss over the colored lips for an extra-shiny finish.

Blusher

1. Apply blusher color by sweeping across the cheekbone area with the airbrush. The cheeks should never look made up. A subtle hint of color is all you need.

2. Use a loose tissue to block off any unwanted color into the hairline, being careful not to hold too close to the skin—this will create a hard line.

PRO TIP

To find the natural contours of the cheeks, have the actor smile while you airbrush the cheek color. Go to www.airbrushmakeup.com for video instructions.

How to Clean your Stencils

By Bradley Look

Productivity and the life of your stencils can be vastly improved with regular cleaning. Just as you should always leave your airbrush clean, so should you treat the rest of your equipment. This is particularly paramount when working as a Makeup Artist who's using an airbrush on talent. After all, you wouldn't use dirty sponges or brushes, would you? A stencil comes in contact with an actor's skin and should be cleaned frequently. Simple steps are all it takes to maintain clean stencils. First, you'll need the basic equipment to get started.

Materials

A solvent-proof tray (such as an enamel butcher's tray, found in most art stores)

Paper toweling

Powder puffs

Isopropyl alcohol, 99 percent

Spray bottle

Synthetic brush (with soft bristles)

To Begin the Whole Cleansing Process

1. Detach two sheets of paper toweling from the roll, and fold so that the toweling will fit inside the butcher's tray (Figure 10.19).

2. Carefully pour the isopropyl alcohol on top of the paper toweling so that it is entirely saturated with the solvent (Figure 10.20). Note: If you are unsure whether the solvent will affect the material your stencil is made of, check a small section before immersing it.

181

FIGURE 10.19: SETUP

FIGURE 10.20: POURING

3. Lay the stencil face down (dirty side) onto the toweling (Figure 10.21).

4. Let it sit there for several minutes so that the solvent can loosen all products on its surface. Note: If both sides of your stencil have dried product on them, then you'll need to flip the stencil over to soak.

5. Now flip over the stencil onto the paper toweling (dirty side up).

6. Saturate a powder puff with solvent, and lightly pat the stencil to remove product (Figures 10.22 and 10.23).

7. Once you're satisfied with the cleaning, rinse the stencil off with tap water in the sink.

8. Lay the stencil down on some clean paper toweling and pat dry (Figure 10.24).

9. Store the now-clean stencil away for the next time you'll need it (Figure 10.25).

PRO TIP

If you have stubborn spots, use the spray bottle containing isopropyl alcohol. Mist those areas. Then take a synthetic brush and use a patting motion to loosen dry material.

PRO TIP

An Itoya portfolio (available in art-supply and office-supply stores) helps keep stencils flat and organized.

FIGURE 10.21: WASHING STENCIL IN TRAY

FIGURE 10.22: CLEANING STENCIL WITH PUFF

FIGURE 10.23: CLEANING WITH BRUSH

FIGURE 10.24: DRYING STENCIL

FIGURE 10.25: STORED STENCILS

FIGURE 10.26: KAZU AIRBRUSH EQUIPMENT

Airbrushing Silicone Prosthetics

By Kazuhiro Tsuji

[Kazu illustrates an example of using the airbrush on a silicone appliance (Figure 10.26). This professional example is for an Old Age Makeup design for film.]

Before Actor Prep

1. Seal your pre-painted appliances with a thinned plastic bald cap material like Mouldlifes and New Baldies, available at Motion Picture FX Company.

2. Powder the sealed appliance.

3. Trim out the flashing where necessary.

4. Clean up the back side of the appliance with 70% or 99% alcohol.

5. Pre-glue the appliance with Telesis or Snappy G. Snappy G is a silicone adhesive from Mouldlife that is stronger than Telesis. You can use this adhesive on the entire face, but if the actor has sensitive skin, use just around the mouth area. If the actor sweats a lot or if you need extra hold for a long shooting day, I would use a stronger adhesive all over to secure the piece.

Note: Whatever you do, do not trap wet glue under the appliance. The solvent in it could irritate the skin. Before you lay the appliance down, let the solvent "flash off" from the glue as much as possible.

Actor Prep and Application

1. Ask the actor to wear a button-down shirt to work. It will be easier to remove clothing after the application is done and will not disturb the makeup. Place a cap or towel over the actor's lap.

2. If using a bald cap, wrap the hair for a bald cap application (see Michele Mulkey's bald cap application, Chapter 8).

3. Clean the surface of the skin with Kiehl's Blue Toner, followed by an application of Michael Davy Sweat Stop, wherever necessary. Make sure that both products are dry before you start to apply the appliances.

4. Lay down (flatten) the eyebrows with KRYOLAN Eyebrow Plastic, and then cover with PAX Paint. If the silicone appliance is thin around the eyebrow area, the PAX Paint will block out the brow color so that it will not show through.

5. Glue down the appliances. I usually use a template of the appliance—a copy of the appliance cast out of the appliance mold in firm silicone. Lay the template on the skin; using a powder wand, trace the edge with RCMA Translucent Powder. This will help guide you in applying the appliances in the correct location. Silicone appliances are very soft. It is easy to apply a very soft silicone appliance without stretching it. After the piece is glued down, make sure the appliance has been glued down all the way to the edges. Melt the "flashing" off the appliance with a small amount of acetone on a paint brush. Be sure to have a fan or hair dryer blowing off the fumes from the actor's face. Do not use too much acetone. If the acetone drips or the actor feels it on the skin, that means you are using too much.

Note: I use Dyson's Air Multiplier. It has a gentle and consistent air flow. You can put it right between the actor and the mirror at your makeup station. The actors can still see themselves and you can control the amount of airflow.

6. Seal the edges with a 50:50 mixture of Duo Surgical Adhesive and Premiere Products Beta Bond Plus. You can change the formula according to your needs. If you want this mixture to be applied to the eyelids as in an old age stipple, add more Duo. You will have a better wrinkle effect for the eyes. Dry with a hair dryer and powder. Apply Ben Nye's Final Seal with a white sponge to get rid of any powdery effect on the edge. If you spray the Final Seal from the spray bottle, you will add too much and not have control over the product.

7. Apply old age stipple (or appliance) on the hands.

Painting

I airbrush with Premiere Products Skin Illustrator and Reel Creations airbrush colors thinned down with alcohol. You should never use these colors as they are; always mix your own colors. You have to know what you want to see and how to paint it. This will decide the silicone's opacity and color. The color you mix and how much you thin down these colors will affect the final outcome of the appliance. Rather than 99% isopropyl alcohol to thin down paints, I use either Premier Product Thinners, or ethanol alcohol 99% or weaker. For additional colors, you can use RCMA's Appliance Foundation, thinned with AF Thinner or 99% alcohol, or both. Any oil makeup that will stay shiny on silicone appliances sometimes can be used, but try to use a minimal amount of oil.

My favorite airbrushes are the Iwata HP-C 0.3 mm and the Paasche H with #3.

For airbrush spattering, I use a vinyl tube fitted over the feeder cup. I came up with this when creating a "larger-than-life" portrait makeup of Dick Smith. Having a hard time spattering under the chin area, since it was too big to move, I added height to the feeder cup. You get a better feed for spattering and there is less of a chance of spillage, especially under the chin.

Put a quick disconnect on each airbrush so that you will not have to carry more than one hose. I use a 25-foot-long air hose. This way you can direct the compressor's noise away from the actor. When you use a small compressor, it works like an air tank to stabilize the airflow.

Use the lowest pressure on the compressor as possible. Of course, put an air filter and regulator on it. It is surprising that many Makeup Artists never have tried an airbrush on themselves. You should—it is uncomfortable, especially around the eyes, nose, and ears. Every Makeup Artist should be airbrushed so that they know what it feels like; this will help them find a comfortable way to use an airbrush on actors and/or other clients.

Note: When you pre-paint your appliances before the application, seal the paint job with a thinned bald-cap material. It should be very thin, mostly acetone. Give an extra coat on the neck area where costumes will rub against your work or the hairline where wigs or hairpieces will be glued down.

Check all of your work before applying any wigs or hairpieces. Use ADM Tronics Pros-Aide paste (mixed with Cab-O-Sil or TS-100 Fumed Silica), W.M. Creations Spirit Gum or Matte Silicone adhesives for gluing any type of wig lace.

Spray using Paasche fine spattering with Makeup International Super Matte Antishine mixed with distilled water over the entire surface. For extra matte, apply Antishine or M*A*C Matte right out of the tube or container.

Finally, check all of your work and final touch or adjust for the camera.

Application of Airbrush Body Makeup

By Bradley Look

The airbrushing of makeup is not exclusively used only on the face. Its use to apply body makeup is becoming just as common. The use of the airbrush has become a standard application tool with spray tanning products across the country. Airbrushing of larger areas speeds up the process and allows for a more even coating of cosmetics than is possible by hand application alone.

Setting Up Your Work Area

As you will be working on a larger surface than just the face, having a separate spraying area set aside for this purpose is advisable, since there will be more airborne particulate matter in the air. It cannot be overemphasized enough that the room or tent (commonly used when many people have to be sprayed) must have an exhaust system, to remove all product from the air. Many Makeup Artists will tape a furnace filter to the front side of a box fan and position it close to a doorway in order to suck harmful particles from the room. Additionally, I have used whole-house air ionizers, which drop airborne particles from the air by sending an electrical charge (negative ions) through the air working with an effect similar to static electricity. A six-foot table should be set up for your airbrushes and compressors along with all necessary makeup products. Other supplies might include a hair dryer with a cool setting, powder to set the makeup, latex sponges, power strip, and appropriate cleaner to remove residual product from airbrushes. A word of warning: Heaters are nice to have but be careful where they are placed when working with alcohol-based products.

Instructions to Give Actors

The day before you are to apply body makeup, specific instructions should be given to actors. For example, if all body hair needs to be removed, it should be done a day or so ahead of time in order to allow the skin sufficient time to recover, in case it breaks out. If the person wishes to moisturize his or her skin before reporting for makeup, a water-based lotion needs to be used in order to allow the makeup to "take" evenly. Another issue to mention to your performer is the use of deodorants. Only roll-on types of antiperspirants should be used because spray deodorants always cover larger areas and the film they leave on the skin will keep makeup from adhering properly. And one last subject that needs to be addressed: Actors need to be instructed not to drink any alcohol the night before the application of body makeup—this is especially true if an alcohol-based product such as temporary tattoo ink (i.e., Reel Creations, Skin Illustrator, or Temptu) is going to be sprayed on the body. Alcohol can seep through the pores causing makeup to lift or even dissolve. I've seen this happen firsthand.

Makeup and Airbrush Supplies

The choice of makeup you use will greatly depend on the durability of the finish you ultimately need. Generally, airbrush spraying for body coverage will consist of the use of spray guns since they can cover larger areas more evenly and quickly. For example, I use Iwata's LPH-50 Spray Gun in the Baby Series since it can be operated on a low PSI setting of 10 to 13. If you only need to spray the arms or legs, Iwata's Kustom Hi-Line TH will work perfectly. The TH works similarly to other spray guns in that it can spray fairly wide using the fan tip or more directly by using the cone tip. The Kustom TH also has the ability to spatter, which comes in quite handy when covering tattoos. Be sure to always operate spray guns at the lowest possible PSI setting to reduce dangerous overspray. On the topic of compressors, always use one that can properly operate the type of gun you're going to spray with.

Applying Body Makeup

To begin, use filter masks to airbrush for long periods of time or when proper ventilation is not at its best. This includes the actors you are working on. Start airbrushing any primer you might use first. Be very careful to take your time and not cause drips or uneven skin tone. Work in long sweeping motions using the whole arm and not just the wrist. It is best to work from the arms inward. When doing the legs, if possible, have the actor step up on an apple box or some other type of platform to save your back from the strain of bending over. If the makeup needs to be more durable, a makeup sealer is advisable.

On-Set Touch-ups

A small tent or designated area near the set to do touch-ups on body makeup will be needed. Ask your AD department to assist you with this setup. You will also need the electrical department to set up power for your compressors, fans, or hairdryers. NEVER plug into any power setup on set: Always ask an electrician to provide you with power and they will plug it in for you. Also, there are battery-operated compressors that work wonders for small areas of touch-up. Be prepared by having whatever you may need on hand.

Removing the Makeup

For removing most tattoo inks or glues, a 50/50 mixture of isopropyl alcohol and isopropyl myristate used on a powder puff breaks down most makeup.

PRO TIP

Shaving cream is a great makeup remover. It removes makeup blood, tattoo inks, cream-based makeup, and water-based makeup. Have available damp hot towels with cleanser or shaving cream for makeup removal.

Cleaning your Airbrush: Paasche

By Paasche

Follow these steps to clean your airbrush (Figure 10.27):

1. Pour any leftover color back into its container.

2. Rinse and wipe color cup or bottle assembly clean. To back-flush color from the airbrush, keep bottle assembly or color cup attached.

FIGURE 10.27: CLEANING STATION

3. If using a color cup, cover the top of it with your thumb or a cloth to keep air from blowing out.

4. Place one finger over the air cap of the airbrush, and release some air by depressing the finger button. This causes back pressure, which induces a bubble action inside the airbrush and container. This helps clean the fluid passage.

Spray excess airbrush cleaning product into a cleaning pot, sometimes referred to as a cleaning station. The cleaning station has a filter system that helps to trap harmful solvent so as not to be introduced into the environment.

—Bradley Look

Safety

Certain safety issues do come up with airbrushing. Having good ventilation is at the top of the list. Although there is little or no proven risk of airbrushing with makeup and low-PSI compressors, you, as a professional, are responsible for knowing all of the current safety recommendations in order to protect yourself and the actor's health. One of the main defensive actions to protect yourself and others while airbrushing is to locate your station near an open door, and/or by having open doors at either end of the trailer. Windows should be open and any built-in ventilation systems running. There should be a limit on the number of Makeup Artists in the trailer who are airbrushing at the same time. Airbrushing has little or no risk, but spray-on tanning is a greater concern. Good websites to research the latest findings on cosmetic ingredients and workplace safety issues, respectively, are the Food and Drug Administration at www.fda.gov and the Occupational Safety and Health Administration at www.osha.gov.

References

187

KTS Effects, Inc.

Tsuji, K., Special Effects Designer and Makeup Artist.

Internet Resources

ARTtalk.com. www.arttalk.com.

Badger. www.badgerairbrush.com.

Evans, K. Krisevansmakeup.com.

Food and Drug Administration. www.fda.gov.

Iwata. Professional Airbrushes and Accessories, www.iwataairbrush.com.

Klasfeld, D., Obsessive Compulsive Cosmetics, www.occmakeup.com.

Look, B., Original articles written for the online magazine, Airbrushtalk.

Mandor, S. www.temptu.com.

Occupational Safety and Health Administration. www.osha.gov.

Ousley, D. www.dinair.com.

Paasche. www.paascheairbrush.com.

11

EFFECTS

Prosthetics is the process of creating an effect in makeup by sculpting, molding, application, and painting. Prosthetic makeup is widely used today for wounds, to simulate illnesses, to change the shape of a face, or to create a whole different face. Countless monsters and creatures are created using prosthetic makeup. Your imagination is all you need, plus skills in the art of mold-making, applying, and painting the final outcome. Finding the right tools and products will help you to create anything the director has asked for. You might find yourself behind and in trouble on occasion if you can't produce or help a department head in making, laying, or painting a prosthetic piece. Directors and Makeup Artists are much savvier and expect high-end, quality work. The process in prosthetics starts with molds, making molds, and casting chosen materials to go into the mold to cure. There are many different ways to do this, and we'll go over the steps later on in this chapter. In today's market, there are many ways to shorten the path of mold-making because of the advances in products being used. There will be many times when you need to rush something out, a request has been made for a last-minute makeup effect, or you need to reuse a prosthetic piece over and over again. Whatever the case, there are easy ways to do this right on location.

As a Makeup Artist, you should also learn where to turn for help in achieving realistic prosthetic applications. Not everyone needs to pour a body cast or to sculpt masks. If you know the process and who to call, then applying the final piece is what counts.

Mold-Making for Today's Market

By Smooth-On

Many products on the market are used for mold-making. Most use a variety of flexible rubber products. These products can mimic fine details, are easy to remove from the original piece being cast, and can be used over and over again,

which makes them cost effective. The following rubber products are often used by Makeup Artists.

Latex: A natural rubber found in rubber trees, mainly in Southeast Asia. Raw rubber is processed with ammonia and water to make the rubber usable as a molding material. Latex is often brushed or slushed into a mold, but not poured. The advantage of using latex is that you don't have to weigh the product. You can use latex right out of the container. It's not too expensive, and has a high elasticity. Latex molds are also good for casting wax and gypsum. The disadvantage of latex is the drying time. Most latex products need to dry for four or more hours between each layer when being brushed on. Some projects can take up to 20 brushed layers. Also, there can be a strong ammonia odor, but there are products out there today that have addressed this problem.

Silicone Rubbers (Smooth-Sil Series): Silicone rubbers are two-component systems, and are available in ranges of hardness from very soft to medium. Silicone can be cured with a platinum catalyst or a tin catalyst. You can make molds that are poured, brushed, or sprayed onto a model. Silicone can have negative results when coming into contact with other products such as sulfur clays. Silicone also must be accurately mixed by using a scale.

Gelatin: Can be poured into a silicone mold. The appliance picks up more detail from the mold if the silicone is slightly heated before pouring the hot gelatin.

Safety Tip

By Smooth-On

Materials are safe to use when following directions by the manufacturer. Federal law requires that manufacturers provide important information in the form of a material safety data sheet (MSDS). The MSDS provides all pertinent information on a product—ranging from directions for proper use to safety precautions, a list of active ingredients, associated hazards, combustion levels, and storage requirements.

Problems That Might Arise When Mold-Making

If the mold has soft spots (partial cure):

1. It was not mixed correctly (premixed).

2. It was not mixed thoroughly.

3. The product was contaminated.

4. It was not correctly measured.

If your mold stuck to the model:

1. The wrong release agent was used, an inadequate amount was applied; or it was not used at all.

2. The model was not properly sealed.

Quick Overview

1. An original model can be made with almost any material. This includes clay, wax, wood, plaster, stone, metal, bone, or cement (Figure 11.1).

FIGURE 11.1: PRODUCT SUPPLIES

FIGURE 11.2: MODEL BEING POURED WITH A CONTAINER WALL

2. If you are pouring, use a container wall around your model (Figure 11.2). If brushing, no wall is needed.

3. Seal all areas of the mold and model if using porous materials: plaster, wood, sulfur, or water-based clays.

4. Use a release agent for all sealed areas. If you are using silicone, a release agent is not necessary.

5. Follow manufacturer directions suited for your project.

Have good ventilation. Do not inhale fumes, rubber products, release agents, sealers, fillers, resins, plasters, and so on. Wear good rubber gloves, and minimize skin contact while working. Wash your hands with soap and water, or anywhere there has been contact with products.

Protect your surfaces from spills with wax paper, brown paper, or your own favorite setup towels. Keep your station clean by keeping utensils clean, and surfaces washed with acetone or alcohol to remove any materials that have spilled. Gelatin can be simply washed off.

What should you have in your kit for mold-making? Smooth-On suggests the following:

Wood or acrylic pieces for container walls (this is for containing any product from spilling over). Mold boxes can be homemade.

Scale

Modeling clay

Mixing containers

Stirring sticks

Sealing agent

Release agent

Mold rubber or molding material of choice

If you find that your mold did not set properly, it could be for one of the following reasons:

1. Wrong mixing measurements

2. Wrong type of scale (should be a gram scale or triple beam balance)

3. Temperature too cold

Steps to silicone mold-making with Smooth-On:

1. Sculpt (Figure 11.3).

2. Release (Figure 11.4).

3. Mix product (Figure 11.5).

4. Apply thin layer (Figure 11.6).

FIGURE 11.4: RELEASE

FIGURE 11.5: MIX PRODUCT

FIGURE 11.3: SCULPT

FIGURE 11.6: THIN LAYER

5. Apply second coat (Figure 11.7).

6. Apply third coat (Figure 11.8).

7. Remove mold (Figure 11.9).

8. Scrape clay (Figure 11.10).

9. Measure out (Figure 11.11).

10. Mix flesh tones (Figure 11.12).

11. Mix A and B (Figures 11.13A and B).

12. Mix quickly (Figure 11.14).

13. Spread in mold (Figure 11.15).

14. Release with powder (Figure 11.16).

15. Done (Figure 11.17).

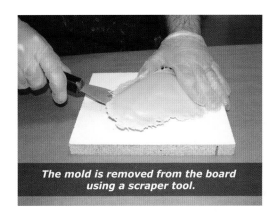

The mold is removed from the board using a scraper tool.

FIGURE 11.9: REMOVE MOLD

The second coat of Shell Shock™ goes on thicker.

FIGURE 11.7: SECOND COAT

The clay from the sculpt is scraped out using a wooden stick.

FIGURE 11.10: SCRAPE CLAY

The third coat of Shell Shock™ builds a (1cm) thickness of material.

FIGURE 11.8: THIRD COAT

Measure out Skin Tite™ silicone 1A : 1B by volume or weight.

FIGURE 11.11: MEASURE OUT

FIGURE 11.12: MIX FLESH TONE

FIGURE 11.15: SPREAD IN MOLD

FIGURE 11.13: MIX

FIGURE 11.16: RELEASE WITH POWDER

FIGURE 11.14: MIX QUICKLY

FIGURE 11.17: FINISHED PIECE

Terms

You should know the following terms as they pertain to mold-making and appliances:

Adding Color: Mixing pigments or flocking materials to a product before being cast into a mold.

Alginates: Seaweed-based products used to take an impression of an object or person to be used in mold-making.

Chavant NSP Clay: Sculpting clay that holds fine details, sculpture free and available in soft, medium, or hard grades.

Casting: A product being used in a mold to create molded reusable appliances.

Cure: A chemical reaction that occurs when you mix two ingredients together that finish.

Cure Inhibition: Certain casting products can be inhibited by contaminants used in or around a work area, causing the molded product to remain tacky or not to cure.

Demolding: When your product has cured enough to be taken out of the mold.

Green Marble SeLr: Makeup sealer, used in aging techniques and for multiple layers.

KRYOLAN Crystal Clear: Protective coating with clear finish that doesn't yellow.

Myristate: An additive for high-grade cosmetics. Also used as an emulsifier or moistening agent.

Mix Ratio: The proper mix of products.

Plastics: Products such as W.M. Creations, Inc. A.M.E.K.-based liquid plastic. Not to be used directly on the skin. Use in stone or silicone molds.

Pot Life: How long the product mixed will last for usage.

Pros-Aide: A prosthetic adhesive that can be mixed with acrylic paints. Has a strong bond.

Pros-Aide Bondo: Pros-Aide mixed with Cab-O-Sil.

Platinum Cure Silicone Rubber: Abrasion and heat resistance in a versatile product for mold-making productions. Materials such as plastics, concrete, wax, low-melt metal alloys, or resins can be cast into silicone-rubber molds.

Release Agent: An agent used to help release the product that was cast from the mold.

Rigid Gypsum Molds: Known as stone molds.

Slush Casting: Products that are to be used in a mold, poured and worked around the inside of the mold until all areas are covered. You can slush several layers on top of each other. Each layer must be cured before applying a new layer.

W.M. Creations, Inc. Soft Sealer: Product used to seal wax, gelatin appliances, and as a sealer on the back of gelatin appliances to prevent moisture from attacking gelatin.

Silicone Mold-Making

By Matthew Mungle

[This is a technique that can be used on location with professional results.]

Silicone is a flexible material, and easy to demold appliances. Once a silicone mold is made, it should last indefinitely. Silicone molds can be made quickly and on location.

What should you have in your makeup kit to be able to create silicone molds and appliances? Components of a mold-making kit follow:

Silicone mold-making materials

Small spatulas

Throwaway brushes

Liquid soap such as Ivory clear soap

Pros-Aide Bondo

W.M. Creations, Inc. Soft Sealer

Medical mixing cups

Chavant NSP Clay

Sculpting tools

Steps to Silicone Mold-Making

1. Set up your station. Make sure there are no latex gloves or sponges near the work area. Wash your hands and lay down setup towels (preferably paper towels).

2. Sculpt the desired form out of Chavant NSP clay (non-sulfur clay). Spray the clay with one light coat of KRYOLAN Crystal Clear, and dry thoroughly (about three minutes). Mix the silicone material (Third Degree molding material or Skin Tite by Smooth-On). These two products are platinum-silicone based, and are affected by latex or sulfur products. Paint the silicone material onto the sculpture with a finger or throwaway brush, making sure not to trap bubbles in the cast. Build the material up at least 1 inch to avoid warpage. Let dry at least 30 minutes, and then demold.

What to Pour into the Mold

Suggested materials that can be poured into the mold would be plastic, Pros-Aide Bondo, and silicone products.

Applying the Finished Prosthetic:

1. Set the appliance in place on the skin area, holding tweezers if necessary (Figure 11.18).

2. Applying a small amount of 99-percent alcohol under the appliance with a brush or cotton-tipped applicator, let the appliance blend (melt) into the skin (Figure 11.19).

3. Blend off any soft sealer edges with 99-percent alcohol (Figure 11.20).

4. Color with Stacolors, activated with 99-percent alcohol (Figure 11.21).

5. Paint with cut example (Figure 11.22).

6. Finished painted cut (Figure 11.23).

7. Adding blood (Figure 11.24).

8. Cut and blood (Figure 11.25).

9. Finished scar (Figure 11.26).

10. Seal with a soft sealer if necessary.

FIGURE 11.19: STEP 2: MELT INTO SKIN

FIGURE 11.18: STEP 1: PLACE ON SKIN

FIGURE 11.20: STEP 3: BLEND OFF ANY SOFT SEALER

FIGURE 11.21: STEP 4: COLOR WITH STA COLORS

FIGURE 11.24: STEP 7: ADDED BLOOD

FIGURE 11.22: STEP 5: PAINT WITH CUT

FIGURE 11.25: STEP 8: CUT AND BLOOD

FIGURE 11.23: STEP 6: FINISHED PAINTED CUT

FIGURE 11.26: STEP 9: FINISHED SCAR

Painting Prosthetics

When an appliance is translucent, there is a realistic quality that shouldn't be painted over. Stacolors, which are activated with 99-percent alcohol, give you the flexibility to paint in thin layers like a wash (translucent) or opaque (dense so it cannot be seen through). Apply Stacolor with brushes, sponges, or cotton-tipped applicators. Stacolors also come in liquid form, which you can use in an airbrush without having to thin the product first.

Remove products with isopropyl myristate, Super Solv, or baby oil. Clean skin first with 70- or 90-percent alcohol. Do not use near the eyes (Figure 11.27).

Silicone Prosthetics

Materials

Plastic wrap

Transparent tape

Black Sharpie

Scissors

Pencil

Formica project board or make-up counter top

Chavant NSP Brown Medium Clay

Sculpting tools

Texture stamps

KRYOLAN Crystal Clear Spray

Mouldlife Sculpt Gel (A, B, and C)

Metal spatula

Black W.M. Creations, Inc. Stacolor Liquid

Epoxy Parfilm

Mold-size cardboard (see instructions, step 15)

99% alcohol

RCMA No Color Powder

Powder puff and straight pin

Procedure

1. Determine what size the prosthetic appliance will be on the face. Create a tracing of the area off the actors face with plastic wrap, covered with transparent tape and a black Sharpie as you would for a beard pattern. Write "top" at the top of the tracing to help in positioning the piece on the board and on the face later (Figure 11.28).

2. Cut the shape out of the plastic wrap with a pair of scissors. Trace the pattern out on the Formica project board or on a Formica make-up counter top with a pencil (Figure 11.29).

FIGURE 11.27: MATTHEW MUNGLE

FIGURE 11.28: STEP 1

FIGURE 11.29: STEP 2

FIGURE 11.31: STEP 6

FIGURE 11.30: STEP 3

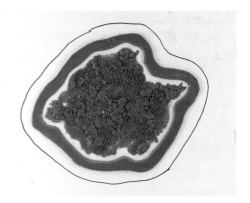

FIGURE 11.32: STEP 7

3. Sculpt the prosthetic using NSP Chavant Clay and Sculpting Tools (Figure 11.30).

4. Make sure the edges of the prosthetic are blended out. This will be the edge that is blended onto the actor's face.

5. Texture the appliance and edges.

6. Spray the sculpting with a light coat of KRYOLAN Crystal Clear Spray. Let dry for 10 minutes (Figure 11.31).

7. Build a flashing wall around the sculpting 1/4" wide by 1/8" tall with additional NSP Clay (Figure 11.32).

8. Spray sculpting and flashing with one more coat of KRYOLAN Crystal Clear Spray. Let dry for 10 minutes.

9. Wash hands and dry.

10. Scoop out equal portions of A and B Mouldlife Sculpt Gel with a metal spatula and mix together thoroughly in a plastic cup. Clean the spatula before dipping into each side of the Sculpt Gel containers to avoid cross contamination. Important note: Sculpt Gel is a platinum-based silicon and will not set up if exposed to a latex product (Figure 11.33).

11. Add 15 drops of W.M. Creations, Inc. Black Stacolor Liquid to the Sculpt Gel mixture and stir thoroughly.

FIGURE 11.33: STEP 10

FIGURE 11.35: STEP 14

12. Carefully paint the Sculpt Gel onto the sculpture with your clean finger, working the product into all the sculpted detail. Use a back and forth motion to prevent trapping bubbles. This first coat should cover the sculpture and past the flashing 1/4". Let this coat cure for 30 minutes or until completely set (Figure 11.34).

13. Mix a larger batch of A and B Sculpt Gel product, twice as much as the first coat.

14. Spatula the material over the appliance and flashing area. Smooth out the top of the mold as flat as possible. Mix one more batch of Sculpt Gel, if necessary, to level the top of the mold (Figure 11.35).

15. Before the last coat of the Sculpt Gel is set spray a sheet of plastic wrap, the size of the mold, with a light coat of Epoxy Parfilm. Place the sheet on top of the wet Sculpt Gel, sprayed side down.

16. Place a piece of cardboard on top of the plastic wrap and press down very lightly to create a flat surface (Figure 11.36).

17. Let the material cure for one hour.

18. Pull off the cardboard and plastic wrap from the mold.

19. Peel the Sculpt Gel mold off of the appliance sculpture. The sculpture should stay intact and will be able to be cast several times if need be (Figure 11.37).

FIGURE 11.34: STEP 12

FIGURE 11.36: STEP 16

FIGURE 11.37: STEP 19

FIGURE 11.39: STEP 22

20. Clean the mold, if necessary, with 99% alcohol and a tissue.

21. Spray the mold with a heavy coat of Epoxy Parfilm and massage the separator into the mold with your finger. Spray one additional coat of Parfilm into the mold (Figure 11.38).

22. Mix a small batch of Sculpt Gel with the addition of part C. Use equal portions of A, B, and C (Figure 11.39).

23. Carefully spatulate the product into the appliance area of the mold. Make sure the edges of the appliance are very thin and no bubbles are trapped in the appliance. Two colors of Sculpt Gel may be used to create depth in the appliance (Figures 11.40 and 11.41).

FIGURE 11.40: STEP 23

FIGURE 11.38: STEP 21

FIGURE 11.41: STEP 23

24. Let product set for at least 30 minutes.

25. Powder the back of the appliance using RCMA NO-Color Powder and a powder puff.

26. Use the tip of a straight pin to peel the appliance out of the mold. There is no need to powder the piece when separating it from the mold (Figure 11.42).

FIGURE 11.43: MATERIALS

Silicon Prosthetic Application
Materials

Sculpt gel appliance

Telesis Silicone Adhesive and Thinner

Makeup brushes

1" chip brush (cut down for spattering color)

Mouldlife Sculpt Gel A, B, and C

Plastic mixing cups

Metal spatula

Tissues

W.M. Creations, Inc. Stacolor Kit (Character and Full Color)

99% alcohol

RCMA No Color Powder

Powder puff (Figure 11.43)

Procedure:

1. Clean the front and back of the appliance with acetone (Figure 11.44).

2. Clean the model's skin with 99% alcohol.

3. Start the application by gluing the middle of the appliance to the skin once the piece is positioned on the model's face with Telesis Silicone Adhesive. Continue to glue the appliance down from the middle of the piece outward. Sculpt Gel can also be used to apply the appliance (Figure 11.45).

4. Mix a small amount of Sculpt Gel A, B, and C and spatulate onto any thick edges that need to be blended into the skin or added to. A powder puff or makeup brush may be used with a slight bit of 99% alcohol to blend out the Sculpt Gel material (Figure 11.46).

EFFECTS

FIGURE 11.42: STEP 26

FIGURE 11.44: STEP 1

FIGURE 11.45: STEP 3

FIGURE 11.47: STEP 5

FIGURE 11.46: STEP 4

5. Color the appliance with Stacolors activated with 99% alcohol. Skin Illustrator or Reel Creation colors may also be used (Figures 11.47, 11.48, and 11.49).

6. Powder with No Color Powder if necessary.

Prosthetic transfers

By Christien Tinsley

Some of the wonderful attributes these prosthetics offer are undetectable blended edges, translucency (so they look like flesh when a proper tone is mixed), and incredible tenacity to hold during the long day of a shoot.

FIGURE 11.48: STEP 5

FIGURE 11.49: STEP 5

In order to set up for a prosthetic transfer application, I first like to prep my station. Materials that I like to have with me at all times when doing a transfer application follow:

Transfer prosthetic to be applied

Transfer paper

Astringent to clean the skin

Cotton pads

Shavers (electric and razor)

Shaving cream

Scissors

Adhesive (Pros-Aide)

Latex sponges

Tissue

Spray bottle (water)

No-color powder

Powder puffs

Q-tips

99-percent alcohol

Brushes

Sealer (BenNye Final Seal)

Hand towels

Isopropyl myristate

Super Solv

Body, hand, or face lotion

smashbox Anti-Shine

Tattoo palettes (flesh tones and primary colors)

Prepping the Skin

Depending on what approach you will take for prosthetic transfer application, you will commonly prep the skin by making sure it is free of hair, oil, and dirt. Hair can be tricky if applying a prosthetic transfer because it won't allow full contact of the piece to the skin. Try to remove all hair if possible. Prep the skin by cleaning it with an astringent of your choice. This removes dirt and oil, and slightly dries the skin for better adhesion of paint or adhesive. Sometimes a layer of adhesive can be applied to the skin before the prosthetic transfer, helping in the adhesion.

Preparation

1. If prosthetic is powdered, gently wash prosthetic transfer with anti-grease soap and water. Note: This step is not necessary if prosthetic transfer is already clean.

2. Stipple a light coat of Pros-Aide over surface of prosthetic transfer all the way to the edges.

3. Let Pros-Aide dry until clear.

Steps 4 to 8 should be done only when ready for application to actor:

4. Place prosthetic facedown onto shiny side of transfer paper.

5. Press firmly onto paper, paying close attention to the edges. This is the most important part of the preparation.

6. Trim as close to the edge of the prosthetic as possible.

7. Peel off plastic top sheet slowly. If parts of prosthetic pull away from paper, lay the whole piece back on paper and repeat step 4 until prosthetic comes off clean.

8. Now you're ready for application.

Application

1. Place prosthetic transfer facedown on skin, and press firmly.

2. Wet back of prosthetic transfer generously with a Tinsley Transfer moistener (filled with water).

3. Continue wetting the paper for approximately 30 seconds, and slice or peel the backing off. Smooth transfer gently with water, and let dry well. Any visible edges can be blended away using 99-percent alcohol.

4. Powder generously with no-color powder of your choice. Gently wipe any excess powder, and seal prosthetic transfer with a spray of makeup sealer (we recommend Ben Nye Final Seal).

Prosthetic Transfer Application Steps

1. Lay down with water (Figure 11.50).

2. Peel (Figure 11.51).

3. Blend visible edges (Figure 11.52).

4. Powder (Figure 11.53).

5. Seal (Figure 11.54).

6. Paint (Figure 11.55).

On-Set

In order to maintain prosthetic transfers on-set, be aware. As with any makeup, things can happen with prosthetics. An actor sleeps hard

FIGURE 11.51: PEEL

FIGURE 11.50: LAY DOWN WITH WATER

FIGURE 11.52: BLEND

FIGURE 11.53: POWDER

FIGURE 11.54: SEAL

over lunch, or he rubs his arms on a table while eating, or the scene requires actors to wrestle or sweat or run, and so on. Always have backup transfers with you, and alcohol, in case you have to remove and apply a new one on-set. Do not remove with oils in the middle of the day because your next one won't stick. For minor repair, have a premixed color or colors to match the tones and to fill in areas that have rubbed away. If an edge has pulled up or rolled over, you can fill it in using any kind of filler

FIGURE 11.55: PAINT

of your choice (Bondo, wax, etc.). Remember, it is always best if you have time to remove and apply a new piece. Things happen—just be resourceful and prepared.

To Remove

Saturate prosthetic transfer with adhesive remover of your choice (Super Solv, isopropyl myristate, Detachol, etc.), and rub gently with remover and dampened powder puff.

Application of Gelatin Prosthetics

By Kenny Myers

[The information contained in this section is presented in good faith. The responsibility for the use of any material in special makeup effects rests solely with the user. The author assumes no responsibility for the use, or misuse, of any material, technique, or informational content discussed within this article.]

What Is Gelatin?

Gelatin is a colorless protein formed by boiling the skin, bones, and connective tissue of animals. It is used in food, pharmaceutical, photographic, ballistics, and cosmetic manufacturing. The end result is a protein derived by rendering the remnants of the animal down to a powder that is composed of about 84 to 90 percent protein, 8 to 15 percent water, and 1 to 2 percent mineral salts, free of additives and preservatives. It also contains about 18 different amino acids joined together in a chain.

In the film and television makeup industries, gelatin appliances are an alternative to foam latex in that gelatin is a gelatin, flexible, and translucent material that simulates human flesh in a more natural way than latex. Gelatin for prosthetic appliances has a much higher bloom, or stiffness (around 275 to 300) than the gelatin used for food consumption (around 200 to 250).

When you purchase gelatin from a supplier for appliance construction, you shouldn't have to concern yourself with the bloom. However, it is useful to know that the gelatin's bloom is the relative strength or rigidity of the brand or grade of gelatin, as well as its water-binding capacity. The higher the bloom number, the denser it will be. Gelatin is hydrophilic, which is a fancy way of saying it likes and absorbs water, swelling to many times its weight of dry gelatin as you mix in liquids, turning the dry gelatin into a slurry. The higher the bloom, the higher the price as well. The bloom scale was created by Oscar T. Bloom. He must have played with an awful lot of gelatin in his time!

How to Make Gelatin

Many companies sell premade gelatin blocks that come in a variety of colors that you can use "as is." As well, many provide a clear block that you can add your own colorants to. This would be the best place for any Makeup Artist to start until you understand the processes and the medium.

Gelatin formulas are as unique as the artists that use the material; however, if you're determined, understand that whatever formula you find that

works for you may not work for your friend across town. Why? There are many reasons. For example, you may not buy raw materials at the same place, so the gelatin may be a little different. Or the sorbitol or gelatin may be formulated differently and your method of processing the gelatin into your mold may differ. Any or all of these things may throw a wrench into your "formula," but you'll learn this as you go.

A general place to begin would be to have on hand some gelatin, sorbitol (which increases the tear resistance while being less affected by humidity; usually sold as a 70-percent solution), and glycerin (which replaces much of the water that would be used in food formulas), along with a good scale to measure your ingredients. These three ingredients are used in most basic formulas, and can be obtained from special-effects supply houses via the Internet or any of the brick-and-mortar special-effects supply houses across the nation. As a side note, sorbitol is sold in two forms: powder and liquid. The liquid is the sorbitol already in solution, and it's the form I like best for its ease of use. The liquid is usually sold as a 70-percent solution.

To reiterate: Ingredients are not necessarily the same from vendor to vendor. The supply of gelatin, the mix of sorbitol, and the gelatin itself can vary. I cannot encourage you enough to make a chart of your ingredients and procedures, and to write down everything— including proportions of ingredients, time of day, time of year, weather conditions, and type and wattage of microwave. All these things can have an effect on the end result. The object of all this work is to create a batch size that works for the appliance you're making—say, a prosthetic nose.

Gelatin, like a lot of makeup processes, came from many artists and many years of contribution and sharing their knowledge with each other. Much of what is outlined here is from the contributions of Dick Smith and Kevin Haney, who did a great deal of experimentation early on, with many successes and failures that many people today take for granted. It's not an exact science, and as an artist you can be surprised by all kinds of problems, usually at the wrong time. There is no shortcut to experimentation and experience. Keep a record of each formula, and network as much as possible.

Here is a starter formula: to 20 grams of gelatin, add 40 grams of sorbitol (70-percent solution) and 40 grams of gelatin. Other ingredients to consider by testing their effect on the finished appliance include water, zinc oxide, face powders, flocking, and pigments.

Caution: Pigments should be Food and Drug Administration approved for use in cosmetics. Pigments from an art-supply house may not be suitable for cosmetic use—so don't use them! Safety is your responsibility.

Heating the Gelatin

Melting the gelatin into a liquid is necessary to both homogenize the mixture and break down the powdered gelatin so that it can be poured and molded. Usually this is done in a microwave for both convenience and speed. *Caution:* Hot melted gelatin is dangerous, and can blister and severely burn your skin. So be extremely cautious, and protect yourself with both gloves and goggles.

Microwaves come in different wattages, so a setting of #4 for 15 seconds on one machine is not the same as #4 on another machine. Read the ratings, usually written on the back of the appliance, and write this information down.

A double boiler can also be used, but will take a bit more time. Remember to put your gelatin into a metal bowl or container, and place it into the water of the lower boiler. Do not use bare hands—it will burn you. Instead, use gloves for hot work, or a long gripping tool (pliers)

to place and remove your container of melted gelatin. If you allow gelatin to boil with either method, the gelatin will break down, making it useless. So don't burn it. Allow your gelatin appliance to cool in the mold. Most artists will put the mold in a refrigerator (not the freezer) to speed up the process.

Molding Gelatin

UltraCal 30 molds are the best place to begin because they are economical, and many people are still using them today. For the advanced user, Epoxical gives a better release and won't break down as easily. But it is more expensive, and needs more time and skill to make. Silicone molds are also used, so there are a variety of techniques to choose from. All have advantages and disadvantages, as with any material—you just have to find what fits your situation, pocketbook, and skill level.

Keep in mind that your molds should be kept warm. A cold mold will solidify your gelatin before it can flow into all the areas you require. It's also best to fill your molds with the negative side down, placing your positive side into it. You will probably have to vent your mold to eliminate voids, air traps, or to prevent hydraulic back pressure from squashing its halves together. Many Makeup Artists use a sealing coat on their UltraCal molds, but some do not. Some use a thin film of Vaseline for a mold release. Others may use PAM cooking spray or Epoxy Parfilm.

Assuming that you've flashed your mold as you would for a foam latex appliance, powder the gelatin as you remove it from the mold. Use no-color powder, talc, or cornstarch. Leave any flashing on the piece after removing it from the mold. This will be a great help in maneuvering the gelatin and handling the piece for application. Gelatin appliances should be kept on a form to keep them from losing their shape, so have either a vacuform copy of the positive or just a plaster copy. Remember to clean the finished pieces thoroughly with alcohol or acetone before application.

What your makeup kit should contain for gelatin applications:

Acetone

Brushes

Sponges

Green Marble Sealer

Pros-Aide

Witch hazel

No-color powder

Skin Illustrator

Prepping the Appliance
1. Flip over the wound so the bottom side is up.
2. Clean the gelatin piece with acetone using a brush or sponge.
3. Let dry thoroughly.
4. Lay flat on underside, and then apply two to three layers of Green Marble, drying each layer.

Applying the Gelatin Piece
1. Cleanse (using toner) the area of the face or body that the gelatin piece is being applied to.
2. Fit the gelatin appliance to its intended position; in this case around the jawline (Figure 11.56).
3. Lift areas of the appliance, and apply Pros-Aide with a sponge (Figure 11.57). Allow to dry most of the way clear. Press into place. It's best to start from the inside pressing outward. If you fold an edge, use a little alcohol on a brush, and lift the edge to replace it correctly.
4. Have chin slightly down, and attach one side at a time (Figure 11.58).

FIGURE 11.56: FIT THE GELATIN: STEP 2

FIGURE 11.57: LIFT AREAS: STEP 3

FIGURE 11.58: CHIN SLIGHTLY DOWN: STEP 4

5. Take flash off with witch hazel (Figure 11.59).
6. Gently blend edges with witch hazel—it's easy to overdo this step and dig a hole in your appliance edge.

7. Blend the edges with stipple sponge and Pros-Aide (Figure 11.60).

8. Apply Pros-Aide over the entire piece.

9. Let dry completely.

10. Use no-color powder around edges (Figure 11.61).

FIGURE 11.59: TAKE FLASH: STEP 5

FIGURE 11.60: BLEND EDGES STIPPLE: STEP 7

FIGURE 11.61: FINISHED PIECE

Painting Gelatin

By Kenny Myers

Now that your appliance is prepped and applied, you're ready to paint. If you've done your homework and have properly made your appliance (including the intrinsic coloring) and paid attention to translucency (the balance on intrinsic coloring to the mass of gelatin), the piece should require only a series of color stipples and wash passes using Skin Illustrator (my favorite). Taking a standard wedge of white makeup sponge and tearing holes in a random pattern on the application side of the sponge gives an excellent pattern on the appliance. Overstippling with this sponge will result in a natural soft skin pattern. Be careful not to use too opaque a mix of color, but instead, soft washes of color on the sponge.

Another favorite technique of mine is a hand-painted scumble, instead of using orange or red stipple sponges. This technique uses a round natural-bristle brush, usually around a #8, and the color is placed on the appliance in what may seem like a random pattern. However, if you closely study most skin, you'll see variations of color density and color placement everywhere. This will help "sell" your paint job! Most Makeup Artists are people watchers—not only for behaviors, but also character traits and, most of all, variations in individual colorations. This is a great pastime when sitting around a mall or at any gathering.

This brings up an issue for those of you wishing to move into the professional end of the industry. I say this only because if you are planning a career in the makeup industry, have a "for sure" before you have a "maybe." I've seen many Makeup Artists ignore a tried-and-true method to keep themselves in the technological limelight—only to fail miserably in the 11th hour, when it was too late to correct the situation, and get themselves a reputation for irresponsibility. This warning cuts across all material usage or processes, no matter what they are. This is an issue of responsibility for your contract with your employer.

Making a Gypsum Mold and Foam Latex

By Gil Mosko

[Gil Mosko created GM Foam in 1987 to meet the needs of the Makeup Artist for a more user-friendly foam latex. Gil has numerous awards and has developed the foam latex that has become Industry Standard. He explains how to approach working with foam latex, and how to make a gypsum mold.]

To make a gypsum mold, the mold-maker needs to take a life cast of the actor and reproduce his or her face in gypsum (the positive mold). The most popular type of gypsum is Ultracal 30 from United States Gypsum, which is bought in 100-pound bags, or in smaller amounts from makeup-supply houses (such as Motion Picture Effects Company, in Burbank, California). The mold-maker would now need to complete a sculpture on the positive. There are many types of clay to sculpt with. Plastilina is the generic name for oil-based clay that never dries out. Common types are Roma Plastilina, and Chavant Clay.

Once the sculpture is completed, it is important to use more Plastilina around the outside of the sculpture to provide "relief" from the negative. In other words, by using this "flashing clay," a thin strip of contact between positive and negative is created. Having a thin strip of contact creates less surface area of contact, and therefore needs less pressure to squeeze foam out of this contact area. The finished foam piece will now have a very thin edge, which is most desirable for the Makeup Artist who is applying the appliance to hide in the final makeup application. The finished sculpture, complete with its flashing and setter points of contact (to prevent rocking), is now sprayed with KRYOLAN Crystal Clear Acrylic Spray. This creates a barrier that prevents the positive and negative from sticking to each other during the molding process. Many mold-makers also use a very light spray of MR 1500 (spray Vaseline) or Parfilm spray.

The simplest form of foam mold is the two-piece squash mold. It has a simple positive, free from undercuts. To match it, there is a one-piece negative, containing all the information from the original sculpture, but in the reverse, or negative. These two mold pieces fit together intimately. The mold-making steps are simply put: Make a wet clay floor and walls around the sculpture, which sits on the mold positive; splash a coat of wet gypsum; add a second splash coat, hemp or burlap coats, and a finishing coat; including three feet.

Our lab has a steadfast rule: "Feet on every mold." Having little feet on the negative means that the mold will sit in a stable manner on the table, without rolling or rocking. This will enable the user to adjust the mold strap without having the resistance of the mold sitting on the strap. This is especially helpful in the context of having a full-foam injector and many molds to fill. The user can save precious seconds by not having to fiddle with mold straps that are rubbing against the bottom of the negative mold.

The most popular form of gypsum for these molds is Ultracal 30, from United States Gypsum. Although many people use burlap as a mold-strengthening fiber, we prefer using hemp fiber. The simple reason is that hemp has many more fibers per inch than burlap, and the number of fibers adds to the strength of the mold. Once the mold is finished, it is always best if you have the time to allow the mold to sit overnight before opening it. GM Foam likes to heat the mold to about 120° F, so the Plastilina inside will be softened. In this way, the positive and negative can be separated with far less resistance from the rock-hard, cold Plastilina.

In extreme cases, preheating before opening a mold will actually save the interior of the negative, which would otherwise be chipped and broken by the hard, cold Plastilina. After opening the two mold halves (positive and negative), all of the Plastilina must be carefully removed. Use wooden tools to scrape away the Plastilina. Never use metal tools, which will scratch the interior of a mold. When the mold is fairly clean, it is time to scrub the interior with 99-percent isopropyl alcohol with a chip brush. This will wash out any remaining Plastilina residue and oil. Your mold is now ready to be prepped for foam use.

New damp molds should be sealed before attempting to run foam in them. Use a thin solution of Johnson's Paste Wax, thinned with 99-percent isopropyl alcohol. The ratio is about four to five parts alcohol to one part wax. Mix well, and then strain out the lumps through cheesecloth or window screen. Paint this "Alco wax" into both sides of the mold, all over the interior. Mop up any pools, and place the mold in front of a fan to dry. After the alcohol has evaporated, repeat this sealing process. It is always wise to bake out wet molds at this point. A convection oven works much better than a plain oven that does not have circulating air. We bake out molds at 140° F, but many of our friends use temperatures as high as 180° F. The moisture will stay in the mold for much longer than you think. It often takes a minimum of six hours to truly bake a mold.

After baking the empty mold, a third painting of Alco wax is done. When that is dry, the interior mold surface can be brushed out with a chip brush, or polished with a towel. This will make the surface shine. Use GM Foam Mold Release around all of the edges, where the mold pieces contact each other. Just paint a very thin layer of the white GM Release all around the perimeter of the piece, and let dry to white film. Your mold is now ready to be used with foam.

Steps to Mold-Making
1. Little feet (Figure 11.62).
2. Little feet (Figure 11.63).
3. Sculpture (Figure 11.64).
4. Clay walls (Figure 11.65).
5. First splash coat (Figure 11.66).

FIGURE 11.62: LITTLE FEET

FIGURE 11.63: LITTLE FEET

6. Second splash coat (Figure 11.67).
7. Hemp coat (Figure 11.68).
8. Finished coat (Figure 11.69).
9. Two pieces (Figure 11.70)

Foam Molds
All of GM Foam's latex kits come with excellent instruction sheets. For this illustration, let it suffice to say that liquid latex and other

FIGURE 11.64: SCULPTURE

FIGURE 11.67: SECOND SPLASH COAT

FIGURE 11.65: CLAY WALLS

FIGURE 11.68: HEMP COAT

FIGURE 11.66: FIRST SPLASH COAT

FIGURE 11.69: FINISHED COAT

FIGURE 11.70: TWO PIECES

the two mold halves are pried apart, and the resulting foam piece is removed, taking great care not to tear it during removal from the mold.

PRO TIP

DO NOT USE YOUR HOUSEHOLD COOKING OVEN FOR FOAM USE!

Please keep in mind that during the curing process, toxic vapors are given off, which will contaminate your oven for food use. Keep these chemicals away from children and pets.

---

ingredients are weighed into the mixer bowl. The mixer is turned on low for a minute to mix all the ingredients, and then turned to a high speed to whip the foam to a desired volume, usually four to five times the original volume. When the foam reaches this height, the mixer is turned down to a lower speed to pop large bubbles and "refine" the foam. All the while, ammonia is escaping from the mixer bowl. As a function of this ammonia loss, the foam will have a steady drop in pH. When a certain point is reached (usually pH 10.4), the user carefully pours in a preweighed amount of gelling agent. This begins an acid-producing reaction in the foam, which will eventually coagulate into a solid mass, or "gel." Before the foam actually gels, the user will have ample time to fill the foam molds and close them. It is important to gel the foam before putting it into an oven to cure, because un-gelled foam will collapse when exposed to oven heat. Cells will start popping, and the resulting foam will look like Swiss cheese.

Curing the foam will cause the rubber molecules to cross-link, or "vulcanize." This transforms the raw foam into a springy sponge. Most small appliance molds will need three to three-and-a-half hours in the oven at 185° F. Then the molds are cooled slowly to a comfortable temperature for handling. When removed from the oven,

It is recommended that you wash the completed foam pieces in warm water and a few drops of baby shampoo, or a few spoonfuls of Simple Green. Then the pieces are gently rinsed, pressed between two towels, and placed on a form that keeps the natural curve of the piece intact. Never wring a piece of foam. If the foam is not allowed to dry in its own natural shape, it will "take a set" from any wrinkles or folds. These set-in flaws will almost always be permanent, ruining the piece, so please be careful to always store foam pieces in their natural curvature.

For long-term storage, foam pieces should be powdered, and then sealed into plastic bags or airtight food containers. If kept in airtight containers, away from light, foam pieces can be successfully stored for years.

A Word about the State of Latex in the World
All foam latex systems are a combination of natural latex (concentrated sap of rubber trees), a soap to make the foam whip up to desired volume (foaming agent), a vulcanizer (curing agent), and a coagulant (gelling agent). Some of the ingredients are extremely safe, such as the foaming agent, and others are toxic. Both the

curing agent and the gelling agent are poisonous. Therefore, the entire system should be treated with respect, and basic safety precautions should be used. It is important to note the following: Up until last year, there was one major plantation in Indonesia that manufactured natural creamed latex. Their largest customer was an elastic-thread manufacturer. When the thread manufacturer went out of business, the rubber plantation chose to discontinue the production of natural creamed latex. Several companies have begun making a replacement product. This new product is concentrated centrifuged latex. Normally, centrifuged latex has a solids content of 60 percent, which is too low for our type of foam making. But now the new evaporated product is a centrifuged latex at about 67 to 68 percent, which is perfect for making foam. To my knowledge, all the major foam companies are using this evaporated centrifuged latex.

At GM Foam, we still believe in natural creamed latex. Through difficult dealings, we have contracted a plantation in another part of the world to start making the original type of creamed latex for us. We believe the physical properties of this type of latex to be superior to the evaporated centrifuged latex. Remember that the centrifuged rubber has been exposed to heat for hours. The latex in the huge drums turns to a thick glop. All of the ammonia preservative has long gone, and we believe that oxidation is occurring during this process. Of course, ammonia is added back into the latex before it is sold, but during the time the latex was a thick paste, it lost some of its physical characteristics due to oxidation of the evaporating process. Our new creamed latex is as good as anything we have seen in the past 20 years. When we see cell structure that is strong and resistant to breakdown, and a smooth, shiny surface on gelled foam, we know that our rubber is performing the way it did back in the 1980s, when we started. Creamed latex is back, and we have it!

Safety

1. Read the instructions before starting. Refer to the material safety data sheet (MSDS) for more information.

2. Have adequate ventilation to remove ammonia fumes.

3. Wear safety goggles and gloves when working with foam.

4. Do not let foam components come into contact with skin. If this happens, wash with soap and water as soon as possible. Clean up spills.

5. Wash your hands after working with foam. Never eat, drink, or smoke without washing first.

6. Anyone working with foam latex should keep a set of material safety data sheets (MSDSs) nearby in case of emergency.

Prepping Ultracal 30 and Other Stone Molds

New, damp molds should be sealed with wax before applying GM Foam Mold release. An effective wax sealer can be made using Johnson's Paste Wax (or any carnauba wax) that has been thinned with 99-percent isopropyl alcohol. We use a ratio of four parts alcohol to one part wax.

Liquid latex and other ingredients are weighed and placed in a mixer bowl. The foam is now whipped at high speed until it rises like whipped cream. When the desired height is reached, the mixer speed is turned down, and the foam is refined to make the bubbles or cells smaller. This also allows the ammonia content of the foam to decrease. At just the right time, gelling agent is added to the slow-turning mixer. After about two minutes of slow blending, the mixer is turned off, and the foam is poured into the negative mold. The positive is carefully placed on top of the negative. Now pressure is applied to squeeze the two mold pieces together. With small molds, simply pressing with the hands will suffice. Larger molds require mold straps to create a good pressing action. Often the negative requires a wooden board to be placed on it and then be strapped. This increases the leverage of the strap, and gives a greater squeezing action.

Filling Molds
Curing
Once the foam has gelled, in a few minutes the mold can be placed into the oven for curing. During this process, vulcanization occurs. The latex molecules chemically cross-link, and give the foam piece a memory. Once demolded, the foam will spring back into shape after being pressed.

Demolding
Specific instructions and product information can be acquired by contacting GM Foam, Inc. at (818) 908-1087.

How to Paint Foam Appliances

By Gil Mosko

The gluing of a foam appliance is more or less a mechanical process. There are many different adhesives, but an appliance is built to sit on the face or body in one specific way, and is never stretched. Let us assume that your appliance is glued to the face, and it is time to paint. The goal of course, is to make the paint job not only look like the surrounding skin, but to also make an opaque medium appear translucent. This is achieved by building up layers of thin wash of color, so you can see through the layers and see depth.

We all learn by watching other artists. In my case, the truth is that the very gifted artist Greg Cannom had me visit his lab, along with my model, and literally showed me how he painted a bald cap. This was during the period in the 1980s when I was studying for my union exam. I applied a bald cap to my model, and Greg painted it. That simple act of generosity has, since that day, changed the way I look at painting.

Everyone has their own style. Todd McIntosh begins with a base coat of reddish color, and paints everything over the red. This lets the painting have the feel that there is blood under the skin, and you can barely see it, once again creating depth. I like to use a base coat of paint that closely resembles the actor's or actress's skin. I use full-strength Pax Paint (a term coined by our dean of makeup, Dick Smith). I might add that GM Foam, Inc., has a complete line of Pax Paints in two palettes: dark flesh tones, and light flesh tones. Each palette also has a red appropriate to the other colors. Once the piece is painted, I gently feather a very thin layer of the base coat onto the skin, using a white makeup sponge. From this point on, I use what artists call "scumble sponges." Take a white makeup sponge, hold it in both hands, and pull until it breaks into two pieces. Pick at this edge with your fingernails until little holes have been picked away. The sponge is now a stamp of sorts, and can be used to create a mottled surface.

Painting steps:
1. After the full-strength base coat, I never again use full-strength Pax Paints. I thin them with water until they are mere washes of color.

2. After the base color, I paint a thin coat of red by dabbing the scumble sponge, constantly turning it as I dab, so the pattern of the sponge cannot be seen repeating itself. I dry each coat after it is applied.

3. After the red, use a shade one or two shades lighter than the base.

4. Next, use a color that is two shades darker than the base.

5. Then I use greens and blues.

6. Finally, apply a last coat of the original base as a wash over everything.

7. Once all the Pax colors are dry, I like to use a thin layer of RCMA Appliance Foundation that matches my base color. Incidentally, my Pax colors are keyed into the RCMA color scheme, with such colors as Olive 1, Shinto 2, and so on, so that when you are ready to harmonize all of your Pax layers, you just smudge a little RCMA over the Pax Paints in the same shade as your base coat. If you use a thin enough layer, it will not hide all of your hard work, and also it will actually bite into the Pax Paint, making the use of powder unnecessary.

8. If there is more shine than you desire, you can use Origins Zero Oil. Use this product in a sweeping motion. Do not use a stipple technique, or it will dry in little white spots.

9. Finally, if you have the time, you can paint freckles and blemishes, either with greasepaints, or aqua colors.

I can tell you in all candor that there is a point, if you are lucky, when the paint job ceases to be layers of paint, and suddenly becomes skin. For a Makeup Artist, I can think of no greater thrill than to have an appliance painted so accurately and artistically that one cannot distinguish it from the surrounding skin. And believe me, the director and the cinematographer will notice.

> **PRO TIP**
>
> As with anything else, this technique requires practice. What I wish for readers is that you have a good time learning these techniques, and someday do a makeup that is so flawless that you earn the respect of your peers.
>
> —Gil Mosko

Theatrical Prosthetics

By Lars Carlsson

The degree of difficulty in using prosthetics in the theatre varies just as it does for other mediums. The size of the theatre, the type of stage, production design, lighting design, and stage blocking all play a part in your choice of design, application, and painting.

The actor may go through an array of different lights and color gels in the course of the show, so choose the lighting that the performer(s) spend the most time in as your guide for application and painting.

The front row seats could be particularly close to the edge of the stage, giving the first few rows an "up-close" experience. For these audience members a careful application of the prosthetics edges is needed, and makeup that is not too garish. Design for the middle of "the house" to ensure the majority of the audience can see the work.

A "quick change" could be a part of the pacing of the show where you need to solve removal issues. These "quick changes" must be rehearsed and timed with adjustments made to accomplish the change.

Wigs and costumes could be involved that are helpful in hiding edges. The staging of the performance could be that they are in the dark and the need to fully glue down the appliance would not be needed. Save yourself and the performers in this case!

You not only have to design an appliance that provides the visual impact needed, you also have to be practical in the application and necessities of the show.

During a theatre production you hardly ever get the luxury of time. As the Makeup Artist, you may be responsible for all the makeup, prosthetics, and the manufacturing of the prosthetics, as well as the maintenance of the show. The most common scenario is a play that runs five times per week for a number of months.

On the Job

A typical day working with prosthetics for the theatre might look like this:

13:00 Cleaning lace fronts of wigs and hair pieces from the night before.

13:30 Styling wigs and hairpieces.

15:30 Demolding prosthetics casted the previous night. Also clean molds.

16:00 Prepainting prosthetics.

17:00 First actor comes in. A normal play would involve four to six makeups.

A normal beauty or character makeup can't take longer than 20 minutes including the wig work. Prosthetic makeup can't be allowed to take longer than 30 to 40 minutes.

19:00 Play starts.

Depending on the play, there are usually makeup changes during the evening. Normally there is a break to cast the prosthetics needed for the next night.

22:00 Show is over. I collect all the wigs and put them on blocks.

Help the actors remove prosthetics.

Theatrical Casting and Mold Making

By Lars Carlsson
Silicone Master Mold

Step 1: Start by making a life cast in plaster using alginate or silicone (Figure 11.71).

Step 2: Try to identify all possible undercuts that can be a problem in the mold-making. Typical examples of these are shown in Figure 11.71. There are several other undercuts that should not be removed, such as undercuts at the nostril or side of the nose. If these are removed, your finished piece will not fit your actor as well as it should (Figure 11.72). Remove all undercuts by filling them with Plasteline clay. Try to mimic the original

FIGURE 11.71: BLUE LIFE CAST

FIGURE 11.72: LIFE CAST WITH UNDERCUTS

texture of the face. All other defects on the plaster cast should be corrected with Plasteline clay (Figure 11.73).

Step 3: On the finished, corrected life cast, create a master mold of the face. Having a negative mold of your actor means you can create many positive molds to work on at the same time. Also you can make smaller molds, such as a nose mold (Figure 11.74).

Making the Mold

Brush on a few layers of thickened silicone. You may use more or less silicone for this. To stay safe, stick with the same sort of silicone that you will cast your final pieces in. For this cast, I used PlatSil Gel-10 from Polytek, thickened with Poly Fiber II, also from Polytek (Figure 11.75).

FIGURE 11.73: FILLING UNDERCUTS WITH PLASTELINE CLAY

FIGURE 11.74: CREATE MASTER MOLD OF FACE BRUSH SILICONE

There are many ways to thicken your silicone depending on which brand you are using, but I have found the Poly Fiber to be wonderful as filler. Poly Fiber blends into most silicones with ease and will not cause too many bubbles. We will also use it later to thicken our urethane plastic.

Step 4: The first layer of silicone should be runny, so add about 10% (by weight) Poly Fiber II to the silicone. This prevents air from being trapped in the details of the second and third layers. As you can see (Figure 11.76), I have drawn a red line on the board around the head. This serves as a guide on how far out my mold should extend. Later, we will be drilling holes through this part to keep the mold together. It is very important to get it wide enough for this.

The finished silicone skin is about one centimeter thick and weighs about 300 grams. The silicone should be fully cured before you go on to the next step (Figure 11.77).

Step 5: Since the silicone is very soft and won't hold its shape, it needs to be supported on the outside with about three layers of plaster bandage. Let the plaster set for at least 30 minutes before taking it apart (Figure 11.78).

The master mold is ready to be cleaned up and filled with urethane (Figures 11.79 and 11.80).

FIGURE 11.75: THICKEN SILICONE

FIGURE 11.76: RED LINE ON THE BOARD

FIGURE 11.77: FINISHED 1-CM THICK, SILICONE SKIN

FIGURE 11.80: PRODUCT PICTURE

FIGURE 11.78: SUPPORT ON THE OUTSIDE

FIGURE 11.79: MASTER MOLD READY TO BE CLEANED UP

Urethane Mold

The urethane used in this demonstration comes from Ebalta and is called SG130 Component A and PUR11 Component B. Sometimes these urethane components are referred to as Mix A and Mix B.

This urethane combination is a very simple one-to-one mixture ratio (weight or volume) with a three minute pot life, which allows you to make your molds with incredible speed. These materials are also incredibly strong and yet still flexible, which makes them more or less impossible to break.

The urethane system does not give off unpleasant odors, so it is easy to think that it is harmless; however, repeated contact may cause allergies. Always work under forced ventilation or use a mask with the appropriate filters. Have your entire work area strongly ventilated so you will not be exposed to any dangerous fumes. Skin contact with the uncured materials can also cause allergies; therefore, gloves should be worn at all times.

Strengthen the urethane so that you will be able to bolt the molds together strongly. I laminate it with two kinds of fiberglass (Figure 11.81):

- Fiberglass flocking. Every little strand of glass is about one centimeter long.
- Fluffy fiberglass tissue that absorbs urethane easily.

The normal boat-making fiberglass mats that you use with polyester will not work with urethanes. They simply don't get enough time to soak into the mat before the material is set.

You should cut the fiberglass in 3- to 4-centimeters wide and 10- to 15-centimeters long strips for easy application later (Figure 11.82).

FIGURE 11.81: STRENGTHEN URETHANE WITH FIBERGLASS

FIGURE 11.83: POSITIVE FACE MOLD

FIGURE 11.82: CUT LONG STRIPS

FIGURE 11.84: SECOND LAYER: STEP 2

221

The positive face mold will be made in four layers of urethane. Since our master mold is made from silicone, there is no need for any release agent, so you can get started right away (Figure 11.83).

Step 1: For the first layer, pour up to 75 grams of SG130 Component A of the urethane in a paper or plastic disposable cup. Thicken it with 10% (7.5 grams) of Poly Fiber II and stir it until it is fully mixed in. Then add 75 grams of PURII Component B, and stir quickly until fully mixed.

Using a disposable brush cover the whole surface with an even layer of urethane. This mixture starts to set very quickly and it takes a little while to get used to working with it.

Step 2: The second layer will include our first fiberglass. For this we will use the fiberglass flocking (Figure 11.84).

After the first layer is dry, allow it to set for about 30 minutes. Mix up a new batch following the same recipe as the previous layer (see Step 1 above).

Apply in the same way as before, but as soon as you have brushed it out, you start adding fiberglass flocking to the surface using your gloved hands to create an even layer of it.

Wearing vinyl gloves, pat the flocking down so that it lies neatly on the surface. Any flocking that is sticking up will cause a problem later. Be careful not to trap any air under the flocking. All air pockets will be weaknesses in the final mold (Figure 11.85).

FIGURE 11.85: WEARING GLOVES

Step 3: The third layer is once again mixed the same as the first recipe (see Step 1 above) and poured into the mold (Figure 11.86).

This time, instead of flocking, take the strips of fluffy fiberglass tissue and push them into the wet urethane (Figure 11.87).

The layers should overlap a little bit and cover the entire surface (Figure 11.88).

Step 4: To soak the fiberglass matting with urethane, prepare a mix of 100 grams of SG130 Component A and 100 grams of PURII Component B (no Poly Fiber in this mix) and simply pour it over the matting, while moving it around with your gloved hands. Vinyl gloves work best for this since nitrile gloves tend to stick to the material too much (Figure 11.89).

The plastic mixture will soak through in seconds. Keep moving the material around until it starts to get sticky. You will at this point feel that you are destroying your mold if the matting sticks to your hand and gets pulled back out. This feeling is your sign to take a step back and let the setting process continue for a minute without touching it (Figure 11.90).

FIGURE 11.86: THIRD LAYER

FIGURE 11.88: LAYERS SHOULD OVERLAP

FIGURE 11.87: PUSH INTO WET URETHANE

FIGURE 11.89: MIX: STEP 4

EFFECTS

FIGURE 11.90: MOVE MATERIAL AROUND

FIGURE 11.92: THICK MIXTURE

Now comes the most crucial moment of the whole procedure. You need to work very quickly. Using your gloved hands, push the material together and get everything that sticks out to lie down. After a couple of times this step will feel like second nature to you.

Keep rubbing the surface until it becomes nice and shiny.

Step 5: If you didn't get nice, smooth surfaces, you can always mix up a thick batch of urethane, adding up to 20% of Poly Fiber (Figure 11.91).

Using the thick mixture as you would patch up a wall, you can get beautiful results and a mold that is nice to handle later (Figure 11.92).

Step 6: After letting the urethane set for about an hour, you can demold it. Remove the plaster bandage support mold and then simply peel off the silicone master mold, gently. Remember that this can be used many times so it should be cared for, cleaned, and placed back in its support mold (Figure 11.93).

As you can see in Figure 11.94, the positive mold came out beautifully, but needs a lot of trimming around the edges.

Step 7: Urethane resins under high temperatures may release toxic fumes. When working with power tools such as saws, drills, or sanding equipment, I always wear a gas mask to make sure that I am not exposed to toxic fumes or particles (Figure 11.95).

See Figure 11.96 for an example of a finished positive.

FIGURE 11.91: STEP 5

FIGURE 11.93: DEMOLDING

FIGURE 11.94: POSITIVE MOLD

FIGURE 11.97: MELTED PLASTELINE CLAY

FIGURE 11.95: TRIMMING THE EDGES: STEP 7

FIGURE 11.96: FINISHED POSITIVE

Sculpting a New Face

Sculpt on the mold by brushing a thin layer of melted Plasteline clay on the positive. This will form a well-adhered clay layer that you can work on top of. One of the best ways to melt clay is in an inexpensive rice cooker. It will melt the clay plus keep it warm for the rest of your sculpting session (Figure 11.97). Do not lock the rice cooker on "cook." This will destroy your rice cooker and may be a danger to you and your entire studio!

Now, the sculpt has been made and holes have been drilled in the eyes and around the outer edge of the mold as shown in Figure 11.98.

To put the molds together, you will need a place where excess material can escape. This is called the overflow area (Figure 11.99). You create a void in the negative mold by adding a thick layer of clay outside of your sculpture.

This clay layer should have a sharp 90 degree cutting edge about two to three millimeters away from your sculpture.

FIGURE 11.98: HOLES DRILLED IN EYES

FIGURE 11.99: CREATING OVERFLOW AREA

FIGURE 11.101: DRILLED HOLES HAVE BEEN FILLED WITH CLAY

The overflow should be as smooth as possible to avoid difficult removal of your prosthetics later on (Figure 11.100).

Almost done!

The drilled holes have been filled with clay (Figure 11.101). The entire positive has been attached to a board with more clay. Make sure that no urethane can leak in underneath the positive. Add small, square, clay pieces that will create nice little holes where you can open the mold.

A thick line of red, made with a permanent maker around the outer edge, will help you find the seam when you are ready to take the mold apart.

Starting the Urethane Mold

Before starting the mold, apply a small amount of release agent to both the sculpture and the surrounding board. You can use Epoxy Parfilm 5 or a wax spray. Both work very well and aid in the cleanup of the molds later. For this mold, I used the same urethane system SG130 Component A and PURII Component B and refer to them below as A and B.

Layer 1: Urethane (Figure 11.102).

Mix 75 grams of A and 7.5 grams of Poly Fiber II mixed with 75 grams of B.

Apply to the sculpture.

Layer 2: Thick urethane (Figure 11.103).

FIGURE 11.100: OVERFLOW SMOOTH AS POSSIBLE

FIGURE 11.102: LAYER 1

FIGURE 11.103: LAYER 2

Mix 75 grams of A and 7.5 grams of Poly Fiber II mixed with 75 grams of B.

When Layer 2 starts to set, add fiberglass flocking and keep patting it down until flat and dry.

Layer 3: Thick urethane (Figure 11.104).

Mix 75 grams of A and 7.5 grams of Poly Fiber II mixed with 75 grams of B.

When the mix has been spread around the mold, add strips of fiberglass tissue mat and push it down.

The negative mold follows the exact same procedure as making the positive mold.

Layer 4: Liquid urethane.

Mix 100 grams of A with 100 grams of B.

Pour the liquid mixture all over the fiberglass mat with gloved hands. Rub and pat until nice and smooth. Add a fifth layer if needed.

Layer 5: Very thick urethane.

Mix 75 grams of A, 15 grams of Poly Fiber II mixed with 75 grams of B.

Apply mixture. When you are done, the mold should be left to fully cure for a minimum of a few (three) hours before proceeding. Rushing will warp your molds and all of your work will be destroyed.

Waste material can run on the sides of the mold. If you followed the advice of sealing the sides, nothing will have run underneath the mold and cleanup will be easy.

When trimming the edges, use a vibrating saw to get the cleanest cuts (Figure 11.105). The red, permanent marker line drawn all around the edge of the positive now comes in handy. As you saw, the line becomes visible.

PRO TIP

When sawing into urethane, the temperature of the material gets quite high. As a precaution, I always wear a full gas mask to protect both my lungs from gases and eyes from debris. Don't forget to protect your hearing, too!

FIGURE 11.104: LAYER 3

FIGURE 11.105: VIBRATING SAW

Before you take the mold apart, it is important that you drill holes through the new negative too (Figure 11.106). Start drilling straight through the clay filled holes on the bottom half and keep drilling all the way through.

Don't forget the eye holes and any other holes that you may have added for stability.

Most face molds should always be opened from the top (Figure 11.107). The reason for this is due to the nose. If you open the mold from the bottom your negative mold will most likely get stuck on the nose, causing damage. Here the little clay squares at the top of the molds come in handy. They provide a perfect place for screwdrivers to fit.

Open the mold evenly. If you open for example from the right you will put unnecessary pressure on the cutting edge on the left-hand side. Rushing this step will only make failure a reality.

Opening a mold can be frustrating and time consuming. The clay inside the mold is hard and needs to be pried open slowly.

Sometimes it can help to submerge the entire unopened mold in warm water to soften the clay a bit.

Finally after about 15 minutes, the mold should open without any damage or undercuts (Figure 11.108). Don't let this be a guide, however; some molds have taken me a day to open.

Final

Clay can stick to the positive and negative. Separate the clay used for your face sculpt from the overflow sculpt. The reason for doing this is to give you a rough idea on how much silicone is needed to fill your mold (Figure 11.109).

FIGURE 11.106: DRILLING HOLES IN NEW NEGATIVE

FIGURE 11.108: MOLDS SHOULD OPEN

FIGURE 11.107: OPEN THE MOLDS

FIGURE 11.109: CLAY CAN STICK

Cleaning the Mold

Cleaning the mold is a very important step in this tutorial. Use soft sculpting tools and wooden spatulas. Scrub the mold clean with dish brushes, tooth brushes, or anything relatively soft. Add lots of Fairy Soap liquid as you are scrubbing. Mostly, try to avoid using any solvents. Sometimes textures refuse to let go of the clay; if this happens, use a bit of solvent to dissolve the clay.

Making the Silicon Piece for Theatre

The sculpture in Figure 11.110 weighs 255 grams, which means that I will need about that amount of silicone too. The silicone piece that I am making here is a theatre piece (Figure 11.111). Silicone is easier to produce and is fast to apply during the performance. When doing prosthetics for theatre, you need to

FIGURE 11.111: SILICONE THEATRE PIECE

have five to seven new pieces every week. Most of the time tomorrow's prosthetic will be made during tonight's evening performance. Being fast and having a high rate of success is of the greatest importance when working for theatre.

Before applying the silicone barrier layer, spray a thin coat of Epoxy Parfilm on both mold halves.

For this demonstration, I used PlatSil Gel 10 from Polytek. This silicone has a very fast cure time and almost never fails.

Step 1: Mix up a small batch of PlatSil Gel, 20 grams of A and 20 grams of B in a small cup. Add a small pinch of 2mm Persian Red (Pantone 187 C) nylon flocking. The flocking will give your pieces a lovely skin tone and that little lovely unevenness that will sell it as real.

Step 2: Using a polyurethane sponge, evenly spread it all over the surfaces of the mold.

FIGURE 11.110: WEIGHING

PRO TIP

It is very important to never use anything (i.e., utensils, gloves, etc.) made from latex when working with silicone. The latex will inhibit the silicone and it will never cure.

228

EFFECTS

This thin silicone layer will form an outer skin on the prosthetic. This also creates thin edges that we will glue onto the skin of the actor.

Step 3: We are now going to make the soft filling for the silicone prosthetic.

For the filling, add a third component to the mix. This is called Deadener and was developed by the very talented Gordon Smith (Figure 11.112). The Deadener is a softening agent and slows the silicone in its reactions. You can add anything from 50% up to 250% Deadener to your mix, but I have found that a mix of 100% Deadener is perfect for most of my uses.

- For 100% Deadener, mix: 1 gram A, 1 gram B (total of 2 grams silicone), and 2 grams of Deadener.

- For 200% Deadener, mix: 1 gram A, 1 gram B (total of 2 grams silicone) and 4 grams of Deadener.

- For 250-grams batch of 100% Deadener: Mix 62.5 grams of A with 125 grams of Deadener.

- For remaining 62.5 grams of B, do not add until adding color to the mix. Pigments will color your silicone into believable skin tones. There are a number of different products for coloring.

Coloring

For a long time my preferred pigment was mashed grease paint makeup and flocking. Sometimes oil paint would be used. Now I mainly use silicone pigments from Mouldlife .co.uk and 2 mm Persian Red (Pantone 187 C) nylon flocking from www.flocking.biz.

Test color intensity by dipping a clean wooden spatula with a black dot drawn onto it into the colored silicone (only Part A and Deadener so far). Lift up until you see the dot. If the edges are clear, then add more pigments. If you can't see the dot at all, you have added too much.

After you are happy with the color, finish mixing the remaining part B silicone. Be careful not to get too many bubbles into the mix. Pour mix into your mold from as high as you can reach, in a small trickle (Figure 11.113). Doing this will break bubbles in the silicone and give you a nice translucent silicone.

Slush the silicone in a thin layer around the mold (Figure 11.114). This will also ensure that you have no trapped bubbles.

Gently put your positive mold down into the negative mold (Figure 11.115). Do not rush this! Let the positive slowly sink into the silicone and push any last remaining bubbles up and out.

FIGURE 11.112: DEADENER MIX: STEP 3

FIGURE 11.113: POURING MOLD HIGH

FIGURE 11.114: SLUSH SILICONE

FIGURE 11.117: LET MOLD CURE

FIGURE 11.115: POSITIVE IN NEGATIVE

These molds are very strong but if you over tighten the bolts it may still break.

When you are done, leave your mold to cure for 30 minutes to an hour, depending on room temperature (Figure 11.117).

PRO TIP

Since the silicone we are using is a platinum cure silicone, it is easy to quicken the cure by raising the temperature—a low heat oven, 60° C (140° F) is usually good. Doing so will decrease the cure time in half.

FIGURE 11.116: SET YOUR DRILL AND BOLT MOLD

Set your drill to the lowest torque setting (Figure 11.116). Bolt your mold together using wing nuts on the back.

Put every other bolt on the opposite side of the molds. This will put an even pressure on the edges of your mold.

Open the mold for the first time. To aid in opening, spray water into the openings; this acts as lubrication (Figure 11.118).

Figure 11.119 shows fitting with the mask. Flashing is still intact.

Pieces Out of the Mold
Once out of the mold, wash the piece with detergent. Put the piece back on the positive to dry.

FIGURE 11.118: SPRAY WATER TO OPEN

FIGURE 11.119: FIRST FITTING

Very important! Never use any powder at any time when demolding a silicone piece. You will lose the piece's transparency and the edges will be very difficult to blend with the skin.

Painting a PlatSil Gel 10 Prosthetic

How much prepainting is needed depends on the size of the prosthetic. A nose or a scar does not need any work until it is ready to be applied to the actor. A large alien mask would need to be prepainted.

Remember, work under forced ventilation, use a gas mask, and under no circumstances should solvents be inhaled. This method of prepainting is done only on the appliance, and never done on the actor/performer.

Make sure the base tone of the appliance matches the skin tone of the actor as closely as possible. Too much paint on silicone and you will lose the wonderful translucent look of the silicone.

Painting

1. Choose your grease paint palette.

2. Take a small amount of grease paint in a plastic bottle, dissolving the paint with generous amounts of heptanes solvent.

Note: You can find this solvent in most paint shops. Using grease paint instead of pure pigments skips a lot of hassle since these colors are already perfectly mixed.

3. Mix a small batch of Smooth-On's Psycho Paint—10 grams of component A plus 10 grams of component B and mix well. Add a small amount of heptane to slow the setting time.

FIGURE 11.120: MOLDS FROM LARS NOREN'S ORESTIEN AT FOLKTEATERN GOTHENBURG, 2010

4. Divide the Psycho Paint into small plastic cups. Add the pigment mix until you get the desired color.

5. Apply the color mix with an airbrush.

Flocking and Beard Stubble

In theatre it is important to simulate the missing blood in a prosthetic; flocking is a great technique for doing this. Add flocking whenever you can. I add flocking into the outer layer of the prosthetic in the Deadener filling. Flocking also helps hide the edges of the prosthetic, so I add a small mix to the glue. Textures created by flocking will blend and mimic the appliance and the surrounding skin. Flocking adds that little extra life to the piece; my preferred flocking is 2 mm Persian Red.

Note: Painting with Skin Illustrator or Tattoo Inks is the same for theatre as it is for film. The only difference is that in theatre you will paint heavier in the red tones.

Should you need beard stubble for your actor, apply with a toothbrush by flicking it off with your gloved hand. This creates a random pattern.

Blood

There will be many times in your career when you will need to create blood effects. What you use and when to use it will have a big impact on how successful the outcome will be. When a scene requires the use of artificial blood, many departments are involved in creating a realistic effect. In some cases, you will need to camera test the color of your artificial blood. Some blood products will register too dark or too bright under certain lighting and film-processing conditions. These situations are classic examples of working with other departments on a film or television set. You will need to coordinate with the costume department, the prop department, the special effects department, and, in some situations, the stunt coordinator. Discussions about the blood effects start during the prep with

the director. Then, at the production meeting, the first assistant director will address any issues, with all departments present and having input.

PRO TIP

Sidebar meetings provide excellent opportunities for fine-tuning conversations and designs with other departments involved, and not subjecting departments that are not involved to a long discussion.

After the production meeting, there are sidebar meetings with the various departments, at an agreed-upon time, to further discuss the issues.

The blood products that the makeup artist chooses should be color checked with the prop department and special effects so that the color of blood will be consistent. A sample of the blood product you have chosen should be given to the costume department, to ensure that it is washable and to check for stain factor. The prop department and the art department will also need to know the products, particularly how to clean the blood products off props and how to remove the blood from the set. If the props or the sets are expensive and cannot be damaged or stained, this will be discussed in the production meeting, and will affect your product choice. In some situations, the makeup department will provide the blood products for other departments (such as the costume department), or will give the other departments involved the name of the blood product and where to purchase it. If the makeup department purchases products for other departments, just note on the invoice or receipt showing which department it is going to, so that the accounting department is able to allocate the cost to that department. Doing so will keep the makeup budget intact.

If you do not coordinate with others, there will be no continuity in the color or texture of the blood, as well as lead to confusion among departments on the set. These are moments in production and on-set when everyone works together to help each other out to achieve the desired effect. Before we talk about choosing the right blood products to use, it is a good idea to understand how blood functions in the human body.

What Is Blood?

The human body contains about five liters of blood. Blood transports oxygen from the lungs to body tissue, and then transports carbon dioxide from body tissue to the lungs. Blood contains red and white blood cells and is about 55% plasma. Plasma is a liquid and contains 90% water. Plasma is a vehicle for blood cells and platelets. Plasma also functions as a carrier of minerals, potassium, and antibodies. Red blood cells also keep blood clean and deliver oxygen throughout the body. Hemoglobin is a protein that is red in color. Blood is constantly recirculated throughout the body. White blood cells fight off infections or germs. Blood platelets are also found in blood. Platelets help to block blood flow around wounds. Clots can form in blood. For example, scabs are clots found on the outside of the body, whereas bruises are clots formed inside the body. Clots that are dangerous form inside blood vessels.

How to Choose

You will need to know the answers to a few questions before making choices on what products to use and how the blood should look. Start with how the script reads. The scene description will get you started with a description of what the action is: car accident, fight, murder, crime scene, gunshot, bloody nose, illness or death, and cause of death.

- Is there a written description of what it looks like?

- Where is the blood coming from, and why?

- What is the medical implication?

- What does the trauma look like in real life?

- What happens to the texture of the skin?

After reading the script, research and think about how to achieve wounds to match the action. This is one example of using your knowledge of the body and medical resource books. If the wounds are extensive, consult with a medical doctor. An emergency-room doctor is always very helpful in researching wounds and trauma to the body. Be organized in your questions when consulting with a doctor. Their time is limited, but they are normally happy to help. Most of the time, you will have to schedule an appointment, either over the phone or at the office. If you need medical slides, you will have to go to the office.

Medical slides and photos are protected for privacy reasons; therefore, you will need to obtain special permission to access them, as well as a designated area within the doctor's office where you can view them in privacy. Not only are doctors great resources for wounds, but also for all illnesses, diseases, and death, including how long it takes to die from certain diseases or wounds.

If you can answer these questions before meeting with the director, you will be able to bring ideas to the discussion of how to achieve the desired effect. After reading the script and doing preliminary research, meet with the director to discuss what he or she wants. Your director will have a visual idea of what the scene or action should look like. The director might also want you to show research on the type of wounds that are required to match the action. In most cases, the producers will want to be involved in discussions. Producers will also have a say in how much blood is used. This is for reasons related to film and television rating issues, as well as creative choice. There will be jobs where you will have a meeting with the director before reading the script. This could be during the job interview. They will be looking for how you would achieve certain effects. Ask questions about the action and story line, and what they want—or do not want—it to look like. In some cases, the director will not know what he or she wants, but they will know exactly what they do *not* want.

Medical Descriptions

Busted Eye: Bruising, swelling, an open cut often are seen if the person has been in a fight. A freshly bruised eye has just happened and is black and blue in color. A days-old eye injury will be green and yellow in color. This wound effect could be used for many different situations.

Abrasion Wound: Abrasions are surface skin lesions, such as scratches or small cuts, where the skin has been scraped. There is usually no need for stitches to close the wound.

Animal Bites: Animal or people bites are laceration wounds where the skin is torn.

Stab Wounds: Stab wounds or penetrating stab wounds are deep, and often fatal because of the harm done to vital organs.

Broken or Fractured Nose: When the nose has been broken, there will be swelling and bruising. There is also a good chance of the nose becoming deformed. Eye hemorrhaging and bruising around both eyes, as well as nosebleeds, are also common.

Broken Jaw: This is a serious wound for several reasons. The swelling of the tongue can affect breathing. With facial swelling and bruising, there is a strong possibility of lacerations in the mouth. Blood from these lacerations can cause life-threatening choking.

Compound Fractures: There is a big concern with compound fractures that a blood or nerve vessel could be injured. Fractures of this nature leave the bone exposed due to skin lacerations.

Hemorrhaging in the Eye: Same as the bruise, but located in the eye. Blood vessels that have broken in the eye area become trapped under the corona and give the eye a bright red stain effect. As the bruise starts to heal, the area will develop a yellow greenish tone.

Burns:

First Degree: Burns that affect the outer layer of the skin. First-degree burns are red with swelling and pain.

Second Degree: Burns that affect both the outer and under layer of skin. These burns cause pain, redness, and blistering.

Third Degree: Burns that affect deeper tissues, resulting in white, blackened, or charred skin that causes numbness.

Airway Burns: These burns can occur when inhaling smoke, steam, or toxic fumes. Symptoms to watch out for are burned lips, burns on head, face, or neck. Eyebrows and hair can be singed. Dark mucus can occur.

Thermal Burns: These burns can occur when scalding liquids, radiation, flames, or hot media come into contact with skin. Symptoms are blisters, peeling skin, red skin, shock, swelling, and white or charred skin.

Gunshot Wounds: Your wound size will depend on the caliber of the gun and shooting distance. The entrance wound is cleaner than the exit wound. The entrance wound is smaller in diameter, with burned edges of skin at the bullet entrance. The exit wound is larger and messier, with the greatest amount of blood and body matter dispersed outward.

What to Use
By Ken Diaz

[Ken Diaz knows the importance of realistic blood. Finding nothing on the market that worked under the many different shooting conditions, he created his own.]

There are always several factors to take into consideration when creating a makeup. First, you need to determine what type of wound you are creating. Does the wound have arterial or vascular bleeding? With arterial bleeding, the blood is oxygen enriched and bright in color. With vascular bleeding, the blood is oxygen depleted and dark in color. How old is the wound? Is the blood dry or starting to dry? Many times you will have a combination of all three types of blood in one makeup. For example, the center of the wound may have bright, oxygen-enriched blood. As you move away from the center of the wound, the blood would become oxygen depleted and darker. As you move to the outside edges or on smudges, the blood would be dry or starting to dry. Weather elements and on-set conditions can also affect the wound. Is the actor sweating? Is it so cold that the blood is freezing? Is it raining so the blood could wash away? To get really good at dressing blood to wounds, you need to start thinking organically. Do your research and study medical books. Watch and record real-life medical-emergency shows, boxing, and full-contact matches. Take photos of real-life injuries.

The following are blood conditions and what to use.

Lighting Conditions

When filming in low light, dark-colored bloods will not show up. You need to use a brighter-colored blood for it to be visible. Also use bright-colored blood when applying the blood to any dark surface. The opposite is true when working with light-colored surfaces. Dark-colored blood looks much more realistic on white porcelain than does bright-colored blood.

Blood Viscosity

There are now many blood products available that come in a variety of viscosities or thicknesses.

Heavy: A very heavy or paste consistency blood (such as K.D. 151 Blood Jam) is used when a nonflowing blood is needed. This type of blood can be applied with a dental spatula, and works very well when used at the base of cuts. You can create very realistic scratches with this type of paste-consistency blood when applied with a coarse stipple sponge.

Less Heavy: A slightly lighter-viscosity blood (such as K.D. 151 Blood Jelly) should be used when a slow-moving blood is desired to help maintain the continuity of a bleeding wound from take to take.

Medium: Medium-viscosity bloods are the consistency of syrup. These are probably the most commonly used type of blood. Some of these bloods have been formulated for specific uses.

Light: Light-viscosity bloods (such as K.D. 151 Pumping Blood) can be used when matching the viscosity of real blood. Also are good to use when pumping blood through small-diameter tubing.

To create a thinner, realistic dry or drying blood, you need to use a medium-viscosity drying blood (such as K.D. 151 Drying Blood Syrup). When a thick, realistically dry or drying blood is required, you need to use a heavy-viscosity drying blood (such as K.D. 151 Drying Blood Jelly).

When applying blood over prosthetic appliances, you will need a blood that contains a wetting agent (such as K.D. 151 Flowing Blood). Blood that contains a wetting agent will help keep the blood from beading up over slick surfaces.

Working outside with conditions that could be hot, cold, or windy, theatrical bloods tend to have an unrealistic skin that forms on the surface. Applying a little bit of glycerin over the top of the blood keeps it looking fresh and wet. To help avoid this problem, you can use a blood that already contains a glycerin base (such as K.D. 151 Stay Wet Blood).

Mouth Blood

Blood that runs into the mouth should be specially formulated (such as K.D. 151 Mouth Blood).

PRO TIP

Always keep a small can of shaving cream in your kit on-set. Shaving cream removes stains on the skin ranging from blood to permanent markers. It is fast and easy.

There are products now available that make all the difference in continuity and how a blood effect can be used, without the mess involved with cleanup. Skin Illustrator, developed by award-winning Makeup Artist Kenny Myers, is a water- and abrasion-resistant, alcohol-activated makeup that is available in palettes and liquids. Makeup products such as Skin Illustrator are a must-have in your makeup kit. Throughout the book, we mention various Skin Illustrator palettes, and for now, we'll talk about the Skin Illustrator FX Palette and a few ways it is used in blood effects (Figure 11.121).

FIGURE 11.121: SKIN ILLUSTRATOR FX PALETTE

FIGURE 11.122: COMPLEXIONS

The FX Palette was designed for just about any injury or illness imaginable. The Skin Illustrator FX Palette can simulate first-, second-, and third-degree burns; cuts; scrapes; scabs; and bruises. The FX Palette seamlessly integrates with the flesh-tone palette to create varying degrees of injuries and illnesses (Figure 11.122).

Blood Tone is a realistic natural blood color that can be easily altered to a deeper, more theatrical color blood with the addition of ultra blue.

Skin Illustrators are made to mix. If you mix yellow and blue, you will produce a different green than what is already in the palette. Remember color mixing? Refer to the color wheel if you need to refresh your memory. Use the burnt orange to provide a rust tone. The aged blood is a mid-ground aged blood that is not too blue or purple. By taking the aged blood and adding it to any of the other colors in the palette, you will get a whole new range of color.

For Continuity: If you have an actor with dripping blood, and you'll need to do the shot over and over again, you'll want to keep track of exactly where you applied the blood the first time or at the beginning of the take. Between each shot, there will be a few moments to clean up the actor so you can start fresh again.

Know what part of the scene each take starts from in order to match the blood, and any changes of the blood, during filming. Sometimes there is a progression to the blood. You will need to take a continuity photo at the beginning of the take and at the end of the take.

wound for a more three-dimensional look, and keeping continuity are all good reasons to use Skin Illustrator FX Palettes in your work.

PRO TIP

Other products that you can use to get the same effect as FX Skin Illustrator are Stacolor and Reel Color.

If you have laid down blood with Skin Illustrator FX color before the wet blood, you have safeguarded exactly where the wet blood needs to go. If, during shooting, the blood lifts, Skin Illustrator colors will keep the wound looking bloody, even without the wet blood or little of it. Skin Illustrator is also a good way to paint blood on a wound when you don't want to get blood on the wardrobe. For example: A female stunt driver had to match the principal actress. The stuntwoman's arm would be in the shot for a long stretch of time. The principal actress did have wet blood applied to the wound, and the costume designer did cut the wardrobe to expose the wound. Shooting the stuntwoman to match became an issue when wet blood was to be applied. The costume designer did not like the idea of the mess that wet blood would make, and the amount of wardrobe that would be used. The solution was to use blood trails made of Skin Illustrator colors, which, on camera, looked just like real blood. Add a little shine on top of the Illustrator color with KY Jelly. This is a product that will maintain its shine without lifting.

Everyone was happy with the results of not having to use wet blood on the stunt driver. This saves you from having to run in over and over again to clean and reapply blood. With this in mind, you can see why distance shots, working in the rain or elements outside, painting your

Temporary Tattoos

By Christien Tinsley, Creator of Tinsley Transfers, Inc.

When approaching a tattoo job, research is always important. You have to consider the character and the character history and time line to where and when they got the tattoo.

Also, with so many themes and mixture of themes, having a good direction or vision from the director can be helpful in scaling down the possibilities. Let's not forget that tattoos are symbols and representations, sometimes of more than just expressive art. Sometimes there are meanings with deep ties to them, and the last thing you want to do is have your actor with something that is offensive or says something about himself that isn't in the character's description. Tattoo books, magazines, tattoo parlors, photography books, and the Internet are all good sources to find thousands of ideas.

Today in feature films and TV, the techniques of HD, bluescreen, and greenscreen are being more commonly used. The trick to a good makeup, tattoo, or prosthetic is to make it look real. If you can fool the eye standing two feet away, you will most likely fool the camera. Don't rely on video monitors—they can be misleading and not a true image for corrections.

Make sure that you have a good relationship with the director of photography (DP). In HD cases, there are digital DPs (not video assistants) monitoring the recording. Go to dailies. Ask to see them even if they give you a DVD copy. Know what you are looking at. Find out from the director or DP how they are processing the film in post, so you can be aware if you need to punch up certain colors. There are no disclaimers in film and television for a Makeup Artist.

Prepping the Skin

Depending on what approach you will take for tattoo applications, you will commonly prep the skin by making sure it is free of hair, oils, and dirt. Hair can be tricky if applying a tattoo decal because the hair won't allow full contact of the image to the skin. If you are drawing the tattoo on, hair can just be in the way. Try to remove hair if at all possible. After hair is no longer an issue, prep the skin by cleaning it with an astringent of your choice. This removes dirt and oil, and slightly dries the skin for better adhesion of paint or adhesive. Sometimes a layer of adhesive can be applied to the skin before the tattoo, helping the adhesion of any image or ink being applied.

Applying the Tattoo

1. Lay the tattoo decal on the skin and apply water (Figure 11.123).

2. Slowly remove the paper (Figure 11.124).

3. Let dry (Figure 11.125).

4. Powder (Figure 11.126).

5. Seal the finished piece (Figure 11.127).

If you are applying tattoo decals, then you first want to cut close to your tattoo image, and then remove the protective plastic coating. This coating protects the adhesive that has been preapplied to the tattoo images. Next, place the tattoo facedown onto the skin and press firmly over the entire surface. Apply water to the back of the decal, and soak the paper. Allow this to

FIGURE 11.123: APPLY WATER

FIGURE 11.124: SLOWLY REMOVING THE PAPER

sit for 30 seconds or so, and slowly remove the paper. After the paper is removed, wet your fingers or a sponge, and gently—without stroking the surface—press over the entire image. Make sure the water is completely dried, and then powder generously.

FIGURE 11.125: LET DRY

FIGURE 11.127: SEALING FINISHED PIECE

FIGURE 11.126: POWDER

I always let the powder stay until last looks. After you are finished with the makeup, you can be sitting for hours before your first shot, and I prefer to let the powder protect the image. What I have found is that after a while, the powder falls away and absorbs with natural oils in the skin. You may find, by the time you get to shooting, that you require very little sealer.

Never put oils such as glycerin on top of a wet or sweaty look. Always use a silicone- or water-based product.

Applying Sealer
When applying sealer, spray into a sponge and first wipe against your own hand. Then take the dampened sponge and lightly rub over the surface of the tattoo until all the powder is removed. You should in most cases not require anti-shine. If your image is too shiny, then a little anti-shine rubbed over the surface can help. Try to avoid powders.

Applying Tattoo Palette Colors or Tattoo Ink Colors
Flesh-colored tattoo paints painted over the surface lightly can help dull the surface and give your tattoo a more aged quality. If you need to add color or image to a transfer, then any sort of tattoo palette paint or tattoo makeup inks will work. I try to do this additional work after the tattoo has been applied and before powdering or sealing. Ideally, you have done your research

and were lucky enough to get approval from all parties (director, producer, and actor) in time, and the transfer you have made should include all the aging and color you require.

Maintaining Tattoos On-Set

In order to maintain tattoos on-set, be aware. Like any makeup you do—but even more like a prosthetic makeup—things can happen. An actor sleeps hard over lunch, an actor rubs his arms on a table while eating, the scene requires actors to wrestle or sweat or run, and so on. Always have backup tattoos with you, and alcohol in case you have to remove and apply a new one on-set. Do not remove with oils in the middle of the day because your next one won't stick. If it is a minor repair, have a premixed color or colors to match the image and to fill in the areas that have rubbed away. Sometimes just throw your hands up in the air, assess the shot, and say: "Hope we don't see that!" Things happen—just be resourceful and prepared.

Removing Tattoos

To remove tattoos, I mix isopropyl myristate and Super Solv 50/50, warm it up in the microwave so that it is comfortable on the skin, and use a powder puff. Continue to apply remover with the powder puff, gently rubbing the area, and periodically use a dampened hot hand towel to break up the rubbing cycle. Continue this until the area is clean. Finish off with a hot towel, and then apply lotion to the area to help moisturize before the next day of shooting.

Terms
Adhesives

Cab-O-Sil Mixed with Pros-Aide: These two mixed together form a thick paste that is often used to blend appliance edges into the skin and to repair damaged appliances. There are other usages, too numerous to mention.

Duo Adhesives: A latex-based product often used for eyelash application. Also used for fixing small areas on appliances, building small wounds directly onto the skin, blending edges, and applying jewelry or decorations to the face and body. This is one of those items you have in your kit that becomes an all-purpose product.

Liquid Latex: Also in clear. Used for many different purposes. Liquid latex can be used to build appliances directly onto the skin, blend the edges of appliances, pour or paint or slush into molds. Is also used as a skin for some foams.

Prosthetic Adhesives: Pros-Aide, for example, is a prosthetic adhesive that has many other uses. You can find Pros-Aide or No Tack Pros-Aide formulas. No Tack Pros-Aide dries without a tacky surface, so the product can be used to blend edges and prepare appliances for painting. It is also used as a Pax, and seals work already done. Pros-Aide Adhesive has a milky white texture and a strong hold, dries clear, is waterproof, and can be thinned with water or thickened but needs a correct remover.

Resin-Based Adhesives: Spirit gum is one of the least expensive resin-based adhesives. It is easy to remove and has a medium hold. Spirit gum does take longer to dry than other adhesives. Spirit gum is good to use for short time frames or in fashion, applying objects to the skin (beads or crystals, for example). You can find spirit gum in different formulas— regular, matte, extra matte, or extra hold. Spirit gum in matte formulas is often used for lace pieces because the adhesive dries with no shine.

Silicone Adhesive: In its raw form, silicone adhesive is composed of minerals. Silicone adhesive is also found under medical adhesives. It has a strong hold and is fast drying. Silicone adhesives in general work well on sensitive skin and are resistant to water. They are used often by Makeup Artists.

Tapes: Can be thin, wide, double sided, textured, and transparent. There are many usages for tapes found in different materials. There are medical-grade adhesive tapes; tapes to apply hairpieces; to secure bald caps; and to hide or protect small cuts, wounds, and body art on the face and body—just to name a few.

Water-Soluble Adhesive: Adhesive that is easily removed with soap and water.

Thinners

Thinners are made to dilute or thin adhesive products. Most adhesives have a matching thinner to go with their product. For example, Telesis 5 Thinner works with thinning Telesis Silicon Adhesives.

Skin Primers

Primers protect the skin from adhesives or products. They set and preserve the makeup.

Removers

Most often, to be safe, you should buy the remover that goes with the adhesive you are using. Many products are made to be used together in this way. Removers can be solvent based, alcohol based, hydrocarbon based, soap based, oil based, nonoily, made with flammable solvents or nonflammable solvents, and can be thinned with water. There are removers that have emollients to protect the skin from drying. They can be odor-free, hypoallergenic, and cream or gel form for easier use.

Reference

Haney, K., In Dick Smith's Advanced Professional Make-Up Course, Update #3, p. 4.

Internet Resources

Burman Industries, www.burmanfoam.com.

Carlsson, L., Makeup-FX Company, www.makeup-fx.com.

Cole, B., www.gelatin.co.za.

The Compleat Sculptor, Inc, www.sculpt.com.

Cybergraphic Design, www.getspfx.com.

Diaz, K., www.kd151.com.

Dow Chemical Company, www.dow.com.

FXWarehouse Inc, www.fxwarehouse.com.

Gelatine Manufacturers Institute of America, www.gelatin-gmia.com/index.htm.

Mosko. G., www.gmfoam.com.

Mulkey, M., www.michelemulkeyfx.com.

Mungle, M., WM Creations, Inc. www.matthewwmungle.com.

Myers, K., www.ppi.cc.

Naimie's Beauty Center, www.naimies.com.

Smooth-On, Inc, www.smooth-on.com.

Tinsley, C., Tinsley Transfers. www.tinsleytransfers.com.

12

HOW TO BE A PRO

Day Checking: Film and Television Industry

Sometimes Makeup Artists work on a day-to-day basis, known as day checking. Working as a daily hire takes a certain amount of responsibility and know-how. If you are talented plus have the ability to think on your feet and are a good observer, you'll go far. Department heads look for someone they can trust on-set to do the job asked and not use the time at work for career advancement. Once you have worked with someone a number of times, you'll get an idea of how department heads run their makeup departments. No matter how chummy and laid back it might seem, try to remember that you are at work and this is a real job. Don't allow yourself to be careless with what you say and too chatty with the Makeup Artists in the main trailer. One of the biggest mistakes a Makeup Artist can make in any situation is failing to follow directions! Please leave your ego out of the equation when given directions on how and what products to use for the job you are on. There have already been many decisions made by the department heads in charge about the look of the shoot. Do as you're told! On top of being called to work without much information, walking into a job that might already be in progress with people who have already established a relationship with each other can be tough. There are ways to make sure that you are on the right track. The following will help you to understand the do's and don'ts of a day checker for daily hire, and how to watch the set.

Day Checking: Daily Hire for Film

When called in to work, ask the production department to fax or email you a call sheet for the day you are working (Figures 12.1 and 12.2). If you have been contacted by a department head or another Makeup Artist, be sure to get the information you need, such as a production phone number.

Sometimes the makeup team already has a full plate, so you can help by contacting the production office yourself for call sheets and maps. Inform production that you will be working as an additional Makeup Artist and give them your contact information. Wait about an hour after production wraps the night before you are to work. If you have not heard from someone by then, call to remind production that you need a call time. Note that it is the assistant director's (AD) department with the help of the production department to give call times, but in some cases a member of the makeup department will make the calls.

Many times department heads will contact you to ask if you have your call times. It is a plus to say yes because that makes one less thing for the Makeup Artist to worry about. They know you will be reliable and able to find your way to the makeup trailer, and on time. Sometimes you can sense a crazy, hectic situation, so be proactive and get the information you need yourself to get to work the next day. Expect a call from an AD. When you do get your call sheet, read it carefully. Take mental notes on what is being shot, how many background players there are, what the time period is, whether it is day or night, and inside or outside.

Why is it important to know these things? If the weather is bad, bring the right things to wear. Are you outside all day? Be prepared to work under any weather situations and for long periods of time. Layered clothing is a must when working outdoors; bring items such as scarves, rain boots, coats, and sweaters. Maybe your set bag needs to be plastic or covered to protect it from the rain. Should you bring an umbrella? What if you are outside all day and it is hot? Sunscreen will be a must to apply on yourself and on the actors you are working on. Hats also protect you from the sun. Sunglasses help with the glare. Working indoors can mean cramped spaces, humid air, and possible excess sweat. Indoors, you might want to stay compact and

| DIRECTOR: |
| PRODUCERS: |
| EXEC. PRODUCER: |

PROD OFFICE: 110 LEROY STREET, 5TH FLR
NEW YORK, NEW YORK 10014
P.O. PH# 212 555 1212 FAX # 212 555 1212

"THE DUMMY"

CALL SHEET

DATE:

DAY: OF

CREW CALL:

SHOOT CALL:

SUNRISE: SUNSET:

Weather:

NO FORCED CALLS OR EARLY CALLS, WITHOUT PRIOR APPROVAL OF U.P.M.

SET	SCENES	CAST	D/N	PGS	LOCATION
				TOTAL	

CAST	PART OF	MAKE-UP	SET CALL	TRANSPORTATION
#1				
#2				
#3				
#4				

ATMOSPHERE	SPECIAL INSTRUCTIONS
SI #	PROPS:
SI # RPT TO LOC @	
BACKGROUND TO INCLUDE:	
	SET DRES:
	ADD. LBR:
	SP EQUIP:

ADVANCE SHOOTING NOTES					
DATE	SET	SCENES	CAST	D/N	PGS	LOCATION

UPM	1ST A.D.	2ND A.D.	2ND 2ND A.D.

FIGURE 12.1: CALL SHEET FRONT

"THE DUMMY"

CREW CALL: DATE:

#	STAFF & CREW	NAME	Call Time	#	STAFF & CREW	NAME	Call Time	#	STAFF & CREW	NAME	Call Time
	PRODUCTION				**MAKEUP / HAIR**				**CATERING**		
1	Director			1	Makeup Dept Head			x	Company		
1	EP/UPM			1	Key Makeup			x	Chef		
1	Prod. Supervisor			1	Makeup				Caterer		
1	1st A.D.							x	Breakfast Ready @		
1	2nd A.D.								Crew:		
1	2nd 2nd A.D.			1	Hair Dept Head				B.G.:		
1	Set P.A.			1	Key Hair			x	Lunch Ready @		
1	Set P.A.			1	Hair Stylist				Crew:		
1	Set P.A.								B.G.:		
1	Set P.A.								**SET OPERATIONS**		
1	Set P.A.							x	Craft Service		
	Addl. P.A.				**WARDROBE**						
	Addl. P.A.			1	Costume Designer						
	Addl. P.A.			1	Asst. Designer				Ready @		
	Addl. P.A.			1	Cost. Supervisor				Crew		
				1	Key Costumer				B.G.		
				1	Costumer				**ASSISTANTS**		
				1	Costumer			1	Assist to Director		O/C
								1	Assist to Producer		O/C
1	Script Supervisor	Mariana Hellmund						1	Assist to Producer		O/C
	CAMERA							1	Assist to Director		O/C
1	D.P.							1	Assist to		O/C
1	"A" Cam. Operator							1	Assist to		O/C
1	"A" Cam. 1st A.C.										
1	"A" Cam. 2nd A.C.								**TRANSPORTATION**		
1	Loader							1	Transpo. Captain		O/C
								1	Transpo Co- Captain		O/C
1	"B" Camera Operator				**PROPERTY**						
1	"B" Cam 1st AC			1	Prop Master				**VEHICLES & EQUIPMENT**		
1	"B" Cam 2nd AC			1	Asst. Prop Master						
				1	Prop Assist				Single Trailer (s)		
1	Stills Photographer								Prop Truck		
	GRIPS								Grip Truck		P
1	Key Grip								Electric Truck		E
1	B.B. Grip				**SET DRESSING**				Camera Truck		R
1	Dolly Grip			1	Set Decorator				Wardrobe/MU Trailer		
1	"B" Cam Dolly Grip			1	Leadman				Honeywagon		T
1	Company Grip			1	On Set Dresser				2 Banger (s)		R
				1	Addl On Set Dresser				15 Pass Vans		A
				1	Addl On Set Dresser				3 Banger		N
									Director's Car		S
									Hair Make Up Trlr		P
1	Key Rigging Grip										O
1	B.B. Rigging Grip				**ART DEPARTMENT**						
	SET LIGHTING			1	Prod. Designer				**PRODUCTION OFFICE**		
1	Gaffer			1	Art Director			1	Prod. Coordinator		O/C
1	B.B. Electric			1	Asst. Art Director			1	A.P.O.C.		O/C
1	Electrician			1	Art Dept. Coord.			1	Prod. Secretary		O/C
1	Electrician			1	Art Dept. P.A.			1	Office P.A.		O/C
1	Electrician							1	Office P.A.		O/C
1	Electrician							1	Offfice Intern		O/C
1	Genny Operator										
1	Base Camp Genny Op.							1	Publicist		O/C
									ACCOUNTING		
1	Rigging Gaffer							1	Production Acct.		O/C
					CONSTRUCTION			1	1st Assistant Acct.		O/C
				1	Construction Coord			1	2nd Asst Acct.		O/C
				1	Constuction Foreman			1	Payroll Accountant		O/C
				1	Key Carpenter						
				1	Key Const. Grip						
	SOUND & VIDEO			1	Const. Grip				**EDITORIAL**		
1	Mixer			1	Shop Electric			1	Editor		O/C
1	Boom				Shop P. A.			1	Editor		O/C
1	Cable							1	1st Assistant Editor		O/C
									LOCATIONS		
1	Video Playback							1	Location Manager		O/C
	SPECIAL EFFECTS				**SCENICS**			1	Asst. Location Mgr		O/C
1	SFX Coordinator			1	Scenic Charge			1	Locations Coord.		O/C
1	SPFX			1	Stand By Scenic			1	Location Asst.		O/C
								1	Location Asst.		O/C
								1	Location Asst.		O/C
								1	Location Asst.		O/C
	VISUAL EFFECTS							1	Location Asst.		O/C
1	VFX Supervisor				**CASTING**			1	Locations Scout		O/C
1	VFX Producer			1	Casting Director			1	Locations Intern		O/C
1	VFX Coordinator			1	Casting Associate				**ADDL EQUIPMENT**		
	MISCELLANEOUS			1	Casting Assistant						
1	Product Placement			1	Extras Casting						
1	Dialect Coach			1	Extras Casting Dir.						

TRANSPORTATION		DIRECTOR & CAST PICKUPS	
			P/U
			P/U
			P/U

FIGURE 12.2: CALL SHEET BACK

bring a small portable fan for a little airflow. How many background players are coming in? Reading this information will tell you how busy it is going to get. The call sheet will also tell you what time period the movie is in for that day. Adjust your makeup kit to what you'll need. Don't bring in natural makeup colors if you are creating 1980s characters. Use common sense. These are just a few examples of why it is important to read the call sheet and to figure out how to prepare for the day.

On the Job

How to Read a Call Sheet

Reading the call sheet gives you valuable information. If you are day checking, reading what scenes are being shot, how many background artists will be working, and what parts they will be playing is important information for preparing what you will need to bring to work. The call sheet will also tell you where to go and what time to be there, who to call in cases of an emergency, and the people who will be working with you. The following numbers correspond to the numbers on the call sheet and explain what they mean. A film call sheet is two-sided; a commercial call sheet typically is one-sided. This is a film call sheet.

- Name of the production company, their location, and phone numbers. In case there is an emergency, you can contact the production office to find out what your call times are or where you are supposed to be.

- Names of all the producers, ADs, writers, and the director. It is good to know who the ADs are. Besides the makeup department, you will be dealing with the AD department. They control the set, the schedule, and the environment on the set.

- The first time listed is the crew call. Also called the general crew call, this is the time that most of the crew reports for work. The makeup department is not included; we have a separate

call time, usually much earlier. Do not confuse the crew call with the makeup call; they are usually not the same. The second time listed is the shoot call. This is the time that production has scheduled to start filming. Makeup call times are on the back of the sheet for film, and on the front of the sheet for commercials.

- Date for the day of work. Number of days the production has already been shooting. This is good to know because you can judge how fresh or tired the makeup department might be when you first start working. The more days they have been filming, the more tired they will be!

Crew Call: The time that the crew is called in to work.

Weather forecast for the day of shooting: Helps you decide what to wear to be comfortable and protected. This would also include any protection you might need for your makeup kits, or for your actors.

Closed Set: A closed set means no visitors. Please remember this rule. You are there to work. It is not a time to show your friends the set. There will be names listed for you to contact to get permission to bring someone on-set.

SC(#): Scene numbers in the script being shot that day.

Set Description: What is being shot and what the shot looks like; whether the shot is indoors or outdoors.

D/N: Indicates if the scene being shot is a day scene or night scene.

Pages: The number of script pages for the scene being shot.

Cast: The cast members appearing in the scene being shot.

Locations: Where the scene(s) is/are being shot.

Holding and Catering: Where the extras are being held, and where the food is located.

Total Pages: Total number of pages being shot that day.

Cast: Actors working that day.

Character(s): Name(s) of the character(s) the actor(s) will be playing. Each character is assigned a number; this number is used to show the character on the call sheet and shooting schedule.

Stat: Work status of the actor. Shows if they work that day or are on hold, traveling, or off.

Reh: Time of rehearsals for the actor(s).

H/MU: The time the actor(s) will go to hair and makeup.

Set Call: Time the actors are expected on set.

Remarks: What time the actors will be picked up from their hotel, or home, or if they drive themselves.

Atmosphere Stand-ins: How many stand-ins and background actors are working that day, and the characters they play.

Report: What time stand-ins and background actors report to hair, makeup, and wardrobe.

Set Call: The time that stand-ins and background actors report to set.

Remarks: Directions on where to report and at what time for stand-ins and background actors.

Department Requirements: Notes on what each department needs to have for scenes being worked that day. Example: Makeup Dept. blood for scene 11.

Advance Schedule: What scenes will shoot and where for the next few days.

Producers, production supervisor, and first AD sign off on (approve) the call sheet. The set phone number and who to contact in case of an emergency.

Flip side of the call sheet: All departments, the names of the crew members listed, and their call times.

Day Checking: Daily Hire for Commercials

Being called in as a daily hire for commercials is similar to film. There are a few changes that you would need to be aware of. Call sheets are not as extensive, and tend to have all information on the front, sometimes with a storyboard attached so you know how the commercial is being shot. You do not have to worry about bringing in copies of your IDs. Copies might be made for you by production, but even that might not happen. A day rate is also decided by you and the producers. What you charge is up to you, but never go below the asking rate. Remember that the less you charge, the more people perceive you as someone who is not in demand. When assisting another Makeup Artist, he or she will tell you what they have in the budget for you. Working with another pro is a good experience. Working by yourself means more responsibility, so remember to keep your rates where they should be. You'll be asking for a flat day rate, with overtime after 10 hours and a kit fee. If you are with a makeup agency, your representative will work out everything for you. After a rate is agreed upon, the agency or producers might ask for a résumé, reel, or CD of your work. This happens mainly if you have never worked with the agency or producers before, and they want to get an idea of what your makeup looks like in print, as well as who you have worked for in the past.

Makeup Kits for Day Checking

Day checking, or daily hire, means you are called in one day at a time. Even though you might get a heads-up on more days, don't count on it. Anything can happen. Although there are people who consider day checking to be the least important part of the crew, that way of thinking is a big mistake. Department heads recognize the importance of their daily-hire crew. In general a department head who values the crew runs a more efficient operation and gets better results in the final outcome of the makeup look desired for the film. As a matter of fact, on a large feature film or project that Makeup Artists want to be involved with, they often work as day checkers. Skill is very important at this level, for often you are left alone to make your own judgment calls.

The right makeup kit for the right job is also important. If a department head has phoned ahead to recommend bringing very little or just what is needed, take notice and heed that request. The department head knows what is going on with the shoot. There is always time to bring in a larger makeup kit if you are hired for more days, or if you are assigned a specialized makeup procedure such as laying down sideburns for a period piece. You most likely have had conversations with the department head on any special makeup to bring with you. Every now and then, a production comes to town and the makeup department has not expressed to you what it is you will be doing or what to bring. Doing a little research on the production gives you a feel for the time period of the movie, and you can bring what you feel is needed.

The following makeup kit will cover you in all your needs as a day checker or union Makeup Artist (Figure 12.3). If you

are working a non-union production, this same makeup kit would apply, but with the addition of hair products. Every Makeup Artist has favorite products, and no one is wrong. The products below are listed because they are popular with other working Makeup Artists—we are constantly trying out or using products that have been suggested by other professionals. I would also suggest that you buy small sizes that can be refilled, or products in tubes, or use small labeled containers to fill with your favorite products. Remember to stay portable!

Note: Most artists have a makeup kit or case, a makeup bag with additional supplies (including a treatment bag), a set bag or case, and a set chair. The average number of pieces is three. Some artists are great packers and have it down to two!

Gretchen's Treatment Bag Contents

- Kiehl's Ultra Facial Moisturizer for all skin types
- Kiehl's Sodium PCA Oil-Free Moisturizer (for those who do not want any oil added to the surface of their skin)
- Kiehl's Cucumber Herbal Alcohol-Free Toner (transfer to a smaller bottle, or use the travel size and refill from the large 16.9-ounce container when needed)
- Kiehl's Blue Astringent Herbal Lotion (transfer to a smaller bottle, or use the travel size and refill from the large 16.9-ounce container when needed)
- Kiehl's Close Shavers Shaving Formula #31-0
- Kiehl's Ultimate Brushless Shaving Cream
- Terax Body Moisturizing Shaving Cream
- Kiehl's Men's Alcohol-Free Herbal Toner
- Clinique Skin Supplies for Men, M-Shave Aloe Gel
- Remington FaceSaver Pre-Shave Powder

FIGURE 12.3: TREATMENT BAG AND FILM DAY-CHECKER BAG AND CHAIR

- Kiehl's Washable Cleansing Milk for Dry, or Normal to Dry, or Sensitive Skin

- L'annine Hand and Body Crème

- Kiehl's Lip Balm #1 with Sunscreen

- Fresh Soy Face Cleanser Makeup Remover

- Lancôme Bi-Facial Double-Action Eye Makeup Remover

- Evian Eau Minerale Naturelle Spray

- DHC Coenzyme Q10 Water Mist

- Travel-size container of witch hazel

- Sephora Makeup Brush Cleansing Wipes

- DHC Makeup Off Sheets

- Wet Ones Moisture Wipes Travel Pack

- Murad Day Reform Treatment (applied to skin before airbrushing)

- Sunscreen SPF 45 or higher

- Rubbing alcohol in a small bottle

- Natura Bisse Sponges

- Small, clean towels

- Eye Tees Precision Makeup Applicators

- Small scissors for cutting cuticles

- Larger scissors for all-around use

- Diamancel Nail File

- Disposable shavers

- No-shred cotton pads

- Sugar-free gum or mints in a variety of flavors and brands

- Norelco trimmer

- Tissues

Set Bag

The contents of a set bag or case are determined by individual preference. You can be on-set for long periods of time, and might not be able to get back to base camp if you have forgotten an item. Also, it depends on if you are watching large background scenes or one or two individuals. Try to keep your set bag lightweight and portable for easy maneuverability while on-set. If you are shooting outdoors, be sure to check the weather conditions. You might need to use a case that is waterproof or covered if rain is expected. A hard, portable gym locker bag works well because it is compact and has a long strap for shoulder use, as well as handles for carrying. It is also waterproof, so it works well outdoors in varied conditions that may include rain, snow, or high temperatures. Indoors or on smaller shoots, use a clear, larger set bag with long straps and that rests close to the body. With a clear bag, the contents are readily visible, which makes it easy to find a specific product. You'd be surprised at how hard it can be finding items when you need them fast!

PRO TIP

Cover your powder puff with a Kleenex tissue for on-set touch-ups. After each touch-up, toss the tissue away and put a new one around the powder puff. This way, you can touch up many people without contaminating anyone.

Along with the products mentioned below, a small, clear cosmetic bag containing the products you will need to use on the actor for touch-ups on-set is useful. Large freezer bags also work. If you have several actors to watch, use individual bags marked with each actor's name, so there is no sharing of products among the actors. Most important of all, individual bags will keep brushes and powder puffs separate.

Gretchen's Set Bag: Contents for Film Set Day Checker

- Kleenex tissues
- Skin Illustrator Grunge
- Sponges
- Powder puffs
- Wet Ones Travel Pack
- Temptu Trauma Pallette
- Evian Eau Mineral Spray
- Pointy Q-tips
- Package of disposable mascara wands
- Remington FaceSaver Pre-Shave Powder
- Small bottle of glycerin
- Small pair of scissors
- Band-Aids
- Small eye pencil sharpener
- Tweezers, Laura Mercier by Tweezerman
- Eyedropper
- Three Cutex Nail Polish Remover Pads
- Refresh Eye Drops Single-Use Containers
- Visine
- Gum and mints of choice (regular and sugar-free)
- Small Jao Antibacterial Hand Refresher
- Small Bliss Body Butter
- Small Lise Watier Equilibre Solution Double Eye Makeup Remover
- Kiehl's Lip Balm SPF 15
- Lancôme Pure Focus
- Carmex
- Small package of flesh-colored ear plugs
- Andrea Eyelash Adhesive
- Two containers of individual eyelashes in dark brown and black
- Two eye shadow palettes with the following colors: black, dark brown, light brown, off-white, rust, gray blue, taupe; eye shadow palettes by Make Up For Ever and Viseart
- Yves Saint Laurent Touche Éclat Radiant Touch
- Natural oil-absorbing rice paper tissues with rice powder and Bobbi Brown Blotting Papers
- No-color powder pressed compact
- Red eye pencil
- Black eye pencil
- Menthol vapor for the eyes
- Small squeeze bottle of Ken Diaz KD151 Flowing Blood Syrup, Drying Blood in Dark and Light
- Skin Illustrator Flesh Tone Palette
- Skin Illustrator FX Palette
- Reel Color Palette Cover-Up/Effects Kit
- Braun electric shaver

The last five items of the above list I store in my set chair (if not needed), and then they are readily available on set. (See Figure 12.3 for photo of film day checker bag.)

PRO TIP

If you need to use powder, switch among several products like anti-shine, blotting papers, and no-color pressed powder to avoid excess build-up.

Gretchen's Makeup Bag for Film Day Checker

The makeup you bring as a day checker on a film set can be contained in a bag or case of some sort. If you are directed to bring makeup for a certain character or time period, you should adjust the contents of your makeup bag to fit the need. If the job is going to entail helping out the department head most of the time, and is not so much about applying a lot of makeup, you won't need to bring a bulky case. A clear bag with a large strap and handle that can accommodate only what is necessary should work. What you do and how you transport your makeup becomes a personal challenge. Changing out your makeup to fit the job at hand happens no matter how well you think you're organized. Having at home a few different makeup bags or cases already set up and ready to go helps cut down the "What to bring?" question.

- Obsessive Compulsive Cosmetics water-based foundation (can be mixed with another brand)
- Kett water-based foundations (can be mixed with other brands)
- Le Clerc pressed powders: Banana and Apricot
- RCMA KO/MB Palette by Vincent Kehoe
- Sephora makeup brush cleaning wipes
- Visiora MV in all colors
- DermaColor Camouflage System
- A few setup towels
- Metal palette to blend makeup
- Book of artist paper to blend makeup
- Palette knife
- RCMA No-Color Powder
- Laura Mercier Secret Brightening Powder
- Iman Pressed Powders
- Guerlain Bronzing Powders
- Tarte Stick Color Stains in all colors
- Eye shadow palettes in various colors (I like to have a compact shadow palette that I can use on anybody for large crowds, containing colors in black, dark brown, taupe, creams, white,

blue, violet, green, and gray. I have every NARS compact that has come out! My favorite for on-set is Skin Deep.)

- Eye shadow palettes in frosty gold tones
- Eye shadow palettes in frosty silver tones
- Blushers (Blushers should be simple. Light pink, coral, burgundy, red if needed, and a warm neutral color. Again, I can usually find this combination of colors in a palette; therefore, I don't need to bring a lot of loose colors. Make Up For Ever has a good combination of colors you can put together. I have one or two creams that I can use if someone has a dry skin tone.)
- Kiehl's Lip Balm SPF 15 in hues 30G and 58B
- Kiehl's Lip Balm SPF 15
- Laura Mercier Brow Powder Duos in all colors
- Bobbi Brown Long Wear Gel Eyeliners in all colors
- Brow pencils in all the brow colors
- Eye pencils in black, dark brown, dark blue, dark green, and white
- Lip Pencils: M•A•C Rosewood, Trish McEvoy Deep Nude, T. LeClerc Tendre, M•A•C Mahogany, Guerlain Rouge #2, By Terry #11 and #12, Lancôme Lip Coloring Stick Inspire, Mauvelle, Lancôme LipColor Cherub, plus a few colors that will work in any situation, such as pink tones, coral tones, reds, burgundy, and a rust color; Yves Saint Laurent Touche Éclat, all colors
- Various lip glosses in tubes
- Bobbi Brown Eye Brighten
- Laura Mercier Secret Brightener
- Laura Mercier Eye Basics Liner
- Lancôme Definicils Waterproof Mascara
- Lancôme Definicils High Definition Mascara
- Trish McEvoy High Volume Mascara
- Brush roll with a variety of brushes

- W.M. Creations, Inc. Stacolor full palette
- Hand-held fan (for those hot days or sets) (See Fig. 12.3 for photo of film day checker bag.)

Set Chair

Having a set chair available is welcome when you will be sitting for long periods of time. In film, it is important because of the amount of time you spend shooting. Everyone has their favorites. Every day, new chairs surface that we all like to check out. I still like my larger chair that has a pocket below that I can stock with extra items. You will find yourself storing extra pieces of clothing for different weather conditions. The chair is compact and easy to move in a hurry. Observe what your department heads are doing. In some cases, the production or makeup teams do not believe in sitting down on the job. Although this is rare, don't assume that everyone brings a chair to the set.

Commercial Versus Film

Makeup kits for the commercial world are similar to those in film. There are a few differences between the two. For one thing, you probably will need to bring a hair kit as well as the makeup kit. In many cases one person does makeup and hair for a commercial. Do not do hair if you are not qualified or comfortable with it. If you are working on a non-union shoot, you most definitely will be doing both. On a union shoot with a budget for two or more artists, they will hire a Makeup Artist and a hairstylist. The union requires that all hairstylists be licensed in cosmetology and keep their license current.

Just as with film shoots, someone should be contacting you with your call times the day before you are to work. Call sheets are usually faxed or e-mailed. Follow the directions and get to work on time!

When you reach crew parking, you'll be escorted by a van to the makeup setups. In commercials, RVs are usually used instead of makeup star trailers. There can be multiple locations in the course of a day, so traveling is easier for production in RVs. Plus, the number of actors you'll be working on at a time can be smaller. Of course, this isn't always the case.

Once you have set up, an AD should start bringing in your actors. Once done, you're off to the set! On commercials, clients who are representing the company that is being filmed are on-set. Clients are there to make sure the company is getting what they need out of the shoot. Be professional at all times. You never know who is listening or who it is that you might be talking to.

At the end of the shooting day, make sure that you've filled out your time card. Turn in your time card to production. Be sure to stay and wait for the actors to help remove any makeup if needed. If there is room, I like to have hot towels available.

Now you can find your way back to crew parking. Drive carefully and slowly going home. You've worked long hours.

Daniela's Makeup Kit

Many Makeup Artists, including me, have separate kits for commercials and photography. Commercials are not only very tiring, but you work with actors, which is different from working with models. Actors need many more products and attention throughout the day. Therefore, I always have a security kit with me that includes eye drops, different bases, a nail kit, body cream, and a first-aid kit, to name just a few items. For photography, the makeup kit contains a lot of products to create effects, such as glitter, different textures of glosses, and all sorts of eyelashes, powders, stones, jewelry, and stencils. I make some of the stencils myself.

Get your start paper documentation in order to bring with you. On union shoots, you will need a copy of your makeup kit rental inventory, which includes a total value and product list, an invoice for your makeup kit rental fee (or box rental), and a copy of your IDs. Whatever you do, don't forget to bring these in. Everyone is busy; production people have no interest or time to hear your reasons for forgetting. They need the information to process your start papers, so you can get paid. Try to make life easier for everyone. I usually have several copies ready to go ahead of time. Fill out the correct information for that job. I put the papers in my makeup kit so as not to forget. The makeup department should have your start paperwork on the first day to fill out and turn in. The combination of the papers you brought in, and the start papers you'll fill out, are turned in together. If the makeup department does not have start papers for you, find the production trailer and get the papers yourself. Again, it looks good for you to know where to go and what to fill out correctly. If you have any questions about your rate or pay, if no one has told you or if they don't know, ask your local union. If the makeup department is from a different local they might not know your rate. Rate of pay fluctuates with regions and union locals. If you think about it, not knowing what your salary will be isn't very professional.

A "kit fee" is also called a "box rental," and is based on a daily fee paid to you to cover the cost of working out of your kit. It covers your makeup brushes and makeup products—your kit. Almost always, expendables are provided by the makeup department (in film), but always pack plenty of supplies in case they are not there when you start work. Always be ready to work!

Expendables include tissue, cotton balls, sponges, puffs, alcohol, brush cleaner, Q-tips, and so on. In commercials you provide everything. If something is needed for the commercial that you

have to purchase, you can turn in the receipt for reimbursement. Kit fees are negotiated for each job; most artists have a standard fee they charge along with their rate. In day checking on a film, the kit fee is determined by production and the makeup budget; it is not negotiable with day checkers (Figures 12.4 and 12.5).

When arriving on-set for the first time, if you do not know where to report, check in with the department head so that he or she knows you are on site. Knock softly and peek in. There isn't really any need to go into the trailer unless invited. Remember, the makeup team may have already been working for hours before you arrive.

FIGURE 12.4: EAST COAST MAKEUP TRAILER—OUTSIDE

FIGURE 12.5: EAST COAST MAKEUP TRAILER—INSIDE

Keep your energy calm and soothing. Makeup trailers bounce, so watch how much you need to go in and out. Do not slam the door. Lift the handle gently to open and close. If invited in, keep most of your things outside the trailer until you get an idea of where you will set up and what you'll need. I usually leave my set chair outside. If you have already been told where to report, do not go to the makeup trailer. You do not need to check in with the department head. They have assigned a member of the makeup department to "run" the additional hires or day checkers, and this is the person you will be checking in with (Figures 12.6 and 12.7).

FIGURE 12.6: WEST COAST MAKEUP TRAILER—OUTSIDE

255

FIGURE 12.7: WEST COAST MAKEUP TRAILER—INSIDE

PRO TIP

East Coast trailers are more stable, and built for cold weather, so they are heavier with less "bounce." West Coast trailers are not built for cold weather so they are lighter and can "bounce" when someone steps inside. "Stepping up" is called out before entering a makeup trailer for this reason. They tend to be wider with more floor space. In Europe, work is done out of customized buses. European buses and trucks are narrower to accommodate the environment—narrow streets and tight parking.

A typical makeup department has the following personnel:

Makeup Department Head (Chief Makeup Artist in Europe) in charge of designing and running the department

Assistant Makeup Department Head

Key Makeup Artist

Makeup Artist

Additional Makeup Artists

There can also be a makeup designer. If there is a makeup designer, the department head will work with them in running the department and implementing their designs.

It is great to get notes or directions on where you are supposed to report and what makeup you will be doing that day. Many times you will be asked to go and set up, and the key Makeup Artist will find you to explain what they want. This could also be the third or fourth Makeup Artist. Whoever is in charge of supervising the additional Makeup Artists and the look of the background artists will be the person to go to with questions.

Crowd Scenes

"Background" refers to background artists (actors) or extras working in a scene. You will hear many terms for background: BG, extras, background players, background artists, and background actors. There can be from 1 to 500 or more background in any given scene. Imagine a park scene with two principal actors sitting on a bench. Everyone around them has been placed by the ADs, with directions from the ADs for their actions and motivations. These background actors have already gone through the costume, hair, and makeup departments before being brought to set.

Instructions you will hear follow:

Working with Background: That means you are hired to do makeup for the actors in the background.

Report to Background Holding or Extras Holding: Where to show up for work, or where to go. Usually a large room or tent away from the set, designated for the background.

Check the Background: You are being asked to look at the background that the AD has assembled for you, and to decide who needs makeup and who is ready to go to set. The department head will decide who has this responsibility.

Working in background, you will often work on many actors in one day. The department head will give you directions on what he or she wants regarding the look for the actors. Descriptions of special background can be found at the front of the call sheet. In some cases, the supervising Makeup Artist will give you a list of the different looks for the background that day. Swiftness is important when working in large crowd situations. Having an idea of what makeup colors and products work or do not work speeds up the process. Always follow specific directions from the department head or supervising Makeup Artist.

On-set note: Never touch up a principal actor on set unless you have been asked to cover that person! You do not know the actor's continuity, so never assume that they need to be powdered or touched up. You are there to take care of the background artists that are around them. So know who the actors are and who you are responsible for, and don't try to impress your department head by being an overachiever and powdering everyone in sight. If you are unsure, ask!

There are certain makeup looks that are used regularly in film and television. A few of those would be police officers, homeless people, drug addicts, pedestrians, diners in a restaurant, waitresses, bartenders, news reporters, news anchors, and children. The other common makeup situations are for period makeup.

Working out of Your Kit

You will need a variety of products and palettes in your makeup kit so that you can create any of these looks. "Working out of your kit" is a term used by Makeup Artists to tell you that you will be creating looks with what is in your kit, and not specially purchased products that are given to you by the makeup department. You rely on industry standards that are in your kit. As we've mentioned before, the palettes from Skin Illustrator, Stacolors, and Reel Creations are industry standards that encourage mixing to create a more realistic makeup that is long lasting and abrasion resistant. They are essential in working out of your kit, and for those unplanned makeup situations where you have to work quickly on-set. There will also be many times that instructions are given to you in "makeup slang" for products. For example, you are asked to "use MV005" or "use Visiora005," or just "use 005." These three terms are referring to the same product; if you do not know what it is, you will not know that you are being asked to apply foundation using a specific color (industry standard). Makeup and film slang abbreviate just about everything, including products, and sometimes instructions. It is confusing at first, but you will get the hang of it. Remember, if you don't know, ask!

Having trouble remembering what colors to use or which looks to create for a certain period makeup? Tape a color chart and notes on each period inside your makeup kit for a quick reference guide.

Remember color mixing from Chapter 3?

Red: You can mix yellow and magenta to get red.

Blue: Mix magenta and cyan.

Green: Mix cyan and yellow.

Purple: Mix violet and magenta.

Black, White, and Gray: Mix white into black until you get the desired shade.

Knowing combinations gives you so many choices to work with!

Now separate the three background actor looks of homeless (Figure 12.8), drug addict (Figure 12.9), and illness (Figure 12.10) to see their differences.

FIGURE 12.9: DRUG ADDICT

FIGURE 12.10: PERSON WITH COLD

Homeless

- Red or sun-damaged skin with various sizes and colors of sun spots.

- Skin tone has rough, leather-like surface due to exposure to the elements.

- Broken capillaries around the nose and cheeks to reflect substance abuse and weather damage.

- Lesions of various sizes due to illness and injury.

- Ground-in dirt on the body, under fingernails, and even built-up grime from lack of grooming.

- Facial hair would be untrimmed, unshaven, oily, and dirty.

FIGURE 12.8: HOMELESS PERSON

- Darkness, puffiness, and redness under and above the eye.
- Small cuts or scabs on the face, with weathered lips.
- In some situations, the feet must be done as well. The soles of the feet should be blackened with heavy grime, cuts, and bruises.

Drug Addict
- The skin tone tends to be pale and clammy from drug abuse.
- Darkness forms under the eye area from lack of sleep.
- Skin lesions form from drug abuse and illness.
- Track marks on the body from shooting up.
- Bruising on various parts of the body, old and new.

Illness
There are many possibilities for illness: cold, flu, high fever, and disease. You will be directed as to what the illness is, and what the desired effect should be, from the department head or supervising Makeup Artist. For this example, your instructions are for a cold/flu.

Cold/Flu: Red tones around the nose with dry, flaky skin. Eyes can appear red and droopy, even watery. Pale skin tone, which could be clammy. Dryness to the mouth.

Would you apply foundation or do any corrective makeup on these characters? No. The worse they look, the better, in all three scenarios; and you do not want an even skin tone.

Red pencil can be used for rimming the eye area or applying right on the lower lash line for irritated eyes. Several shades of red makeup colors are used for broken capillaries, red noses, and lesions. Have on hand various colors of brown or colors to mix browns for dirt and grime. One black is used to deepen or darken an existing color, plus one white to lighten any

existing color or to make grays. Yellow is used for nails, skin tones, and festering lesions or old bruises. Care needs to be taken when working around the eyes. Use a cream-based makeup or a freshly sharpened pencil.

Police Officers
One of the first things you'll do is clean shave all law-enforcement characters. There should be no facial hair, with exceptions given only by your department head. Moustaches are allowed for most police departments. Sometimes sideburns need to be trimmed. The back of the neck needs to be clean shaven. The officers should have a clean-cut appearance. On all shoots, be prepared with a good electric razor, shave powder stick, astringent of choice, and a small groomer for eyebrows, ears, and nose.

News Reporter and News Anchors
News anchors and reporters usually have a clean-cut appearance as well. If there is a time period issue, you will be told to address that. If it is present time, the anchor look is what to aim toward. Work quickly, and spot cover up only the problem areas. Apply a slightly heavy beauty makeup to achieve a matte, perfect look. Most of the time, lipstick, blusher, eye shadow, and brows are all you will have to do to achieve a news anchor look. The hair department will pull the look together. Reporters and anchor types sometimes are pulled ahead of everyone else to go through the makeup department because they are usually featured in the scene.

Period Makeup
This refers to a specific time period for the look or trend of that time. Assume that you are asked to do a period makeup, taking five minutes for each actress because the actresses are in a large crowd scene. If you could do only three things on the actress, what would you do to execute the makeup properly for the following time periods? And what sets each time period apart

from the others? We will give you some very general looks for each decade. You must do your own research for each decade to recognize and know a more detailed history of the trends.

1950s (Figure 12.11): Red lips, pale eye shadows applied to the upper eyelids, nice liquid eyeliner across the upper eyelid next to the lash line, no eyeliner on the lower eye lash line, beautifully shaped and filled in eyebrows. Apply lipstick, eyeliner, and brows. This is a very clean, sometimes innocent, classic look. Note the shape of the lips.

1960s (Figure 12.12): Pale, flat or frosty (but never glossy) lipsticks, strong upper and lower eyeliners, contrasting eye shadows on the eyelids. For example: light shadow on the lid; a deep, dark eye shadow in the crease; followed by a light eye shadow applied on the brow bone. The look is about eyes, so note the style in eye shadow, eyeliner, eyelashes, and brows, as well as the lips. Apply lipstick, eyeliners, and eye shadows.

1970s (Figure 12.13): Women and men in the early 1970s were riding the wave ushered in by the counterculture from the 1960s. Freedom of

FIGURE 12.11: 1950S MAKEUP LOOK

FIGURE 12.12: 1960S MAKEUP LOOK

FIGURE 12.13: 1970S MAKEUP LOOK

expression through fashion and makeup was seeping into mainstream society. Men had cast off the "above-the-collar" hair restrictions of previous decades, and began wearing their hair much longer. In addition, facial hair had become popular, which included long sideburns that often widened as they extended down the face, as well as full moustaches. Hence, facial hair is a large part of re-creating the 1970s look for men. By the mid 1970s, women kept their hair natural whether long or short. Natural, meaning that it was devoid of hairspray, hairpieces, and setting gels of any kind. Eye shadow was colorful and warm (greens, blues, brown) with or without eyeliner; blush and lips in corals, pinks, and frosts. Sun-tanned skin.

Example of a Decade in Makeup

Makeup varies from the early 1970s to the late 1970s, so questions should be addressed to the makeup department head on what look they are trying to create. In general blues, greens, and brown colors were worn as eye shadows. Makeup was applied, but not heavy or over-the-top. Dark brown tones or black would be used around the eye area as liner, but much softer than in earlier years. Lipstick colors were found in corals, pinks, oranges, and soft reds. If you had only three things to do to create a 1970s makeup, what would they be?

1980s (Figure 12.14): In the 1980s, no matter what colors you were using, makeup was applied heavily. Makeup and hair were used as an art form. Depending on who you hung

FIGURE 12.14: 1980S MAKEUP LOOK

out with, everyone today has a different take on what colors were used in the 1980s. The colors ranged from the punk look (with black liners and dark eye shadows) to the preppy look (girls with rust or fuchsia-colored lipsticks with purple eye shadow). Of course, Madonna always comes to mind when one thinks of a 1980s look. Three things to use for a 1980s makeup: colorful lipstick, full eye shadow, and blusher. Use lipsticks in pinks, purples, fuchsia, rusts, and reds. Apply eye shadows all over the lid and crease, with a dramatic but lighter shade to the brow bone. Complete the look with a dramatic contouring blusher across and just under the cheekbone in a matching color to the lipstick.

PRO TIP

There is a transition for each decade in the looks and trends. It does not happen at the beginning of each decade, but a few years later. So there is an overlap of trends between the beginning of one decade, and the end of the previous decade. Lifestyle, environment, economics, and character play into it as well. Know the year to achieve the look. If the project is not being year specific but wants a general feel of a period, choose to go for the obvious trends associated with the decade. Research, research, research! Know the trends by heart—it puts you at a great advantage.

On the Job with Daniela Eschbacher

When I started out in the fashion industry, I contacted as many photographers and stylists as possible to do "test shooting" first to build up my portfolio and contacts. In the beginning, it's hard contacting everybody and running after magazines. But all that hard work pays off. After working for magazines and commercials, people will get to know you and pass your name and number along. That's what happened to me. Still, in a city like Paris, it is hard to break in. In fashion, sending out your newest editorials to Photographers and magazines will keep them updated on your work.

Preparing for the Shoot

For commercial shoots, it's important to have all the information necessary from the client or photographer. The client normally knows exactly what they want, and they expect the Makeup Artist to realize it. When I get a call for a commercial shoot, I will ask the theme of the shoot, the makeup look wanted, if it's an inside or outside shoot, and how many models. For beauty, it is important to ask the photographer for the model's reference. The photographer can either send her portfolio to you by email, or you can look on the agency's website for the model's portfolio book. Once you have all the information, it is time to start thinking about the makeup and products, and to double-check to make sure you have everything you'll need for the shoot. Many times, the photographer, or even the client, does not know how to express themselves in the form of makeup and colors, so it's up to me to find the right look. Working in fashion is different from cinema. It can be spontaneous.

Even if you agree on a certain look before shooting, it might all change on the actual workday. On larger, more complicated shoots, there are meetings before the job. The stylist knows the clothes, so he or she gives direction and theme for the shoot. It can be really helpful to work with an art director or stylist because they see the overall image. Sometimes a simple makeup works much better than one too sophisticated or creative. Meetings are important for meeting the team—it makes the whole process interesting, fun, and human to take the time to sit down and discuss the project. Of course, for commercial jobs, meetings do not always happen.

FIGURE 12.15: BEAUTY SHOOT, ISTOCKPHOTO

Madonna Theme Shoot

The challenge was to create color combinations that would express and strengthen the atmosphere and theme of the shoot. I found my inspiration from religious paintings and books. The colors dark red, golden, gray, white, and silver were used. Because wardrobe and hair had such a strong look, I didn't want to complicate the makeup. When this happens, use a matte, lightly applied foundation, no blush, and no contouring. White eyeliner applied on the inside of the eye will accentuate any color just under the eye. In this case, a red and yellow matte eye shadow from Make Up For Ever was applied on the eyelid and below the lower lashes. No shaping or contouring was used. Shadow was just posed on the lid. When such strong colors are used, a tissue laid under the eye you are working on protects the rest of the face from falling shadow. Loose powder can also be used. Natural lip colors help keep the makeup from being overwhelming. Shape the lips with a nude lip liner. Mix beige, purples, and pink lip glosses to achieve a natural look. Don't forget to finish off with a strong brow (Figure 12.15).

Remember, you want to work in layers. Work the shapes and slowly go darker. It's like working on a painting. To create something luminous and strong, it's always the combination of colors that accentuate the intensity of another color (Figure 12.16).

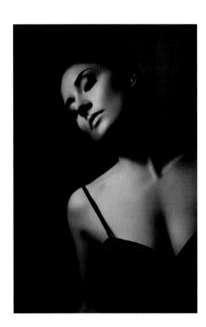

FIGURE 12.16: BEAUTY SHOOT, ISTOCKPHOTO

Things to Know

Makeup Brushes
Types of Bristles

Badger: One of the most popular and easiest to find. Badger hair quality depends on an array of factors. The highest quality is the neck hair, which is the softest and most expensive of all badger hair.

Blue Squirrel: Soft in texture can be mixed with another hair like goat.

Boar: Stronger and thicker than badger hair.

Canadian Squirrel: Very expensive but a favorite among Makeup Artists.

Goat: Strong and soft. It's used alone or mixed with other hairs in makeup brushes. Goat hair can be found in white, brown, or red.

Kazakhstan Squirrel: Softer than blue squirrel. Kazakhstan squirrel is rare and expensive.

Pony: Also known as camel hair. This is a term for brushes made from a variety of hair such as squirrel, goat, ox, or pony. Usually brushes made with these bristles are inexpensive and are made in large quantities.

Raccoon: North American animal with a multicolored tail in grays and browns. Raccoon brushes have a really soft texture.

Sable: An animal from Siberia and Japan. Sable is strong, flexible, and takes to products well. Sable can be found in brown, white, or yellow. Kolinsky sable is a mink found in Siberia and China, and is considered the best. Red sable is from the weasel family, and is often used in place of Kolinsky sable.

Squirrel: Hair that is soft and holds water effectively. It works best with liquids.

Synthetic or Taklon: Brushes that are made of nylon or polyester. Synthetic brushes are considered reliable and strong.

Tree Squirrel: Most like weasel brushes that have stiff bristles. Used most often for liquids and creams.

Weasel: Weasel hair will hold up over time. Weasel hair can be used with liquids and powders.

Types of Brushes

Angled Brush: These are cut to use at defined angles. Blush brushes, shadow brushes, brow brushes, powder brushes, bronzers, and contour brushes are examples of brushes that can be found cut at an angle. In some cases, the bristles are stiffer.

Blush Brush: Soft, wider, rounded brush used to apply blusher color. Blush brushes are made from a variety of bristles.

Brow Brush: Angled or slant brushes with a stiff bristle for application of brow powders. It's also possible to find lash combs and brow brushes as duos.

Concealer Brush or Flat Brushes: Concealer brushes are usually flat brushes in a variety of sizes used for cream-based products. These brushes are good for spot touch-ups, heavy coverage with multiple products, under-eye concealer, and blending products. Many flat brushes can be used wet or dry.

Contour Brush: Is used to get under edges and contours of the face to create definition. The bristles are usually cut blunt or at angles.

Crease Brush: Smaller, with a blunter cut in the bristles. Crease brushes are used to apply eye shadows in the crease area and to blend existing work.

Eyelash Combs: Wire or plastic combs that are used to separate the lashes after mascara has been applied.

Eyeliner Brushes: Come in a variety of sizes and bristles. Bristles usually taper to a point, which works well for lining, detail work, powder, liquid, or water-activated makeup such as KRYOLAN or MAC. There are liner brushes that have several different bristles that can be used effectively wet or dry. Also, flat eyeliner brushes can be found.

Eye Shadow or Fluff Brush: There are many different sizes and shapes of a shadow brush. The brushes are used to apply eye shadow colors. The bristles are usually soft, with a rounded shape at the top.

Face or Foundation Brushes: These brushes are usually larger, flatter, with a rounded or oval bristle shape. Bristles can be made in a variety of hair, including synthetic to sable. Foundation brushes can cover wide areas of the face and body, and work well with liquids and creams.

Fan Brush: Shaped like a fan and come in a variety of sizes. Fan brushes disperse powdered makeup and add color with a sheer application. They can be used for applying mascara, as a powder or blush brush, a stipple brush, or as a blending brush.

Kabuki Brushes: Brushes that are often used with mineral-type powder makeup. They come in a variety of sizes and shapes. The most common shape is a fan or dome.

Lash Combs: Lash combs are made to separate the lashes after applying mascara.

Lip Brush: There are many choices of lip brushes, from shapes of the bristles to what the bristles are made of. Lip brushes are used to apply lip treatments and lip colors.

Paddle Brushes: These brushes are shaped like a small paddle with a lamb's wool covering on one side. They are used for blending blush or makeup colors.

Powder Brush: Larger brushes with rounded, softer bristles, often made with goat, sable, or badger hair. They are good for dusting large areas of the face with loose color or with powder makeup to dust off any excess powder.

Puffs: These are found in so many different brands, shapes, and materials, but all types are used in basically the same way for makeup and powder application, setting the makeup, and touch-ups on-set.

Pump Brush: Brushes made with the product inside the stem of the handle. When the brush is pumped, the product disperses into the bristles.

Retractable: Brushes that can retract back into the handle of the brush. Some lip brushes and blush brushes are made retractable.

Smudger: Any brush that is used to blend and smudge the makeup.

Sponges: Are used for just about anything you can think of. They come uncut in squares or pre-cut and as a brush form. Good sponges are gentle on the face, do not soak up your liquid or cream makeup, and aid in blending. Different brands of sponges are made from different materials.

Stipple: Several blends of bristles in the brush, plus the shape of the brush works to create textures or as a blender.

Wet and Dry Brush: Brushes that are made with several different kinds of bristles that can be used effectively wet or dry.

Industry Standards

Anti-Shines

Many products are available. Anti-shine creates a matte look to wherever you apply product. We all have our favorites. One that's been around for a while is Make-Up International's Face-to-Face Super Matte. It works well for large crowd scenes.

Adhesives

Telesis Beta Bond Plus by Premiere Products, Inc.: Acrylic adhesive for prosthetics.

K.D. 151 Ultra Matte Lace Adhesive: Strong adhesive hold for action-packed situations.

KRYOLAN Water-Soluble Spirit Gum: Removes with soap and water.

Pros-Aide: Acrylic based, waterproof, strong hold, used mostly for appliances.

Telesis 5 Adhesive by Premiere Products, Inc.: Silicone-based adhesive.

Very Flat Matt Gum by Naimie's: Used in the industry for lace fronts, facial hair, or wherever you don't want to have shine.

Xtra Hold Spirit Gum and Extra Hold Plastic Spirit Gum by W.M. Creations, Inc.: Two of the most popular spirit gums in the industry. They are used for fine lace fronts, foam, gelatin, and silicone appliances.

Brush Cleaners

Cinema Secrets: Fast drying.

Naimie's: Fast drying.

Effects Products

AM.E.K. Liquid Plastic by W.M. Creations, Inc.: Use in stone or silicone molds for wounds.

Gelatin in Bulk: Burman Industries carries gelatin products.

Latex Products in Bulk: Burman Industries carries a wide range of latex products.

Old-Age Stipple

Old Age Stipple A, B, C, Crusty by W.M. Creations, Inc.

Green Marble SeLr by Premiere Products, Inc.: Developed by RSD Inc. and CMI. Seals the makeup, is very durable, safe for sensitive skins, and also works as an aging product.

RCMA Old Age Stipple

PAX Paint

Thom Surprenant PAX Paints

PAX Paint by GM Foam: Premixed PAX paint colors that match up to RCMA.

Foundation Colors

Plastic Sealers A, B, Soft, Extra Soft, Shiny by W.M. Creations, Inc.

Scab Materials Light, Medium, Dark, and Brown by W.M. Creations, Inc.: Pigmented, silicone-based liquid that is used for building up three-dimensional scabs.

Scar Material by W.M. Creations, Inc.: Acetone-based plastic material used to build things such as keloid scars and blisters.

Silicon Product in Bulk

Smooth-On Inc.: Easton, Pennsylvania–based manufacturer of silicon products. Their website sells direct.

Burman Industries: Carries a good inventory of silicone-related products. Based in Van Nuys, California.

Tattoo Ink Type Products

All of the products mentioned are industry standards. It's difficult to remember what it was like before these products existed.

Reel Creations Palettes by Reel Creations.

Reel Creations Liquids by Reel Creations.

Skin Illustrator Palettes by Premiere Products, Inc.: Created by Kenny Myers/CMI.

Skin Illustrator Liquids by Premiere Products, Inc.: Created by Kenny Myers/CMI.

Stacolor Palettes by W.M. Creations, Inc.

Stacolor Liquids by W.M. Creations, Inc.

Tear Products

Burman Industries Menthol Blower and Crystals: A must for any makeup kit.

KRYOLAN Tear Stick

Makeup Products

Foundation or Correction Makeup

Ben Nye Mellow Orange: Neutralizes blue and green.

Ben Nye Mellow Yellow: Red neutralizer.

KRYOLAN Dermacolor Mini-Palette: This makeup covers well, has a large selection of colors, and is easy for doing quick makeup or touch-ups on-set.

Iman: Excellent makeup line for a range of skin tones from light to dark, including yellow. Great pigment in shadows, blushers, and lipsticks.

RCMA: Without question, a makeup line we could not do without. Foundation colors come in every possible range for any beauty or character makeup. This is one of the few makeup lines that understands skin tones.

Visiora: A sheer makeup that has a good coverage. Colors have been formulated to match our industry lights and different media. Visiora is also a wonderful makeup to use on men.

Water-Activated Makeup

Ben Nye: Good for theatrical use.

Mehron: Good for theatrical use.

Studio Fix by MAC: Good for flesh tones, editorials, and stylized beauty makeup.

Makeup Palettes

Viseart Palette of Neutrals: A simple palette of neutral colors. This palette is perfect for your set bag.

Powders

Kett No Color: Pressed powder.

No Color Powder by RCMA.

Removers

It's always a safe bet to buy the remover made for a particular adhesive.

Adklen Cleanser by RCMA: No travel-safety issues.

Beta Solv Remover: Works to remove PAX Beta Bond by Thom Surprenant.

Ben Nye Bond Off: Removes spirit gum, medical adhesive, and Pros-Aide.

Delasco Detachol: Removes Pros-Aide; mild and hypoallergenic.

PAX Remover by GM Foam: Removes PAX paint.

RJS Adhesive Remover: No travel-safety issues.

Super Solv by Premiere Products, Inc.: Non-oily. It is extra strength, but safe for sensitive skin. Gentle enough for lace fronts.

Sealers, Primers, and Fixers

Sealers protect your work, act as a stronger bond for adhesives, and act like a shield between the skin and product.

Green Marble SeLr Spray: Also can be used as an aging product.

RCMA Matte Plastic Sealer

Soft Sealer by W.M. Creations, Inc.: Also can be used as an aging product. Can be sprayed or stippled over makeup.

Top Guard by Premiere Products, Inc.

Internet Resources

Dick Blick Art Materials: www.dickblick.com.

Eschbacher D: www.danielamakeup.com.

Hakuhodo: www.hakuhodousa.com.

Indeutsch Industries: www.indeutsch.com.

Makeup Artist's Choice: www.makeupartistschoice.com.

Makeup Creations: www.makeupcreations.com.

Naimie's Beauty Center: www.naimies.com.

Daima PS, Sons: www.psdaimaandsons.com.

Sephora: www.sephora.com.

Solo Makeup: http://www.solomakeup.com.

United States

California

Cimuha, Inc.
Erwin H. Kupitz
7618 Woodman Ave.
Panorama City, CA 91606
E&G@cimuha.com
818 769 6465

Cinema Secrets, Inc.
4400 Riverside Dr.
Burbank, CA 91505
www.cinemasecrets.com
818 846 0579

Coast Airbrush
312 N. Anaheim Blvd
Anaheim, CA 92805
714 635 5557

Frends Beauty Supply
5270 Laurel Canyon Blvd.
North Hollywood, CA 91607
www.realcolorwheel.com
818 769 3834

GM Foam, Inc.
14956 Delano St.
Van Nuys, CA 91411
www.gmfoam.com
818 908 1087

Hair Goods by Teresa
Teresa Valenzuela
7618 Woodman Ave., Unit 1
Panorama City, CA 91402
www.hairgoodsbyteresa.com
818 668 7229

Krembs, Inc.
420 East Easy St., Suite 1
Simi Valley, CA 93065
www.krembs.com
800 835 8267

KRYOLAN Corp.
132 Ninth St.
San Francisco, CA 94103
Info-usa@kryolan.com
www.kryolan.com
415 863 9684

Mark Davenport
Creature Effects Inc.
3325 Cahuenga Blvd.
Los Angeles, CA 90068
323.850.3228

Motion Picture F/X Company
(Mark Traynor Facial Lifts)
123 South Victory Blvd.
Burbank, CA 91502
www.monsterclub.com
818 563 2366

Naimie's Beauty Center
12640 Riverside Dr.
Valley Village, CA 91607
www.naimies.com
818 655 9933

Nigel's Beauty Emporium
11252 Magnolia Blvd
North Hollywood, CA 91601
www.nigelbeauty.com
818 760 3902

Premiere Products, Inc.
10312 Norris Ave., Suite C
Pacoima, CA 91331
www.ppi.cc
800 346 4774
818 897 2440

Professional Vision Care Associates
14607 Ventura Blvd.
Sherman Oaks, CA 91403
www.fx4eyes.com
818 789 3311

Reel Creations, Inc.
7831 Alabama Ave
Ste. 21, Canoga Park, CA 91304
Tblau@reelcreations.com
www.reelcreations.com
818 346 7335

Silpak
10611 Burbank Blvd
North Hollywood, CA 91601
www.silpak.com
818 985 8850

TriEss
Burbank, CA
www.tri-esssciences.com
818 848 7838

Tinsley Transfers, Inc.
P.O. Box 10011
Burbank, CA 91510
info@tinsleytransfers.com
www.tinsleytransfers.com

W.M. Creations, Inc.
5755 Tujunga Ave.
North Hollywood, CA 91601
Mmungle@nu-products.com
www.matthewwmungle.com/wmcreations
800 454 8339

Make-Up Designory
212 925 9250
129 South San Fernando Blvd.
Burbank, CA 91502
www.mud.edu
818 557 7619

Florida
FX Warehouse, Inc.
1575 Aviation Ctr. Pkwy., Suite 414
Daytona Beach, FL 32114
order@fxwarehouse.info
www.fxwarehouse.info
386 322 5272

Le Cosmetique
2338 Immokalee Road
Naples, FL 34110
866 477 6928

Silly Farm
11870 West State Rd. 84
Suite C12
Davie, FL 33325
954 472 5000

New York
Alcone Company, Inc. (store location)
322 West 49th St.
New York, NY 10019
www.alconeco.com
212 757 3734

Alcone Company, Inc. (headquarters and warehouse)
545 49th Ave.
Long Island City, NY 11101
718 361 8373

Make Up Forever
8 East 12th Street
New York, NY 10003
212 941 9337

Make Up Mania
182 Allen Street
New York, NY 10002
212 533 5900

Make-Up Designory
(New York and Los Angeles school and store)
375 W. Broadway, #202
New York, NY 10012

Manhattan Wardrobe Supply
(Some makeup supplies; great bags
   and accessories)
245 West 29th Street, 8th floor
New York, NY 10001
www.manhattanwardrobesupply.com
212 268 9993

Pennsylvania
Smooth-On, Inc.
2000 Saint John St.
Easton, PA 18042
www.smooth-on.com
800 762 0744
610 252 5800

Australia

Barnes Products Pty, Ltd.
53 King Street
Newton NSW 2042
Australia
sales@barnesonline.com.au
www.barnes.com.au
61 (02) 9557 9056

Hub Makeup
40 King Street
Prahran, Victoria 3181
Australia
613 8520 5500

Makeup & Glow
1/189 Kelvin Grove Road
Kelvin Grove, QLD 4059
Australia
00 30 21 0505 5829

Media Makeup
Mezzanine Level, Shop 17
Renaissance Arcade
Pulteney St Adelaide South 5000
Australia
08 8223 3233

Showface
10 Arglye Place
Millers Point
NSW 2000
Australia
612 9247 4736

JMB FX Studio
Unit 3 13–15 Ereton Dr.
Labrador, QLD 4215
Australia
www.jmbfxstudio.com.au
61 (0) 7 5528 8500

KRYOLAN Australia Pty, Ltd.
147 Little Collins St.
Melbourne, VIC 3000
Australia
sales@kryolan.com.au
www.kryolan.com.au
61 3 96544147

Brazil

BelleSkin Cosmetics
Rua Brig. Tobias 356, 11 Andar
Centro
São Paulo SP
Brazil
55 11 3315 0733

Canada

Complections International
85 Saint Nicholas St.
Toronto, ON M4Y IW8
Canada
info@complectionsmake-up.com
www.complectionsmake-up.com
416 968 6739

3D Plastics
12304 Garibaldi St.
Maple Ridge, BC V2W 1N2
Canada
3Dplastics@intergate.ca
www.3dplastics.net
604 462 7755
604 465 6569

Fernanda's Beauty Products
1225 Aerowood Drive
Mississauga, ONT L4W 1B9
800.862.1447

R. Hiscott Beauty and Theatrical Supplies
435 Yonge St.
Toronto, ON M5B 1T3
Canada
416 977 5247

Silithane
14855 Du Froment St.
Quebec, QC J7N 2J7
Canada
Silithane@supernet.ca
514 8241 587

Studio F/X
108–1055 W. Georgia St.
Vancouver, BC
Canada V6E 3P2
604.685.5509

Studio Makijaz
4030 Rue St. Ambroise
Montreal, Quebec
514.934.6254

Takara PBG Group
(Highest-quality handmade Japanese brushes)
244 Elson St.
Markham, ON L3S 3B9 Canada
Info@takaracanada.com
www.takaracanada.com
905 472 6105

France

Boutique Plein Fard
7 Rue De Courcelles
75008 Paris
33 0 1 42 56 34 28

Paris Berlin
56 Boulevard Richard Lenoir
75011 Paris
France
info@parisberlin.com
www.parisberlin.com
33 0 1 43 38 35 90

Germany

Bela Kosmetik
Birnauerstrasse 12
D-80809 Munchen
Germany
www.bela-kosmetik.de
49 0 89 35652223

E&G Hair Goods
Gerhard A. Zeiss and Erwin H. Kupitz
Cologne
Germany
gerdizwiss@aol.com (Gerhard)
E&G@cimuha.com (Erwin)

Fischbach-Miller
(Wig-making supplies)
Info@fischbach-miller.de
www.fischbach-miller.de

KRYOLAN GmbH
Papierstr. 10
13409 Berlin
Germany
Info@kryolan.de
www.kryolan.de
49 30 499 8920

Greece

Beautyworks
Kolokotroni 8
Kifitssia
Athens, 145 62
Greece
30 210 8089070

Hong Kong

May's Co./Gala Gold Ltd.
Unit G 19, Tung Ying Building
100, Nathan Rd.
TST Kowloon
Hong Kong
galagold@netvigator.com
852 2367 5332

Ireland

Nue Blue
7 South William Eriu St.
Dublin, 2
Ireland
www.nueblueriu.com
dublin@nueblueriu.com
353 01 672 5776

Israel

Boaz Stein, LTD
7A Derech Hashalom St.
Tel Aviv Israel 67892
03 6916061

Italy

Kiehl's Milan Store
Corso Di Porta Ticinese, 40
Milano, 20123
Italy
www.kiehls.com
39 0 2 832 41084

Mexico

Kiehl's Mexico City
Centro Comercial Perisur
Periférico Sur #4690 Local 179 PB
Col. Ampliación Jardines del Pedregal
Mexico City, DF
Mexico
www.kiehls.com
52 55 5171 4505

New Zealand

Gelita NZ Ltd.
(Gelatin and related products)
135–145 Connal Street
Christchurch 2
New Zealand
www.gelita.com
64 3384 3093

Philippines

Sprint Asia
Unit 302 Quadstar Bldg.
No. 80 Ortigas Ave
Greenhills
San Juan City 1500
Phillippines
744 6210

Romania

Beauty Shop Bucuresti
55–59 Calea Vitan
Bucuresti
Romania
40 21 327 7532

Russia

Freeline Cosmetics
4A, Chernyahovskogo St.
Moscow
Russia
495 601 2264

South Korea

KRYOLAN Korea
1F, Sungdo Bldg.
336–1, Seogyo-Dong
Seoul
South Korea
Kryolan@kryolan.co.kr
www.kryolan.co.kr
82 0 2 3143 2732

Spain

Stick Art Studios
C/Comtal, 20 Pral. 1A
Barcelona
Spain
34 93 412 4361

Sweden

Goteborgs Perukmakeri

Stora Nygatan 11
5–411 08 Goteborg
Sweden
Info@perukmakeri.se
www.perukmakeri.se
46 0 31 15 7881

Mapont & Co.

Odelbergs vag 9B
134 40 Gustavsberg
Sweden
Info@Mapont.se
www.mapont.se
46 0 70 3523109

MB Sveda

(Glycerin and sorbitol)
Box 48, Marieholmsgatan 56
410 20 Goteborg
Sweden
www.mbsnordic.com
KJell.Johansson@mb-sveda.com
0046 31 838168

Taiwan

Kiehl's Taipei Store
No. 97 Fu Shin Road
Taipei, 105
Taiwan
88 6227125005

United Kingdom

Charles H. Fox Ltd.

22 Tavistock St., Covent Garden
London WC2E 7PY
United Kingdom
Makeup@charlesfox.co.uk
www.charlesfox.co.uk
44 0 20 7240 3111

Creature Effects

Unit 2, 549 Eskdale Rd.
Uxbridge Middlesex UB8 2RT
United Kingdom
Creatfx@dircon.co.uk
44 0 1895 251107

Impet2us, Ltd.

Abbotswood, Evesham
Worcestershire WR11 4NS
United Kingdom
01386 765365

Makeup Artist Provisions

6 Goldhawk Mews
Shepherd's Bush
London W12 8PA
United Kingdom
44 0 20 8740 0808

The Makeup Artist Boutique

33 Conway Court
Clarendon Road
Hove BN3 3WR
United Kingdom
00 30 21 0505 5829

Mouldlife
Tollgate Workshop
Bury Road, Kentford
Suffolk CB8, 7PY
United Kingdom
Justin@mouldlife.co.uk
www.mouldlife.co.uk
44 0 1638 750679

Screen Face
20 Powis Terrace
Westbourne Park Rd.
Notting Hill, London W11 1JH
United Kingdom
Info@screenface.co.uk
www.screenface.com
+44 (0)20 7221 8289

The Makeup Shop
4 Devonshire Rd.
Hounslow W4 2HD
United Kingdom
www.themakeupshop.co.uk

Who's Who

Makeup Artists: Makeup Artists perform the art of makeup, which includes:

- Application of all moustaches, chin pieces, side burns, beards, false eyebrows, and lashes.

- Application of any facial or body appliances, masks, etc., used in the art of makeup, whether made of rubber, plastic, or any other material.

- All body makeup (except on network broadcasting productions, i.e., NBC, CBS, etc.).

- May apply wigs or toupees, or cut the hair on male performers.

- May also do hairstyling on legitimate theater and opera productions.

Assistant Director (AD): An AD is a person who helps the director in the making of a movie. The duties of an AD include setting the shooting schedule, tracking daily progress against the filming production schedule, logistics, preparing daily call sheets, checking the arrival of cast and crew, maintaining order on the set, rehearsing cast, and directing extras.

First Assistant Director (First AD): The first AD is directly responsible to the producer and "runs" the floor or set.

Second Assistant Director (Second AD): The second AD creates the daily call sheets from the production schedule, in cooperation with the production coordinator. The second AD also serves as the "backstage manager," liaising with actors and putting cast through makeup and wardrobe, which relieves the first AD of these duties. They supervise the second second assistant director, third assistant director (third AD), and assistant director trainees, The setting of background (extras) is part of the second AD's duties.

Second Second Assistant Director (Second Second AD): The second second AD deals with the increased workload of a large or complicated production. For example, a production with a large number of cast members may require dividing aspects of "backstage manager" and the call sheet production work to two separate people.

Third Assistant Director (Third AD): The third AD works on-set with the first AD, and may liaise with the second AD to move actors from "base camp" (the area containing the production, cast, and hair and makeup trailers), organize crowd scenes, and supervise one or more production assistants (PAs).

Key Production Assistant (Key PA): The key PA may have a number of duties assigned to them by the AD staff. A key PA is the lowest on the crew's hierarchy in terms of salary and authority. They perform various duties required by the ADs. The subroles of assistant directors differ by nation. For example, the distinction between second second and third AD is more common in North America. British and Australian productions, rather than having a second second AD, will hire an additional second AD to fulfill the same duties. In Britain and Australia, third ADs have different duties from a second second AD, and the terms are not synonymous.

Note: Definition of Makeup Artists derives from the IASTE, Local 706.

Terms

Calling the Roll: One of the first AD's responsibilities is to "call the roll" when all of the relevant heads of department (HODs) and above-the-line people seem ready to perform, the first AD initiates the take. Over the years, special procedures have been developed for this task in order to achieve maximum efficiency during shooting, which is usually some variant on the following:

1. **"Waiting on ..."** First ADs are constantly calling out which department is responsible for delays. If the lights need to be adjusted, the first AD calls out, "Waiting on gaffers." If the actors are still in their trailer, the first AD calls out, "Waiting on talent." If a mascara smear needs attention, the first AD calls out, "Waiting on makeup."

2. **"Last looks, please."** Once everyone is in place, and rehearsals and blocking have finished, the first AD calls out, "Last looks." This allows for last-minute finishing touches, whether to the set, to hair and makeup, to lights, or anything else.

3. **"Quiet on the set."** The first AD calls out, "Quiet on the set" to alert everyone that the take is ready to be filmed.

4. **"Roll sound."** The first AD waits for complete quiet, then signals the production sound mixer to "Roll sound," after which the mixer rolls his sound gear, verifies its status, and replies, "Rolling" or "Speed."

5a. **"Roll camera."** The first AD then signals the camera department to "Roll camera." The camera assistant starts the camera, verifies its status by watching the time code for three seconds, and replies, "Rolling" or "Speed."

5b. **"Lock it down."** Sometimes the first AD will also call out, "Lock it down" to ensure that all objects on the set are "locked down" and will not drop during the take. At this point, everyone must be totally quiet and

move out of frame. This can also be called when the camera is locked down. In some filming situations the camera body needs to be "locked down" (no touching and no movement around the camera) because the focus is critical or the stunt is dangerous so the camera is unmanned.

6. **"Marker."** The first AD signals the clapper loader, or assistant camera (second AC), by saying, "Marker" or "Slate it." The second AC marks the shot by clapping the clapper board, or slate, and announces the scene for editing purposes ("Scene 67, Take 4").

7. **"Action."** The director says, "Action," although a first AD might perform this function if the director prefers it. Only the director is allowed to say, "Cut."

The Low-Budget First AD's Eternal Dilemma: On low-budget productions, the means are often not enough to realize the director's vision. It is the first AD's task to work between the director and heads of department (HODs) to call the necessary compromises when they need to be made, without jeopardizing the integrity of the director's vision. This process can begin as early as the scriptwriting phase, with the AD suggesting such practical compromises as combining sets or reducing the number of story days. The process may progress through to the actual shooting of a scene, at which time the AD may call for the director and the head of photography to refine the blocking of a scene in such a way that it can be adequately shot within the time available. This can be the most indirectly creative an AD gets, and requires great understanding of the conflict between resources and vision. This can prove a useful skill to ADs who move on to produce.

Script Supervisor, or Continuity: A script supervisor, or continuity, is a member of a film crew responsible for maintaining the film's internal continuity and for marking the production unit's daily progress in shooting the film's screenplay. In preproduction, the script supervisor creates a number of reports based on the script, including a one-line continuity synopsis providing basic continuity information on each scene. These reports are used by all departments in order to determine the most advantageous shot order and quantities of supplies, materials, or crew support needed. Example: A character who wears a particular shirt that (in different scenes) progresses from clean to dirty to dirty and torn may require at least three sets of that shirt in order to ensure that continuity can be properly managed.

During production, the script supervisor acts as a central point for all production information on a film shoot, and has several responsibilities.

Script: The working text of the project. The script supervisor is responsible for ensuring that everyone involved has the most current copy of the script. Once the script is finalized, changes are made on a different color of paper. The script supervisor is given any changes, and ensures that they are printed on the correct colored paper and distributed to all necessary parties. This will on many productions lead to a multicolor working script. The actual progression of colors can vary. One such progression is (starting with the original script) white, blue, pink, yellow, green, goldenrod, buff, salmon, cherry, tan, gray, and ivory.

Continuity: The script supervisor takes notes on all the details required to re-create the continuity of a particular scene, location, or action. The supervisor is responsible for making sure that continuity errors do not happen. For every take, the script supervisor will note the duration of the take (usually with a stopwatch), and meticulously log off information about the action of the take, including position of the main actor(s), screen direction of their movement, important actions performed during the shot, type of lens used, and additional information that may vary from case to case. When multiple cameras are in use, the script supervisor keeps separate notes on each. The script supervisor will also keep track of dialogue as it is spoken, and ensure that if it varies from the screenplay, any variation made is known to the director and noted.

Slating: The script supervisor interacts with the second assistant camera (second AC, or clapper loader) and the production sound mixer to make sure that each take of exposed film has a consistent and meaningful slate, and that the sound and picture slates match. The script supervisor also notes the sound roll of each sync take, and the state of all MOS takes (a film take without sound recording: mit out sound).

Lined Script: The script supervisor is responsible for keeping the most current version of the shooting script, and for keeping a copy of it, as the lined script for the shoot. A lined script is a copy of the script with vertical lines drawn down the pages, indicating which takes cover which parts of the script.

Production Reports: The script supervisor is responsible for preparing daily reports for the production team. These reports vary in form depending on the studio or production company; however, they generally include a continuity log; a log of the actual times that shooting and breaks started and stopped; and a breakdown of the pages, scenes, and minutes that were shot that day, as well as the same information for the previous day, the total script, and the amounts remaining to be done. Also included are the number of scenes covered (completely shot), the number of retakes (when a scene has to be reshot), and the number of wild tracks (tracks with sound recorded separately). The AD staff also is responsible for preparing daily production reports regarding scheduling and the crew, noting delays in filming, scenes shot, and payroll (call times and out times), as well as accident reports and actors' times.

Anatomy

Anatomy is a complex field, but we'll concentrate on the areas that Makeup Artists most likely will use as references. The following terms outline only a few of the examples found in the skeletal, muscular, and circulatory systems.

The Skeletal System

The skeleton is divided into the axial and appendicular skeletons. The axial comprises the skull, vertebral column, sternum, and ribs. The appendicular is made up of the upper and lower extremities. The skull consists of cranial bones, which form the cranial cavity. The cranial cavity houses the brain and facial bones, which in turn form the face.

The Skull

Frontal Bone   Bone located at the forehead that helps define the orbits of the eye.

Mandible   Bone that forms the lower jawbone.

Maxilla   The upper jawbone.

Nasal Bones   There are two nasal bones. The vomer bone separates the nasal cavities.

Occipital Bone   Large bone that makes up the base of the cranium.

Zygomatic Arch   Bone that defines the cheekbone.

The Spinal Column

The spinal column is made up of 26 bones. The bones protect the spinal cord. The spinal cord is strong and flexible, allowing movement, supporting the head, and serving as the attachment for the ribs and muscles.

Upper Body

Carpal Bones   Wrist bones.

Clavicle   Collar bone.

Humerus   Upper arm bone.

Metacarpals   Hand bones.

Phalanges   Finger bones.

Radius   One of two lower arm bones. The radius is narrow at the end that connects with the humerus, and wider at the joints that it forms with the wrist bones.

Ribs   Curved bones connected to the thoracic vertebrae.

Scapula   Helps to form the shoulder joint with the humerus.

Sternum   Breast bone.

Ulna   One of two lower arm bones opposite in shape to the radius.

Lower Body

Femur   Thigh bone, the strongest bone in the body.

Fibula   One of two bones that form the lower leg bone. The fibula is the smaller of the two.

Joints   When two or more bones come together to either aid movement and/or to keep the skeleton together.

Metatarsals   Foot bones.

Patella   Knee cap.

Pelvic Bone   Attaches the lower body to the axial skeleton.

Phalanges   Toes.

Tarsals   Ankle bones.

Tibia   One of two bones that form the lower leg bone. The tibia is the larger of the two.

279

The Muscular System

Muscles are described by size, shape, origin, and function. There are over 700 known muscles in the body.

Facial Muscles
Jaw Muscles
Masseter Muscle   Raises the jaw and clenches the teeth.

Temporalis Muscle   Helps the masseter muscle to raise the jaw and clench the teeth.

Mouth Muscles
Buccinator   Draws the corners of the mouth backward, flattens and tightens lips.

Caninus   Raises the corner of the mouth.

Mentalis   Raises and tightens the chin, thrusts lower lip up and outward.

Orbicularis Oris   Circles the mouth and purses the lips.

Risorius   Pulls the corner of the mouth sideward and outward.

Triangularis   Pulls the corner of the mouth downward.

Zygomaticus Major and Minor   Raises the mouth upward and outward.

Eye Muscles
Corrugator   Assists the orbicularis in compressing skin between the eyebrows. Vertical wrinkles form.

Orbicularis Oculi   Closes the eyelids and compresses the opening of the eye from above and below the eyes.

Procerus   Tightens the inner eye by wrinkling the skin on the nose.

Face Muscles
Frontalis Frontal Part   Draws the scalp to the front, wrinkles the forehead, and pulls the eyebrows upward.

Platysma   Muscles on the neck that draw the lower lip downward and upward.

Circulatory System and Veins

The circulatory system is made up of two different systems: the pulmonary (the right side of the heart receives deoxygenated blood from the body and pumps it to the lungs) and the systemic (the left side of the heart receives oxygenated blood from the lungs and sends it to the body; arteries carry blood from the heart to the tissues and organs; veins return the blood to the heart).

Arteries
Aorta   Largest artery in the body.

Brachiocephalic Trunk, Right Carotid, and Right Subclavian Arteries   Provide blood to the neck, head, and upper limbs.

Celiac Trunk, Superior Mesenteric Artery, and Inferior Mesenteric Artery   Supply blood to the abdominal internal organs.

Coronary Arteries   Supply blood to the heart.

Left and Right Common Iliac Arteries   Abdominal aorta divides into left and right common iliac arteries.

Left Carotid, Left Subclavian Arteries   Provide blood to the left side of the head, neck, and upper limbs.

Renal, Suprarenal, and Gonadal Arteries   Provide blood to internal organs at the back of the abdominal wall.

The Veins
Brachiocephalic   One of two veins that form the superior vena cava.

Hepatic Portal Vein   Vein that leads from intestinal veins to the liver.

Inferior Vena Cava   Receives blood from the pelvis, abdomen, and lower limbs.

Internal Jugular   Receives blood from the head and neck area, including the brain.

Portal System   A set of veins that deplete blood from the intestines and the supporting organs.

Splenic Vein   Vein leaving the spleen.

Subclavian   Empties blood from the shoulder area.

Superior Mesenteric   Blood returns to circulation by way of the small intestine.

Superior Vena Cava   Receives blood from the upper body by way of the internal jugular, subclavian, and brachiocephalic veins.

Additional Terms

AD   Assistant director.

Adding color   Mixing pigments to a product.

Additive Color   Adding primary colors to come to white light.

Additive Color Mixing   Color mixing with lights.

Airbrush   A small, air operated tool that sprays various media such as ink, dye, or paint, through the process of atomization.

Air Regulator   Adjusts air pressure.

Alginate   A thickening agent derived from seaweed and giant kelp that absorbs water quickly and is used as a mold-making material in makeup effects and prosthetics, life-casting, and textiles.

Analogous   Colors next to each other on the color wheel.

Atomization   To reduce to fine particles or spray.

Background   Background artists (actors) or extras working in a scene.

Black   Absence of all color.

Blank Out   To start with a blank canvas.

Blending   Applying makeup using tools to achieve a smooth seamless finish.

Bloom   The strength or rigidity of the brand of gelatin.

Bondo   Cab-O-Sil (silica) that is mixed with Pros-Aide to form a thick paste.

Brightness   Percentage of transmission of the full spectrum of energy.

Bull Pen   Working the line with many other makeup artists painting for the crowds with little time to do it.

Cab-O-Sil   A silica substance that is mixed with Pros-Aide (adhesive) to form a thick paste.

Cast   Actors appearing in the scenes.

Casting   To assign an actor a role.

Casting   To form (metal, plaster, rubber, etc.) into a particular shape by pouring it into or brushing it onto a mold, while it is in a fluid or liquid state, and letting it harden.

Center of Gravity   The point of the body that dictates where the weight is distributed.

CFM   Measurement of airflow.

Characters   Names of the characters that the actors will be playing.

Chavant NSP Clay   Sculpting clay.

Chiaroscuro   An Italian term meaning light dark. The term originated as a type of Renaissance drawing on colored paper.

Chief Makeup Artist   What a makeup department head is called in Europe.

Closed set   Means there are no visitors allowed on the film set.

Complementary   Any colors 180 degrees apart on a 360-degree color wheel.

Complementary Colors for Light   Complementary colors are also called secondary colors.

Contour   Darker colors that are applied to any area the Makeup Artist wants to set back.

Correction Filters   To balance a given light source.

Crew Call   Time the crew is called into work.

Cure   A chemical process that allows materials such as plaster, rubber, and gelatin to change from a liquid or fluid state to a solid form.

Dark and Halftones   Halftones divided into light and dark.

Deadener   Smith's (Gordon J.) Prosthetic Deadener is an additive designed to work in concert with Platsil Gel-10 (or any platinum silicone) to create a complete theatrical prosthetic design system for the motion picture industry (www.fxsmith.com).

Demold   Taking hardened product out of a mold.

Digital   Using data in the form of numerical digits in a computerized format.

Digital Cinematography   When film is substituted with a digital format for recording images.

Digital Motion Pictures   Images that are captured and stored in a digital format, in this case motion pictures.

Digital Photography   Images captured in a digital format that records the images and stores them on a computer chip, until they are to be printed or viewed on a screen or monitor.

Digital Television   Pictures and sound that are captured and stored in a digital format for recording, viewing, and/or broadcasting images.

D/N   Means day or night on a call sheet.

Dominant Wavelength   Apparent color of the Light.

Dot Method   Placing dots instead of straight lines in makeup application. For example to create a stronger lash line.

DP   Director of photography.

Dual Tone   A pigment that changes hue from mass tone (pure color straight from a tube or powder) to top tone (adding white to a color).

Extra   Background actor or artist.

Fairy Soap   A brand-name, gentle bar soap for hygiene, used widely in Europe and can be used to clean molds and/or prosthetics.

Foundation Primers   Makeup used to even out the texture of the skin.

Gaffer   Lighting designer.

Gel Filters   Filters are used in front of a light source to change what the light is putting out.

Gelatin   A colorless protein formed by boiling the skin, bones, and connective tissue of animals to form a glue-like substance, used by makeup artists for a variety of reasons, such as mold-making.

Green Marble SeLr   A makeup sealer created by Kenny Myers and Richard Snell for Premiere Products.

Half tones   All of the value (degree of lightness or darkness) variations in a color.

High-Definition Television or HDTV   Television broadcast using higher resolution formats.

Highlight   Lighter colors that are applied to any area the Makeup Artist wants to have stand out.

Holding and Catering   Where the extras are being held, and where the food is located on a film set.

Hue   Any color in reference to the color spectrum and/or a gradation or variety of shades of a color tint.

Imaginary axis   An imaginary axis used by artists to determine where the weight of the body changes.

Licensed Aestheticians   Expert in skin care.

Makeup Department Head   The person in charge of designing and running the makeup department.

Mass Tone   Color right out of the tube or pure powder pigment.

Mattifying Products   Products that are made to take down shine.

Media   Plural for medium used in fine arts to refer to the material or technique with which an artist works, and/or a liquid with which pigments are mixed.

Moisture Filter   A filter for the purpose of removing water from air.

Monochromatic   Any color mixed with white. The various shades of a single color.

Nitrile Gloves   Gloves made of nitrile rubber, a synthetic rubber resistant to fuel, oil, and other chemicals. Nitrile gloves can be worn when working with platinum-addition RTV silicone (used in prosthetic making) since they will not react negatively with the silicone.

Oil Filter   A filter made for the purpose of removing oil from air.

Opaque   Not transparent (see-through/clear glass) nor translucent (semi-see-through/frosted glass); not allowing light to pass through.

On the Clock   Official time record of work being done for payment.

Pantone 187C   A brand name paint color created by Pantone, Inc., using their Pantone Matching System for creating specific colors for various uses, such as painting prosthetics.

PAX Paint   Acrylic paint mixed with Pros-Aide adhesive used for painting prosthetic appliances.

Plasteline Clay   A type of modeling clay that can be used in mold-making.

Platsil Gel-10   A fast-curing rubber that can be used as an adhesive to adhere a prosthetic to the skin.

Poly Fiber II   A brand-name compound used to thicken polyurethane rubbers and plastics for making brushed molds and shells. The level of thickening can be easily controlled to make thin gels to thicker pastes.

Pot Life   The open or working time for how long you can manipulate a material before it starts to set or cure (harden).

Primary Color   Three primary colors that can be mixed together to make all other colors.

Pros-Aide   A prosthetic adhesive.

PSI   Pounds per square inch, a measurement of air pressure.

Purity   The intensity of a distinctive hue or saturation of a color. Similar to chroma, which is the purity of a color or its freedom from white or gray.

Rays   A wave of radiant energy in the form of beams of light, such as ultraviolet rays.

RCW Color Wheel   In Don Jusko's color wheel, every color has an opposite color to be used in mixing neutral darks.

Reflected Light   A light source that is produced by bouncing off of objects in the surrounding environment.

Releases   Products that help to remove cast items from their mold.

Removers   Products that come in many different formulas used to remove adhesives, eye makeup, or a variety of makeup applications.

SC#   Scene numbers in the script.

Secondary Colors   Colors made by mixing together two primary colors.

Secondary Colors in Light   The combination of two primary colors.

Set Call   The time that stand-ins and background actors report to the set.

Shadow   When a form turns away from the light source, half-tones become darker until the light completely goes away.

Silicone   Inert, synthetic compounds with a variety of forms and uses. Typically, heat-resistant and rubber-like, used in sealants, adhesives, lubricants, cosmetics, and so on.

Smith's Prosthetic Deadener   A prosthetic additive developed by the special effects Makeup Designer, Gordon J. Smith, as part of Smith's Prosthetic System (see *Deadener*).

Soft Box   A photographic lighting device used to create a soft, diffused (made less brilliant) light by directing light through a diffusing material, or by bouncing light off a second surface.

SPF   Sun protection factor.

Spot Paint   A technique used to balance out the skin tone.

Stippling   To use an up-and-down motion while applying makeup with a brush, sponge, or textured sponge.

Stipple sponges   Textured sponges used for different stippling effects.

Superior Mesenteric   Blood returns to circulation by way of the small intestine.

Swinging   Caused by the center of gravity being shifted from one leg to another.

Textures   The surface properties of a color.

Thinners   Thinners are products made to thin adhesive products.

Tints   Adding white to any hue.

Top Tone   Adding white to a color.

Translucent   Permitting light to pass through but diffusing it so that persons, objects, and so on on the opposite side are not clearly visible (e.g., frosted glass).

Transparent   Easily seen through; having the property of transmitting rays of light through its substance so that bodies or objects situated beyond or behind can be distinctly seen (e.g., clear glass). Dyes that are clear.

Triadic   Any three colors that are 120 degrees apart on the color wheel.

Undertone   Adding clear media.

UVA Rays   Light rays that penetrate the surface of the skin and damage the connective tissue.

UVB Rays   Light rays that cause damage to the surface of the skin such as burning.

Vertical Axis   The centerline that correctly defines proportions of the facial features when the head is moved in different angles.

Value   Refers to the tone (tonal value) which is the degree of lightness or darkness of a color, as it appears on object.

White   The presence of all colors in the light.

Working Out of Your Kit   An expression used by Makeup Artists to refer to the products that they will be using from their own makeup kit.

Wrap   Term called by the assistant director at completion of the day's filming.

Books

Alex Box, by Rankin

Art of Makeup, The, by Kevyn Aucoin

Atlas of Clinical Dermatology, by Anthony du Vivier

Atlas of Clinical Gross Anatomy, by Kenneth P. Moses, John C. Banks, Pedro B. Nava, and Darrell Peterson

Atlas of Pathophysiology, published by Lippincott, Williams & Wilkins

Beauty of Color, The, by Iman

Bloom Book, by Li Edelkoort and LisaWhite

Body Painting: Masterpieces, by Joanne Gair and Heidi Klum

Brown Skin, by Susan C. Taylor

Clinical Dermatology, by Thomas P. Habif

Color Atlas of Forensic Pathology, by Jay Dix

Costuming for Film: The Art and the Craft, by Holly Cole and Kristin Burke

Crew Freelancing 101: A Guide to Building a Career in Film and TV Production, by Gena Seif

Cyclopedia Anatomicae, by György Fehrér and András Szunyoghy

Digital Cinematography, by Paul Wheeler

Don't Go to the Cosmetics Counter without Me, 6th ed., by Paula Begoun

Face Forward, by Kevyn Aucoin

Fashions in Makeup: From Ancient to Modern Times, by Richard Corson

Fine Beauty, by Sam Fine

Forensic Pathology, by David J. Williams, Anthony J. Ansford, David S. Priday, and Alex S. Forrest

Milady's Skin Care and Cosmetics Ingredients Dictionary, by Natalia Michalun and M. Varinia Michalun

Milady's Standard: Fundamentals for Estheticians, by Joel Gerson, Shelley Lotz, and Janet D'Angelo

Serge Lutens, by Serge Lutens

Skin Care Beyond the Basics, by Mark Lees

Stage Makeup, 10th Edition, by Richard Corson

Vintage Face, by Angela Bjork and Daniela Turudich

Magazines

Hollywood Reporter, www.hollywoodreporter.com

Make-Up Artist Magazine, www.makeupmag.com

Make-Up Artist International, www.makeupinternational.eu

Web sites

www.9mmsfx.com

www.a-squirrel.com

www.adacosmetics.com

www.airbrushmakeup.com

www.anatomical.com

www.badgerairbrush.com

www.beautyhabit.com

285

www.beccacosmetics.com

www.benefitcosmetics.com

www.bennye.com

www.blackminerals.com

www.blincinc.com (lash primer)

www.bluescreen.com

www.bobbibrowncosmetics.com

www.braun.com

www.Brushupwithbarbara.com

www.burmanfoam.com

www.cinemasecrets.com

www.clinique.com

www.cm-beauty.com

www.cosmeticmall.com

www.creativeartistryfx.com

www.dangheno.net

www.Danielamakeup.com

www.dhccare.com

www.dickblick.com

www.dow.com (product information)

www.edwardfrench.com

www.eefx.com

www.eeyelash.com

www.flaxart.com

www.folica.com (brushes, tools, etc.)

www.fxsmith.com (Smith's Prosthetic System)

www.fxsupply.com

www.fxwarehouse.com (products)

www.gaenterprises.net

www.gerdaspillmann.com

www.getspfx.com (adhesive information)

www.greatfacecafe.com

www.gretchendavismakeup.com

www.hakuhodousa.com (brushes)

www.hollynorth.com

www.Ilfordphoto.com

www.imancosmetics.com

www.imdb.com (professional film site for production information, résumés)

www.immune.com (chemical reaction information)

www.indeutsch.com (brushes)

www.japonesque.com

www.jcerilla.com

www.joeblasco.com

www.kanebo.com

www.kd151.com (blood products, effects)

www.kettcosmetics.com

www.kiehls.com

www.lancome-usa.com

www.lauramercier.com

www.loraccosmetics.com

www.maccosmetics.com

www.macpro.com

www.makeupartistschoice.com (brushes)

www.makeupcreations.com (brushes)

www.makeupforever.com

www.makeupmania.com

www.mallatts.com (products)

www.marshallelectronics.com

www.mehron.com

www.michelemulkeyfx.com

www.monsterfx.net

www.monstermakers.com

www.murad.com

www.narcosmetics.com

www.occmakeup.com

www.oshunsupply.com (oils, chemicals, clays, salts, botanicals, etc.)

www.paascheairbrush.com

www.paintandpowderstore.com

www.pauladorf.com

www.paulwheelerbsc.com (HD cameras, crews, technical information)

www.photocrew.com

www.ppi.com

www.prosanity.com

www.psdaimaandsons.com (brushes)

www.realcolorwheel.com

www.reynoldsam.com

www.rdean1028@mac.com

www.rickysnyc.com (beauty supply, NYC)

www.robert@robertrevels.com

www.ronjo.com (products)

www.screamteam.com (masks)

www.screenface.com

www.sculpt.com

www.sephora.com

www.shopofhorrors.com (effects)

www.smooth-on.com

www.solomakeup.com (brushes)

www.stagesupply.com

www.takeupmakeup.co

www.temptu.com

www.topshop.com

www.vwr.com (international chemical supplies)

www.worldwidebeautystore.com

Darla Albright

Emmy Award winner and Makeup Artist, Darla Albright, has worked on numerous TV, film, and music industry events. Her credits include the Academy and Emmy Awards, department heading, and working on the hit TV series *Scrubs*, *Justice*, *That '70s Show*, *General Hospital*, *Ghost Whisperer*, and *The Riches*. Her film work includes *The Good Girl*, starring Jake Gyllenhaal; *Dr. Dolittle 2*; and working with Tyra Banks on *Coyote Ugly*. Darla has also toured the world with her personal client, Neil Diamond, for all of his stage, TV, and personal appearances.

Matiki Anoff

Matiki Anoff is a native of Ghana, West Africa, educated in England, and currently resides in New York. After graduating from the University of Arts in London, England, she embarked on a career in fashion and editorial makeup in Europe; working on spreads for *Vogue*, *MariClaire*, and *Elle* magazines.

Matiki moved to New York to pursue her passion, working on feature films. After a few years in the independent film world, she had a chance meeting with director Spike Lee; that meeting led her to her 20-plus years as a makeup artist in film.

Currently, Matiki also designs the HD makeup for the world's leading sopranos for the New York Metropolitan Opera HD Live Performances, which are viewed throughout the world.

Lars Carlsson

Lars Carlsson is the Department Head of the Wig and Makeup Department for Folkteatern Theatre and the owner of the Makeup-FX company in Gothenburg, Sweden. He has been working professionally since 1989. His early career started in amateur theatre and local TV in his hometown of Boras, Sweden. Lars continued with formal training in an apprenticeship at Gothenburg City Theatre, Gothenburg, Sweden.

Lars continues to freelance as a Makeup Artist, Special Effects Makeup Artist, and Wig Maker with his company, Makeup-FX—all while maintaining his on-staff position at the theatre. His many credits include film, television, print, theatre, and opera, and he is an experienced lecturer and educator.

J.C. Cerilla

J.C. Cerrilla was born and raised in Manila, Philippines. He studied in an art school which eventually introduced him to the world of photography. Fascinated by the craft he made a career out of it. At the age of just 22 years, he was already shooting for magazines such as *Cosmopolitan* and *Playboy* in the Philippines.

Not wanting to settle for mediocrity, J.C. moved to New York and was able to assist photographer, Andrea Blanch, a protégé of the legendary photographer, Richard Avedon. J.C. is now doing freelance work and concentrates on commercial beauty and fashion photography.

Richard Dean

Richard Dean has painted some of the most unforgettable faces in the world, including Nicole Kidman, Uma Thurman, Madonna, Eva Mendes, Amber Valletta, Demi Moore, Glenn Close, Diane Lane, Tom Cruise, Michael Douglas, and Bruce Willis. Richard has collaborated with Julia Roberts on 16 movies—from *Sleeping with the Enemy* and *My Best Friend's Wedding* through *Erin Brockovich*, *Closer*, and, most recently, *Charlie Wilson's War*. Richard's first movie experience was on the tiny independent film, *Union City*, starring Deborah Harry. Currently, he is shooting *Baby Mama* with Tina Fey in New York. With a master's degree from the University of Michigan focused on theatrical design, Richard began doing makeup in the fashion and print arena before moving on to television and then 50-some feature films—among them *Desperately Seeking Susan*, *The Cotton Club*, *Something Wild*, *Fatal Attraction*, *Mona Lisa Smile*, and *Hitch*.

Kenneth Diaz

When Kenny Diaz was young, his father would go all out for Halloween. He would make Kenny and his younger brothers very elaborate costumes. That paved the way for Kenny to make costumes for kids in the neighborhood, and even winning an award for his efforts. Who knew that would lead to an exciting career working extensively as one of the top Makeup Artists in the motion picture industry today? Kenny has two Academy Award nominations and is a two-time Emmy Award winner. He is founder of K.D. 151 Blood Products, an industry standard. Kenny had a special interest in pyrotechnics after watching a television special on the subject. He inquired about pyrotechnics classes at schools located in the Los Angeles area. He enrolled in a makeup school, finding no other avenues that could help him. This included classes in Salon

Makeup! By the end of the one-year course, Kenny knew he would become a Makeup Artist for the entertainment industry. He continued his career working for student and independent films such as *Roar*, starring Tippi Hedren and her daughter, Melanie Griffith. After the film completed, Diaz became an instructor, developing the skills and confidence that have contributed to his success today.

Daniela Eschbacher

Daniela Eschbacher is one of today's newest Makeup Artists. She lives in Paris, and works for international magazines and commercials in places such as Switzerland, Germany, Sweden, Holland, England, Austria, and Japan. She started out assisting various artists before branching out on her own projects with photographers, stylists, and independent movies. Daniela has always been fascinated by photography, fashion, and the creation of illusion. After graduating from Economy High School, she went to Vienna to become experienced in hairdressing and acquire a degree. At the age of 20, Daniela moved to Paris and attended an international artist's school. By this time, she had already started to work with established Makeup Artists and Hairstylists. Daniela's work has been featured by such publications as *Make-Up Artist Magazine*.

Kris Evans

For over 20 years, Kris Evans has created unique makeup designs in the world of entertainment. Kris has worked on everything from *Saturday Night Live* to large production films, creating characters in such movies as *X-Men: The Last Stand* and *National Treasure*. She has also used her skills on Broadway in *The Phantom of the Opera*. Kris is used to traveling worldwide in the NBC Olympic broadcast team or for couture runway shows and fashion shoots.

Kim Felix-Burke

Kim Felix-Burke grew up in the film business. She wanted to be a fashion illustrator, but her stepfather, Ed Levy, a successful film producer, suggested that Kim try makeup instead, reasoning that "[p]ainting a face is just another form of a canvas." This sent Kim off to basic training at the Joe Blasco School in Los Angeles. Kim was fortunate to continue her education in makeup by working for some of the great "old-timers" in Hollywood. Twenty years later she still loves "slinging dirt" and "primping pretty faces." Kim lives in the Los Angeles area with her family.

Dan Gheno

Dan Gheno teaches and lives in New York City. Professor emeritus at the Lyme Academy College of Fine Arts in Old Lyme, Connecticut, he lectures and teaches at The Art Student League and the National Academy School in New York City. Dan has been featured in numerous national and international publications, including *American Artist*, *Drawing*, and *Drawing Highlights*. Gheno studied at Santa Barbara Art Institute, Art Students League, and National Academy of Design. His work is featured in exhibits nationally and in the collections of several museums.

Steven Horak

Steven Horak graduated with degrees in vocal performance from Washington State University and the Cincinnati College-Conservatory of Music, intending a career as an opera singer, but always having an interest in and an affinity for the field of theatrical makeup and wigs. Steven began singing for Detroit's Michigan Opera Theatre (MOT) in the old-man roles often assigned to young bass-baritones, "doing my own makeup in all cases, as no real makeup department existed." Observing that he appeared to have some talent in this area, the company offered to pay a large portion of his tuition to the San Francisco Opera (SFO) Wig and Makeup Training Program, on the condition that he return to MOT and establish a department for them. After receiving his certificate from the program, which was led by SFO's Wigmaster, Richard Stead, he fulfilled his commitment to MOT and returned to Detroit to accept the staff position, which he held for 12 seasons. During the off-season, he represented several wig and makeup companies (Theatrical Hairgoods Co., Bruce Geller Associates, and Tom Watson Associates) at opera companies across the nation, including the Greater Miami Opera, Opera Co. of Philadelphia, and Opera Theatre of St. Louis, among many others. He also began building his own wig stock and client list, which included the Chicago Opera Theatre. In 1994, a staff position in the Makeup Department at the Metropolitan Opera was offered. He continues to do wig rentals and wig building, most notably for Studio EIS, a company in Brooklyn that fabricates realistic human figures to museums across the United States, including the recent, extensive exhibit illustrating the life of George Washington at Mount Vernon, Virginia. He also takes one summer opera job in the NYC area each year, where he hones his skills at cranking out full makeups, including wig application, in 10 to 15 minutes, recalling his early days "on the line" at SFO.

Don Jusko

Don Jusko was an artist before art college. After college in 1962, during the Cuban Crisis, Don was a part of Naval Photo Squadron VFP-62, based in Jacksonville, Florida. After four years in the Navy, he worked as the Art Director for an advertising agency in Jacksonville. He then opened his own agency in San Francisco. For the past 30 years, he has been painting Maui scenes on location, capturing the island's history. Don's work continues to be admired by all. While painting on location with his own choice of transparent primary pigments, the Real Color Wheel was born. By 1996, a printed copy was being sold on the Internet. Today, his color site garners 1.7 million hits a month, with free printable downloads of his color wheel. This color wheel has given artists the ability to paint natural-looking dark shadow colors by mixing real color oppositions together and not using black pigment.

Devon Keene

Devon Keene is a current student and working artist originally from Tampa, Florida. She is currently a junior studying at Ringling College of Art and Design located in Sarasota, Florida, where she will receive her degree in fine arts. Devon works in various mediums, most commonly sculpture, painting, and photography. Since she first started out using photographic mediums, most of her work is heavily influenced by the image. She is involved in various artistic organizations and her work has been exhibited in a variety of shows throughout Sarasota, Florida.

Erwin H. Kupitz

Erwin Kupitz is a professional Hairstylist, Wig Maker, and Makeup Artist, with more than 25 years of experience in the fields of opera, theater, film, media, and management. He has been the owner of the wig-making business Custom Made Hair Goods for the past 12 years. Erwin is the president and founder of Cimuha, Inc., which has been in operation for the past three years. He is also the Designer of Hair Replacement, EHK, for the hair-replacement company J.A. Alternatives, Inc., located in New York and New Jersey. Erwin completed his education and corresponding apprenticeships in Germany. In addition, he has expanded his professional training by attending workshops

and seminars at various institutions in the following fields: special effects makeup, hair coloring, and modern hair-cutting techniques. Erwin's professional affiliations include membership in the Chamber of Handcrafts, Germany, and the IATSE Local Makeup Artists of Hollywood. Erwin embarked on his career in Europe, and from 1982 to 1992 held the positions of Makeup Artist, Principal Makeup Artist, Wigmaster, Vice Department Head, and Department Head in performing-arts productions ranging from the Bavarian State Opera and Theatre in Munich, Germany, and the Royal Opera in Belgium to the Salzburg Festival in Austria. From the onset of his professional work in the United States in 1992 to the present, Erwin has had a prolific career that has encompassed the following: 59 major motion pictures (including Academy Award–winning films *Forrest Gump*, *Titanic*, and *Dreamgirls*), 22 television shows, and eight stage productions. Erwin received Emmy nominations in 1994–1995 for Outstanding Achievement in Hairstyles for a Mini Series (*In Search of Dr. Seuss*, TNT), and in 1998–1999 for Outstanding Achievement in Makeup for a Television Series (*Buffy the Vampire Slayer*, FOX TV). The list of accomplished actors who Erwin has worked with include Academy Award winners, screen legends, and contemporaries such as Jack Nicholson, Shirley MacLaine, Warren Beatty, Sir Anthony Hopkins, Angelina Jolie, Anthony Quinn, Diane Lane, Michael Caine, Patrick Stewart, Gene Hackman, Diahann Carroll, Edward Norton, Plácido Domingo, Jane Seymour, Hugh Jackman, Andy Garcia, James Woods … and the list goes on and on. Erwin's body of work reflects his flexibility to traverse the diverse media of the performing arts with a degree of technical expertise and professional experience that future Makeup Artists and Hairstylists can respect and aspire to in their own careers.

Bradley M. Look

Emmy winner for *Star Trek: Voyager* ("Threshold" episode) and eight times nominated, Makeup Artist Bradley Look has written numerous articles on makeup, including co-writing the book *Star Trek Aliens & Artifacts*. Born in Peoria, Illinois, Brad now lives in Southern California, where he works in the entertainment industry. Besides teaching The Art of Film and Television Makeup at national and international universities, Brad has worked on productions such as *Pirates of the Caribbean: At World's End, The Santa Claus 3: The Escape Clause, Boston Legal, Poseidon, Star Trek: Deep Space Nine, Star Trek: Voyager,* and *Star Trek*—just to name a few.

Gil Mosko

Gil Mosko, president of GM Foam, Inc., created GM Foam in 1987 to meet the needs of the Makeup Artist for a more user-friendly foam latex. Gil Mosko has numerous awards, including 10 Emmy nominations, and five Emmy Awards for Outstanding Achievement in Makeup for a Series. He was also director of the Star Trek Makeup Lab. Mosko has developed foam latex, which has become the standard of the industry. He started his career with a major in environmental biology and a minor in chemistry at the University of Colorado. From there, he worked at Mattel Toymakers for two years as a designer in the Preliminary Design Department. For the next 15 years, Gil owned and operated Gil Mosko Pottery and worked as director at R&D Nearly Me Corp., holding patents for revolutionary designs for prostheses for mastectomy patients.

Michele Mulkey

Michele Mulkey has been a special effects Makeup Artist and prop maker for over 11 years, working in both Los Angeles and New York City. While attending college in Pennsylvania, Michele discovered her love of makeup while taking independent study classes for theatre makeup with her mentor, Professor Brenda C. Eppley. Upon receiving her degree in the performing arts/theatre, Michele moved to California to continue her professional training as a Makeup Artist through classes at Make-Up Designory. Starting her career in Los Angeles, Michele honed her skills working both in-house and on-set for many special effects shops, including Keith Vanderlaan's Captive Audience, Crisis FX, Alterian, Inc., and Film Illusions.

Working out of her own Special Effects shop and traveling back and forth between Los Angeles and New York City, Michele continues to work as a special effects Makeup Artist and prop maker in film, television, and theatre, as well as serving as a member of the faculty for Make-Up Designory's New York campus. Michele's credits have a combined total of over 34 feature films and television shows, including *Petunia, The Last Samurai, The Chronicles of Riddick, Venom, Son of the Mask, Blood Junkies, Charmed, C.S.I. Miami, Joss Whedon's Firefly, Law and Order: Criminal Intent*, and the Off-Broadway production of *Beast*.

Matthew Mungle

Academy Award and Emmy Award winner Matthew W. Mungle is regarded as one of Hollywood's premier special effects Makeup Artists. With over 100 film and television projects to his credit, Matthew has earned accolades and recognition as one of the industry's top masters of makeup illusion. Born in Durant, Oklahoma in 1956, Matthew was one of five children. As a boy, he was fascinated by makeup. Matthew credits the film *7 Faces of Dr. Lao* as a factor in him deciding to become a Makeup Effects Artist. In 1978, Matthew applied to and was accepted into Joe Blasco's Makeup Center, the premier academy responsible for training many of the film and television industries' elite Makeup Artists. Matthew's impressive list of film, television, and theater credits include the box office hits *The Perfect Storm*, *Bedazzled*, *The Polar Express*, *The Omen*, *X-Men*, *The X Files*, *CSI: Miami*, *Six Feet Under*, *The Fast and the Furious*, and the Broadway hit *Wicked*—just to name a few. Matthew, founder of W.M. Creations, Inc., along with John E. Jackson, has developed products for the Makeup Artist that no one should be without. Matthew wanted to give the working Makeup Artist a chance to create and buy products he would use himself. Matthew continues to educate and influence new Makeup Artists today worldwide.

Kenny Myers

Nominated twice for Emmy Awards and Department Head on the Academy Award–nominated picture, *Star Trek VI: The Undiscovered Country*, Kenny Myers has mastered many projects and has had many successes over the years. Kenny graduated from William Paterson College in 1976 with a master's degree in communication arts-theatrical design. In 1976, Kenny moved to Los Angeles and began to work as an apprentice to Chris Walas. During the past 20 years, Kenny has been involved with many pictures, including *The Prestige*, *X-Men: The Last Stand*, *War of the Worlds*, *Collateral*, *The Last Samurai*, *Home Alone*, *Star Trek*, *Back to the Future Part III*, *The Return of the Living Dead*, and *Austin Powers: The Spy Who Shagged Me*. In 1999, Kenny, in conjunction with his company Cine Makeup, Inc., created an effects makeup line of highly pigmented flesh tone inks called Skin Illustrator. Shortly after, Kenny teamed with industry manufacturer Premiere Products, Inc., and is continually expanding the product line. Kenny was truly honored when asked to become a member of the Academy of Motion Picture Arts and Sciences.

Dina Ousley

Over the past 15 years, Dina Ousley, president and founder of Dinair Airbrush Makeup Systems, Inc., has guided and directed the development of a sprayable glamour makeup and glamour makeup application system. Of even more significance, during that time, she pioneered "the new art of airbrush makeup." The artistic makeup techniques she has developed go far beyond the boundaries of traditional application, and more fluently and vividly express the Makeup Artist vision. The new art of micropointillism makeup is a futuristic version of pointillism where one dot of color at a time is applied to depict images. The 15-year proving ground for the makeup and techniques occurred during her work as a Hollywood Makeup Artist. Over the past 20 years she has worked on feature films, TV specials, national and regional commercials, music videos, and star still-photo shoots. Her Makeup Artist career followed her earlier career as a film and television actress.

Cristina Patterson

Born in Madrid, Spain, Cristina Patterson came to Los Angeles at the age of one. Cristina was introduced to the film industry by her mother, Raffaelle Butler, a Hollywood Makeup Artist. Following her mother's example, Cristina dove into makeup for motion pictures. In 1995, she joined Professional Vision Care Associates as a Contact Lens Technician. In 2002, Cristina was promoted to Special Effects Coordinator. She is now designing and painting contact lenses for film and television, and prosthetic lenses for patients. Cristina is an accomplished, self-taught painter in the fine arts. She is always working to find new ways to paint contact lenses.

Robert Revels

Robert Revels graduated from the Academy of Art University with a BFA in illustration. Robert has worked in the illustration and graphics industry since 1994. Mr. Revels has worked on a variety of projects ranging from children's stories to large concert backdrops for artists such as Carlos Santana and U2. Since graduating from the Academy, he has garnered numerous awards. Revels was chosen as one of two artists to represent the Academy in the San Francisco International Arts Festival. He was also the recipient of a Judges Choice Award from the San Francisco and New York Society of Illustrators annual shows. He is also the founder of the greeting card company, Rockfish Designs. Mr. Revels has returned to teach at his alma mater to give back to the next generation of artists.

Christien Tinsley

Christien Tinsley is an Academy Award–nominated Makeup Artist who grew up in Auburn, Washington. At the age of 21, Tinsley moved to Los Angeles after receiving his first job as an effects artist. Working at Steve Johnson's FX Shop, Christien developed a range of materials and was soon overseeing and supervising effects for several films. Tinsley's first union job was applying prosthetics to Clint Howard in *How the Grinch Stole Christmas*. Tinsley continued on to his next film, *Pearl Harbor*, which ultimately launched his signature product, Tinsley Transfers. Christien developed "prosthetic transfers" when creating the look for Jesus in *The Passion of the Christ*. Today, Tinsley Transfers, Inc., has emerged into a leading provider of tattoos and prosthetic transfers effects for some of Hollywood's biggest stars, including Brad Pitt, George Clooney, Vin Diesel, and Justin Timberlake. Tinsley accredits his influences to such individuals as Rick Baker, Greg Cannom, Steve Johnson, Rob Bottin, and Dick Smith.

Joseph N. Tawil

Joseph N. Tawil is founder and president of GAM Products, Inc., the Los Angeles–based theatrical lighting and special-effects company. He is a graduate of Carnegie Mellon University, a fellow of the United States Institute of Theater Technology, and an associate member of the American Society of Cinematographers. Tawil has authored a dozen articles on lighting that have been published in industry trade journals. He often guest lectures at universities on the subject of color, and is a frequent speaker for the International Photographers Guild about color measurement. Tawil holds more than a dozen patents in the lighting field, and has created many special-effects and projection devices (including the patented Film/FX and SX4 film loop) that have become standard production tools for the entertainment industry. They include the first deep-dyed polyester color filter, the first off-the-shelf, stainless-steel pattern, and Black Wrap, the original, for which he received an Academy of Television Arts & Sciences Award.

Nancy Tozier

Nancy Tozier went to Salem State University, majoring in psychology. She attended cosmetology school in Massachusetts. In the 1980s, she owned her own spa and managed another spa with 22 styling chairs, heading the makeup and skin care department. Nancy graduated from the Catherine Hinds Institute in Woburn, Massachusetts in 1989, valedictorian and winner of the Marietta Hinds Award. She has studied the art of skin tones, color theory, and skin care with mentors such as Glen Lockhart of Bion Research Skin Care, James Vincent, and Nancy Feliciano. Tozier is a respected educator and innovator.

Kazuhiro "Kazu" Tsuji

Kazuhiro Tsuji was born in Kyoto, Japan. Throughout his childhood he was interested in art, movies, science, and technology. Later Kazuhiro started corresponding with Dick Smith (*Amadeus*, *The Exorcist*, and *The Godfather*). After Tsuji graduated, Smith invited him to work on the Japanese film, *Sweet Home*. Tsuji started his own business and has worked on numerous Japanese movies including *Rhapsody in August*, directed by Akira Kurosawa (*Seven Samurai*, *Ran*, *Yojimbo*). Tsjui has also taught makeup at the Yoyogi Animation Institute.

In 1996 he was sponsored by Rick Baker (*An American Werewolf in London*, *The Nutty Professor*) to work on *Men In Black*. This started the collaboration between Tsuji (as project supervisor and makeup artist) and Baker that has lasted over 10 years. The projects include *Batman and Robin*, *The Devil's Advocate*, *Mighty Joe Young*, *Nutty Professor II*, *How the Grinch Stole Christmas*, *Planet of the Apes*, *Men In Black II*, *The Ring*, *Hellboy*, *Norbit* and many more. Tsuji also won a BAFTA award for *How the Grinch Stole Christmas*, and was nominated for *Planet of the Apes*. He won the Hollywood Makeup Artist and Hair Stylist Guild Awards for *Planet of the Apes* and *How the Grinch Stole Christmas*. He received an Oscar nomination for *Click* and an Oscar nomination for *Norbit*.

Tsuji started his own company, KTS Effects, Inc., in 2007. Tsuji continues to be one of the top respected Makeup Artists for designing and executing exciting and new makeup techniques.

Paul Wheeler

Renowned cinematographer, director of photography, and writer are only just the start of a list of titles that outline Paul Wheeler's career. He was twice nominated by BAFTA for a Best Cinematography Award, and has twice been the winner of the Indie Award for Best Digital Cinematography. Paul is the author of several popular books on cinematography. He also lectures at establishments such as The London International Film School and the Royal College of the Arts. He is a member of the Guild of British Camera Technicians, a Fellow of the British Kinematograph, Sound and Television Society, and a Member of the British Society of Cinematographers.

Patty York

Patty York wanted to be involved in movie making since she was a little girl. Being a big dreamer, movies activated her imagination; she was a natural at creatively expressing herself. Patty worked as a commercial artist in her early years, moving to New York City where she worked with fashion designers, all the while stimulating her lifelong obsession with the beauty industry. A need to generate more income in New York City sent Patty back to school to earn a degree in business. Patty became a "suit." The stagnation was killing her spirit and she craved and missed being creative; she woke up one day to realize that being a suit was not her! Time to put her brush strokes to a living breathing canvas. She appreticed with several professional Makeup Artists in New York City, learning everything she could from them. She worked as a print Makeup Artist before moving to Hollywood to pursue her dream. With additional training in the film industry to fine tune her instincts as an artist, she learned film techniques and set protocol. Today, Patty still lives in Los Angeles, and enjoys a successful career as a makeup department head and personal Makeup Artist to the stars!

International Alliance of Theatrical and Stage Employees (IATSE): Theatrical Stage Employees, Moving Picture Technicians, Artists, and Allied Crafts of the United States, its Territories, and Canada, AFL-CIO.

The IATSE is the labor union representing technicians, artisans, and craftspeople in the entertainment industry, including live theater, motion picture and television production, and trade shows.

LOCAL 706: Makeup Artists and Hair Stylists
828 N. Hollywood Way
Burbank, CA 91505
Tel: 818-295-3933
info@ialocal706.org
Web site: www.local706.org

LOCAL 798: Make-Up Artists and Hair Stylists
152 West 24th St.
New York, NY 10011
Tel: 212-627-0660

Note: Page numbers followed by *b* indicate boxes and *f* indicate figures.

INDEX

301

305

INDEX

THE MUD PONY

A traditional Skidi Pawnee tale

Retold by Caron Lee Cohen

Illustrated by Shonto Begay

SCHOLASTIC INC.
New York Toronto London Auckland Sydney

Acknowledgments

THE MUD PONY is one of a number of ancient boy-hero stories told among the Skidi band of the Pawnee Indians of the American Plains. These stories exhibit the Pawnee belief that no matter how lowly one's origin, the path to honor is open through adherence to virtues such as constancy and a humble spirit. This version of *The Mud Pony* was adapted from a longer story in the collection of George A. Dorsey, who recorded the traditions and tales of the Skidi Pawnee between 1899 and 1902. It was told to him by Yellow-Calf.

The author gratefully acknowledges the research assistance of the Nebraska State Historical Society, the Museum of Science in Boston, the American Museum of Natural History, and innumerable branches and services of The New York Public Library in the preparation of this book. Special thanks to Dr. James Smith at the Museum of the American Indian in New York City for his invaluable help.

ISBN 0-590-41526-3
Text copyright © 1988 by Caron Lee Cohen.
Illustrations copyright © 1988 by Shonto Begay.
All rights reserved. Published by Scholastic Inc.

13   4/9

Printed in the U.S.A.   08

For my husband Bill with love
—C.L.C.

In memory of my brother, Nelson
and my sister, Dorothy.
—S.B.

THERE WAS ONCE a poor boy in an Indian camp who would watch by the creek as other boys watered their ponies. More than anything, he longed for a pony of his own.

So at last the boy crossed the creek, dug the wet earth, and shaped a pony out of mud. He gave it a white clay face. He loved his mud pony. Every day he went to it and took care of it as if it were real.

One day while the boy was with his mud pony, scouts rode into camp. "We've sighted buffalo several days' journey west," they said. The people broke camp, for they would starve in the months ahead if they didn't hunt the buffalo. The boy's parents looked everywhere, but they couldn't find him. Finally, they had to leave without him.

When the boy got back to camp, he saw that everyone was gone. "My people!" he cried out. "I will never find you! I am all alone!" He wandered, heartsick and hungry, around the empty camp, picking up scraps of dried meat and a tattered old blanket someone had thrown away. He ate, then huddled up in the blanket and cried himself to sleep.

As he slept, he dreamt his mud pony was alive and spoke to him: "My son, you are not alone. Mother Earth has given me to you. I am part of her."

When the boy woke at daybreak in the empty camp, he cried for his people. Then he went to his mud pony and could hardly believe his eyes! The white-faced pony was alive, tossing her mane and pawing the ground.

She spoke like the pony in his dream: "My son, you are not alone. Mother Earth has given me to you. I am part of her. You must do as I say, and someday you will be a chief among your people. They are far away. Get on my back, and I will take you to them. But do not try to guide me, for I know where to go."

For three days they journeyed over the plains. The boy was worn and hungry, but he would not give up; he let the pony guide him.

Then at the third nightfall, the boy saw smoke curling up from tepees in a camp. They had reached his people.

"Go and find your parents," said the pony. "But leave them before dawn; it is not time yet for the others to see you. I will be waiting in the hills. Now cover me with the blanket to protect me from the rain, for I am part of Mother Earth."

The boy went into the camp. He wandered among the tepees until he found the smallest one. He went in and threw dried grass into the fire, so a blaze went up. In the fire's light he saw his mother and woke her.

"Here I am," he said.

She touched him and tears came into her eyes. Then his father woke and marveled at how the boy had found them when they had gone so far away.

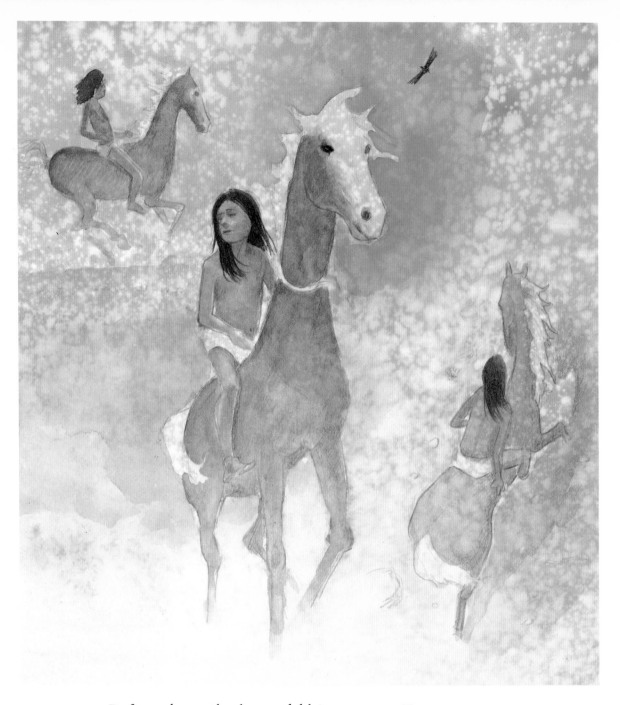

Before dawn the boy told his parents, "I must go now.
On my own." He left them, but from the hills he turned and
watched as the people broke camp to continue on their
way to the buffalo. At last they disappeared.

For three more days the boy and the pony journeyed
over the plains. The boy was weary and had no food at
all, but he kept on going.

Finally at the third nightfall, he saw a camp in the distance. "There are your people," the pony said. "It is time that you join them. Ride me into the camp."

The boy did. And all the people came out of their tepees, astonished to see him.

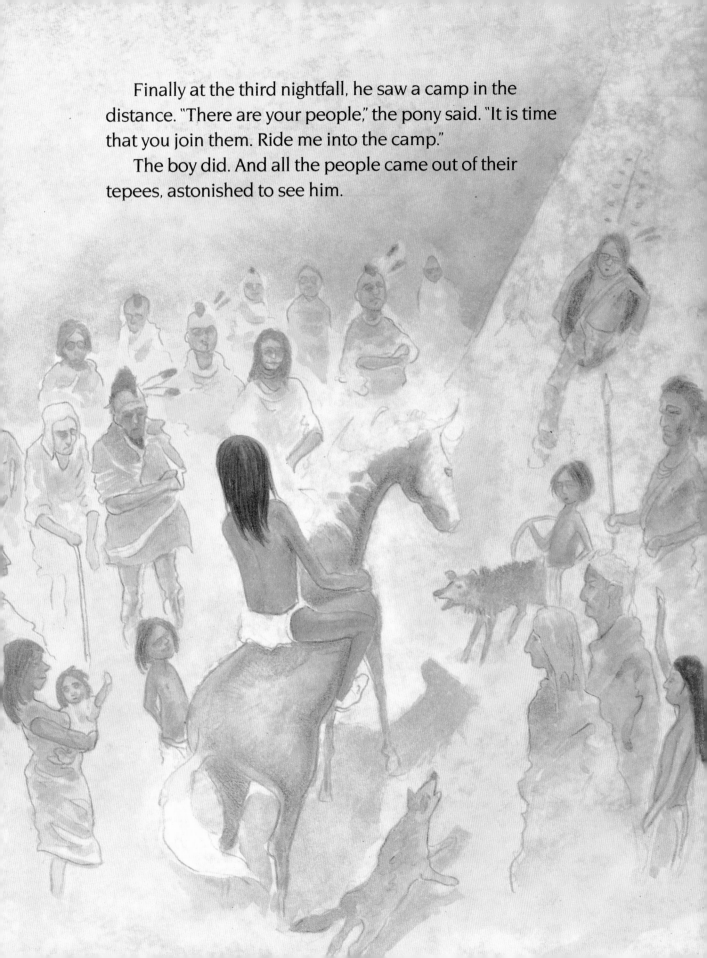

A war chief invited him into a big tepee. There was soup and dried meat and two buffalo horn spoons in a wooden bowl. They ate together.

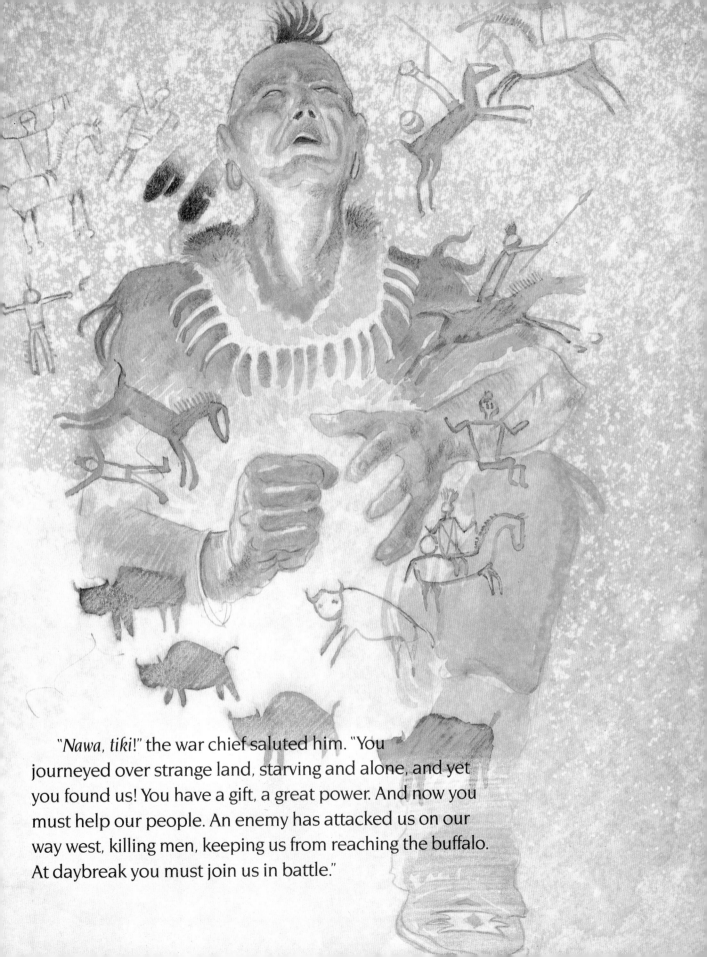

"*Nawa, tiki!*" the war chief saluted him. "You journeyed over strange land, starving and alone, and yet you found us! You have a gift, a great power. And now you must help our people. An enemy has attacked us on our way west, killing men, keeping us from reaching the buffalo. At daybreak you must join us in battle."

When the boy left the big tepee, he trembled. But the pony spoke to him: "My son, do not be afraid. For I am part of Mother Earth. And the enemy's arrows can never pierce the earth. Put earth all over your body, and you will not be hurt."

At daybreak he covered his body with earth and rode the pony straight into the fight. There was a fierce battle, but he led his people to victory. At last the people were free for the hunt, and the boy on the white-faced pony showed the way, capturing more buffalo than any of the grown men.

Years passed, and always the boy let his pony guide
him. Always he was a powerful leader. Finally, he was made
a chief! As a chief, he had a corral full of fine horses, but the
white-faced pony was his great gift. He tied many eagle
feathers into her mane and tail. And every nightfall he carefully covered her with a blanket to protect her from rain.

Then one night while he slept the pony came to him in a dream: "My son, now you are a chief among your people, a chief with the power of Mother Earth. It is Mother Earth who gives you the power, and not I. I am part of her, and it is time that I go back to her. You must let me go."

The chief got up in the dark and went to his pony. She pawed the ground and tossed her mane in the wind.
"Take my blanket," she said. He did. Then he went to his tepee.

Just before daybreak, he woke to shrill winds and rushing rain. He ran to his corral, and looked everywhere for his white-faced pony. He couldn't find her.

Then as the morning light broke over the wet earth, the chief saw a patch of white clay. And through the wind, he heard a voice:

"I am here, your Mother Earth. You are not alone!"